TESTING
FOR
TEACHERS

SECOND EDITION

· BRUCE W. ·
TUCKMAN

Florida State University

HARCOURT BRACE JOVANOVICH, PUBLISHERS

San Diego   New York   Chicago   Austin   Washington, D.C.

London   Sydney   Tokyo   Toronto

*To Christa McAuliffe, the school teacher who
was killed in the explosion of space shuttle Challenger
on January 28, 1986*

ISBN: 0-15-591435-9

Library of Congress Catalog Card Number: 87-80736

Printed in the United States of America

Preface

Testing for Teachers, Second Edition, is a revised version of *Measuring Educational Outcomes: Fundamentals of Testing*, first published by Harcourt Brace Jovanovich in 1975—shortened, updated, reorganized, and geared more directly to prospective and practicing teachers whose need for knowledge about testing is both practical and immediate.

Testing for Teachers has been written for the practitioner, not the researcher or theorist. It is an accurate, straightforward, and comprehensive guide to testing. Because good and meaningful testing must have a clear purpose, one is provided here as the framework of this textbook. That purpose is simply to measure students' attainment of instructional objectives, a purpose that serves as the basis not only for test construction but for test evaluation and interpretation as well.

Regardless of a classroom teacher's philosophy of education, testing is an integral part of teaching. This is especially true given the "back-to-basics" educational climate of today. All teachers should be able to build useful classroom tests, relate those tests to their instructional objectives, and interpret the results of those tests as well as the results of published achievement tests given on a district-wide basis.

It is my hope that through the use of this book future teachers will discover the valuable place testing has within the context and content of the curriculum, as well as the necessary "how-to" skills of testing that are so important for implementing meaningful testing in the everyday classroom setting.

I would like to acknowledge the contributions made to this book by reviewers Michael Subkoviak, University of Wisconsin, and Norman Mulgrave, University of Pittsburgh, and my colleague John Hills. In addition, many thanks to the staff at Harcourt Brace Jovanovich who worked with me in the production of the book: Julia Berrisford, acquisitions editor; Kenneth F. Cherry, manuscript editor; Amy Dunn, production editor; Robin Risque, art editor; Diane Pella, designer; and Sharon Weldy, production manager.

Bruce W. Tuckman

Contents

11   GETTING THE MOST FROM A TESTING PROGRAM

1

Putting Measurement and Evaluation in Perspective

OBJECTIVES

- Identify reasons for giving tests to students in the classroom.
- Describe, in nontechnical terms, how tests are constructed and evaluated.
- Define some common terms used in describing tests.

WHY DO WE MEASURE?

Observations are always subjective. They reveal most often what is in the eye of the beholder, not what actually exists. The teacher and the scientist, however, must obtain information that is accurate or **veridical**—information that reflects what is happening, not what we would like to have happen. Tests, and other forms of measuring instruments, are designed to replace subjective judgment with objective measurement to the greatest degree possible; for without the detachment and impartiality of a well-designed, properly used test, the teacher is left compounding and confounding judgment with more judgment, never having any independent basis for assessing the behavior of students. (However, it must be remembered that even tests can be misused to help make a point.)

Sometimes we are faced with the necessity of not merely observing a behavior as it happens but of stimulating the behavior or finding out if the person is capable of performing that behavior. In these situations, we must not only measure the behavior but, in a sense, sample it from among the individual's total repertoire. For all of these purposes we use what are commonly called tests.

Teachers will find tests useful because they are faced with the responsibility of recording, measuring, and evaluating the behavior and performance of their students. With the aid of tests they can monitor and evaluate student learning and diagnose strengths and weaknesses as they occur.

Reasons to Assess

There are four principal reasons for assessing students. The first is **to identify student strengths and deficiencies as a prerequisite to placing a student in an instructional experience.** We'll call this the *diagnostic* function of assessment.

The second reason is **to identify what has and has not been learned during instruction so that subsequent decisions can be made about additional instruction.** This is the *prescriptive* function of assessment.

The third reason is **to assess individual student performance in order to assign a grade.** All teachers have to evaluate and grade their students; tests, as we shall see, can help accomplish this. Let's call this the *grading* function of assessment.

Finally, teachers may want **to evaluate the quality of a unit of instruction so that they can decide whether to teach it the same way the next time.** Let's call this the *instruction-evaluation* function of assessment.

Thus, we have the four reasons for collecting information about student performance:

- to diagnose
- to prescribe
- to grade
- to evaluate instruction

Diagnosis comes first, guiding the initial choice for instruction. It provides information about individual learning needs. Just as physicians must diagnose medical needs, teachers must diagnose learning needs. Should this student be in an advanced class or a regular class? Should she take Spanish II or III? Should she be given additional remedial instruction?

The second set of decisions, the prescriptive ones, are much like the first except that they occur during the course of instruction and may involve students collectively rather than individually. If only a few class members seem to understand a particular point, then the teacher had better spend more time explaining it. Just as the physician may prescribe rest or medication after seeing a patient, the teacher may prescribe more homework or another lesson.

Grading follows instruction and shows what the student has or has not learned. Grades represent conclusions or outcomes which can be used to evaluate students. Unlike diagnosis and prescription which are **formative** (that is, they help form or decide what will happen next), grading is **summative;** it is a summation of progress.

Instructional evaluation, like grading, is also a kind of summative evaluation, but it is an evaluation of the instruction rather than of the student. It is done *across* students rather than *on* students, although their performance, taken collectively, provides its basis.

Some Reasons for Using Tests to Assess

There are a variety of ways to assess or collect information that can be used to diagnose, prescribe, grade, and evaluate. Testing is only one of those ways. You might simply observe your students' reactions during the course of teaching. However, there are a number of good reasons for using tests as a basis for judgment, such as those described below.

To Give Objectivity to Our Observations. As educators we are used to making observations. Since we are concerned with shaping human behavior, we must constantly be observing it. At times we evaluate the behavior we are observing in terms of a set of criteria or standards that may be unspecified and operate only within our minds. These observations often lack specificity, but in some situations that is not necessarily a problem.

However, there are occasions in all endeavors—education being no exception—when reasonably precise observations are needed. Precision in observation refers to the accuracy with which we are able to capture a particular quality or component of the behavior before us. To measure behavior objectively we need measuring instruments. We need measuring instruments that *record* behavior from a *neutral* vantage point so that we can apply our own standards and values in *evaluating* it.

To Elicit Behavior under Relatively Controlled Conditions. Can we judge student performance from homework? From classwork? Such judgments must be limited by the many variables that operate in these situations. Were there distractions? Was the student given help? Did he or she look up the answer in a book? Did he or she have enough time? Too much time? And so forth. These kinds of variables will not only change for different assignments but will change for different students on the same assignment. How then is a teacher to know about student performance? The testing situation occurs under conditions the teacher can reasonably control. By controlling some of the conditions, the teacher can eliminate the influence of many variables that may bias the outcome being sought.

To Sample Performances of Which the Person Is Capable. A person does not demonstrate all of his or her skills and characteristics in all situations in ways that are evident to an observer. To find out certain things about a person, we create a situation in which we can sample specific capabilities or tendencies. Whenever we ask a person, "Can you do this?" or "Do you like this?" or "Do you know this?" we are testing him or her. We could conceivably watch this person for a long time without ever knowing whether he or she could do a particular thing, and if so, how well. It is far easier and more efficient to pose the question or create the situation for him or her, thus providing the opportunity to sample the relevant performance from his or her repertoire. Measuring, therefore, is sampling. The test or measuring device helps us find what we want to know.

To Obtain Performances and Measure Gains Relevant to Goals or Standards. It is often not enough to know whether a person can do something. The question more typically put is *how well* he or she can do it, particularly after being instructed in it. Simple observation is insufficient here. We must have a performance sample that can be judged in some way as to its appropriateness, accuracy, correctness of fit, timeliness, or some other standard or criterion. For this to happen, the performance must be obtained in a form that makes *evaluation* or comparison possible. Again, the mere observation of behavior does not render it in a form or size suitable for comparison to some standard. We must create a situation that will allow us to evaluate behavior or performance, particularly that which results from learning and instruction. It is this process that lets us determine whether sufficient learning has taken place.

To Apprehend the Unseen or Unseeable. Scientists long ago abandoned the naked eye in favor of the microscope for detail work. The naked eye can see neither microbes nor molecules, the constructs of science. Similarly the naked eye cannot fully see attitudes or values, developmental levels or social patterns. For these we need instruments—instruments that help us tap what is inside people. The complexities of life force people to present themselves in complex ways. The proper measuring instrument gives us insight that the naked eye may rarely afford.

To Detect the Characteristics and Components of Behavior. When we are given the opportunity to isolate behavior, to explore the performances of which a person is capable, we can often gain information about behavior in small units, not necessarily differentiable by normal observations. Achievement partitions itself into math, social studies, and so forth, and math into algebra and geometry. Character becomes aggressiveness, warmth, sociability, and frustration tolerance. Classroom climate becomes esprit de corps, openness, support, and structure. Leadership becomes consideration and initiating structure. And so it goes.

To Predict Future Behavior. Certain tests have been found to relate to future outcomes or events thus creating the possibility of being able to predict future performance based on test scores. While this is the most controversial aspect of testing, there is some basis for saying that if we can detect characteristics, we can predict related behavior, and in some instances prevent undesirable outcomes.

To Make Data Continuously Available for Feedback and Decision Making. In education we test in order to improve instruction. Testing provides data about outcomes that can serve at least two important functions: to inform students about the quality of their performance, and to help teachers make instructional decisions. For the teacher, all the other reasons for testing feed into this one: to facilitate student learning and growth.

Thus, testing in the classroom is a *controlled* and somewhat *objective* procedure by which the performances of which a person is *capable* may be sampled and evaluated against *standards,* such performances often being *unseen* and representing the *components* of behavior. It is this procedure that makes possible the availability of data for student feedback; the diagnosis of learning disabilities, of past failures, of present weaknesses; the detection of mastery, of competence, of the acquisition and possession of skills, knowledge, creativity; the discovery of character, of temperament, of values, of attitudes, of interests; all that and much more. But the success of any measuring venture by teacher or scientist depends on how well the test is constructed, how well it is used, and how reasonably it is interpreted. Such considerations are the subject of this book.

HOW DO WE MEASURE?

Because detailed information on the techniques and procedures of measurement will be presented throughout the book, this section is intended merely as an overview of the measurement process.

The first step in measurement is to decide what it is you want to measure. Measurement requires a fairly precise set of goals or objectives that will guide the measurer in choosing his or her procedures. Trying to measure something that has not been clearly stated is like trying to put together a jigsaw puzzle without first seeing a picture of what it will look like when completed. It is hard to know which pieces to combine unless you know how the end result should look.

Once you have your objectives you are ready for your measuring instrument (within the limitation that all of your objectives may not be immediately measurable). Starting with objectives, the test developer uses a set of rules such as those described later in this book to develop test items. Such items may be short-answer or open-ended (for example, essay); they may involve paper and pencil or actual physical performance; they may deal with what we know or how we think; they may be designed for the student to fill out or for the teacher or other observer to fill out. The test items are the critical mass of the test. They are the controlled situations, each aimed at sampling some aspect of human behavior. Success in sampling will always be determined by how good the items are.

The test user cannot make valid judgments with a test that is imprecise or inaccurate. The worth of a test is measured in terms of its **validity** and **reliability. Validity means whether the test measures what it is supposed to measure.** To establish validity it is often helpful to have some independent way of assessing the property that the test is supposed to measure. Sometimes, in the absence of any such independent criteria, tests must be evaluated in terms of their fit to the objectives of which they are supposed to be a measure. In this book, we will refer to the fit between a test and its objectives as the validity of the test. **Reliability refers to the test's consistency.** Whatever a test measures, it must measure the same thing on each occasion it is used. It must give us as error free an estimate of the property to be measured as is possible. Thus, the test developer must not only write test items, he or she must also evaluate them against certain criteria.

Tests must also have some basis for interpretation. That is, the test must provide the user with a way of evaluating the performance of a student. What does the student's score mean? What does it tell us about him or her? The score itself cannot be considered to be the final product of a test. It must be interpreted. There are two ways of interpreting test scores. One way is in terms of the scores that other people get on the same test. We can talk about the fact that a score is higher than 65 percent of all the scores obtained on a test, or we can talk in absolute terms about how good a score is by virtue of some other criterion. If a test represents what a person should know to become an accountant, then we may demand that a person get 75 percent of it right without regard to how many or how few attain this level of performance. At any one testing, it is possible that no one may attain this predesignated level.[1]

---

[1] We refer to the first kind of test interpretation as *norm-referencing* and the second kind of test interpretation as *criterion-referencing*.

The art and skill of measurement also include test administration. To be able to measure you must be able to give a test under controlled conditions and you must be able to report the results of a test in an understandable and useful way.

There is also the matter of **ethics**. The taker of tests must be afforded certain safeguards such as confidentiality so that the power of testing will not be abused. Those of us who give tests to human beings, particularly children, must be aware of and sensitive to their rights and undertake all necessary steps to protect them. This protection is as much a part of testing as the construction of test items.

A CLARIFICATION OF TERMS

Because the terms **evaluation, measurement,** and **testing** are used throughout this book, it is important that their meanings be clear.

Evaluation is a process wherein the parts, processes, or outcomes of a program are examined to see whether they are satisfactory, particularly with reference to the program's stated objectives, our own expectations, or our own standards of excellence. The assessment of a program's outcomes or results is facilitated by measurement. In other words, tests may be used constructively in the process of evaluation. Essentially, tests are *tools* that are useful in a number of *processes* such as evaluation, diagnosis, or monitoring.

The entire field of inquiry with which this book deals can be called measurement. Measurement is a broad term that refers to the systematic determination of outcomes or characteristics by means of some sort of assessment device. A test can be considered to be a kind or class of measurement device typically used to find out something about a person. Moreover, it is the kind of measuring device in which the person provides samples of his or her own behavior by answering questions or solving problems.

In this book a test will be regarded as a measuring instrument whose intent is to determine changes or gains resulting from a particular educational experience.

The term **objective** will appear frequently. An objective is an intended outcome for learners as a result of certain experiences. Where possible, objectives are generally stated in observable, hence measurable, terms. When so stated they serve as a description of the intended behavior of the learner rather than that of the teacher.

Norm-referenced and **criterion-referenced** are terms used to describe types of test score interpretation. Scores from norm-referenced tests are interpreted on a relative basis in terms of the performance of a "test" or sample group (called a *norm group*) while scores from criterion-referenced tests are interpreted on the basis of some absolute performance criterion such as, "does she know it," or "can he do it." Criterion-referenced tests are built on the assumption that tests are tools that provide an accurate representation of absolute performance. Often called proficiency tests, they are used to determine which objectives a student has acquired competency in. The tests that teachers themselves build are essentially criterion-referenced tests.

ORIENTATION OF THE BOOK

The subject of testing has usually been treated in such a highly technical way as to remove it from the level of understanding of many teachers and thereby render it into the domain of jargon. This situation is bad because every teacher must do some testing, and testing, like other teaching activities, requires training. Thus, the first tenet of this book's orientation is that **testing must be presented in a manner that can be understood.**

The second is that **testing must have a purpose.** You cannot test nothing; you must test something. The development of measurement instruments of any kind must be preceded by the preparation of objectives. In other words, before a teacher can prepare a test, he or she must have decided what it is he or she wants to measure, that is, what the objectives are.

The third tenet is that **testing is a tool that can help teachers help their students.** Thus, usefulness and ease of interpretation are important criteria in test construction and selection. And, test results should be used as part of the instructional process.

Fourth, **feedback and evaluation often require testing as a source of data.** Teaching methods that involve individual student progress typically use testing as a means of monitoring student performance. Testing can help teachers identify areas in which more emphasis is needed.

Fifth, **testing need not be restricted to those things that are easy to test.** When this happens, the easy-to-test things tend to become the most important criteria for evaluation to the exclusion of equally or more important criteria. Creativity (that is, the formulation of original yet appropriate solutions) gives way to intelligence; problem solving gives way to simpler forms of achievement based largely on memory; attitudes and feelings about self and school give way to reading level. This need not be the case. Measurement can itself be creative, enabling the more complex and, in many cases, more meaningful criteria to enter the classroom.

Sixth, **tests need not be used to compare students to one another** (although sometimes comparative information is useful). Put more positively, tests can be used to determine the level and degree of performance of individual students by comparing their performance against independent criteria. For example, if a youngster can add two fractions and get the right answer on two occasions, we might reasonably conclude he or she knows how to add two fractions. We need not always be concerned with the percentage of students nationally who have mastered this skill. It is often sufficient to have determined the degree of mastery of an individual child as a basis for determining whether that child is ready to proceed to new learning.

Seventh, **tests must be consistent with the kinds of instruction and the kinds of learners they are being used to evaluate.** New methods such as computer-assisted instruction require tests that are consistent with the goals and objectives of these programs. Students with different backgrounds or different learning patterns often require different kinds of tests to measure their capabilities. An hourglass would not be an effective instrument for measuring the acceleration of a jet plane. Modern instruction requires modern testing.

PLAN OF THE BOOK

Planning a Test

The first step in testing is to plan the test you will need. This is done by specifying the objectives to be measured and then relating these objectives to specific test items. Before you can write or select test items, you must prepare objectives. Accordingly, Chapters Two and Three deal with the actual procedures for writing objectives and for relating these objectives to test items.

Constructing a Test

Later chapters of the book will describe how to construct tests in different areas and of different types: paper-and-pencil tests, performance tests, short-answer tests, essay tests, checklists, and other types that may find their way into a classroom. These chapters show how to build, use, and interpret different kinds of tests.

Evaluating a Test

A test is a tool for evaluation that must itself be evaluated or "tested" for its suitability as a prerequisite to using it. Within this process of evaluating or judging a test's suitability, the following questions may be asked:

1. Does it measure what I am using it to measure, that is, mastery of my objectives—is it **valid**?
2. Does it measure consistently and accurately—is it **reliable**?

In order to answer these questions, one must understand and be able to apply the skills and concepts of content validity and test reliability which are presented in Chapters Seven and Eight along with their means of implementation. Moreover, information acquired in evaluating a test, such as through item analysis, can also be used for improving it. This, too, will be covered in these chapters.

Published Tests

The alternative to building a test is finding one. Teachers are often called upon to administer and interpret tests that someone else has selected. When this is the case teachers may be at a marked disadvantage. To overcome or offset this disadvantage this book deals with existing tests in the area of *achievement*, the primary area in which district-wide testing is undertaken. Later chapters offer descriptions of the various concepts measured by published achievement test batteries, telling what they mean, and providing instructions for administering tests.

Interpreting Test Results

The last two chapters deal with interpreting test results. In explaining test interpretation, both norm-referencing and criterion-referencing are covered along with descriptions and examples of the different types of scores generated by each. It is here that we encounter the *stanine*, *percentile rank*, and *grade-equivalent score*.

Testing programs and procedures can be used for a variety of purposes, such as assessing student progress, providing student feedback, evaluating instruction, and determining whether the district's program is working. The last chapter deals with programmatic uses of tests so that their procedures and results can be better understood. Applications by teachers will be outlined with respect to the test performance of both individuals and groups.

Because the ideas about testing and test-item writing presented in this book are organized around measurable objectives, it will be necessary to first understand and be able to write objectives. Therefore, before we turn to test-item construction, we will deal with the matter of writing objectives.

Proficiency Test

1. Mr. Carlson tests all of his students the first day of class. Which of the following reasons for testing would be unsuitable?
   a. to get an indication of a student's proficiency
   b. to assign grades
   c. to plan class assignments
   d. to diagnose a specific deficiency
2. Observation is sufficient to judge the extent of a person's knowledge or the depth of his or her feelings.
                    TRUE   FALSE
3. What is the first step in measurement?
4. The final outcome of a test is a (an)
   a. series of items.
   b. score.
   c. interpretation of a score.
   d. performance.

5. In this book, the fit between a test and its objectives is called _____.
6. Criterion-referenced tests are used to determine
    a. how a student's performance compares to that of a sample group.
    b. whether a student likes coming to class.
    c. how successful he or she will be in college.
    d. which objectives a student has acquired competency in.

_____

(Answers to all Proficiency Tests are given at the back of the book.)

2

Constructing Objectives

OBJECTIVES

- Describe a classroom system model and the role of objectives in it.
- State the purposes for objectives in education.
- Identify the three parts of an objective: action, conditions, and criteria.
- Construct measurable objectives containing these three parts.
- Identify and describe the criteria for evaluating objectives, and the application of these criteria.
- Use the cognitive taxonomy to classify objectives.

A CLASSROOM MODEL

We can conceive of a simple model of the classroom as shown in Figure 2-1 below.

If we consider the classroom as a system, our description of it must include a statement of its goals and objectives. The following may be some of the goals of the classroom system:

- to develop the reading and writing skills of students
- to help students gain knowledge of math and science
- to help students master the concepts of social studies
- to enable students to develop independent study skills

Each of these objectives can in turn be broken down into other, more detailed, objectives; but as they are, they help us define the classroom as a system. If we want to measure the success of teaching in meeting these objectives, we need some measurement instruments, but if we select measurement instruments without regard to the teacher's objectives, then the information these instruments provide will bear little relation to the classroom system's successes or failures.

Figure 2-1
The Classroom as a Simple System

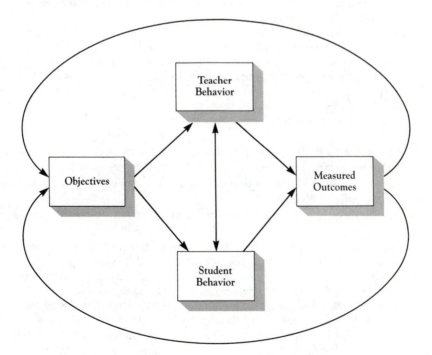

Applications of the Model

Consider the following occurrence in the light of the systems model.

> Miss Logan wanted to teach the students in her ninth grade social studies class to be better consumers. She wanted them to develop the knowledge and skills needed to identify the characteristics and evaluate the quality of a product. She was also anxious to see them actually *buy* items of better quality and greater usefulness and be willing to spend the time shopping around to get something at the lowest price without sacrificing quality. Her last objective was that they would learn to critically evaluate advertisements. She did not know how to help her students learn these things so she began making inquiries of her colleagues.
>
> Her inquiries brought a class unit about consumer education to her attention along with a game called *Consumer*. She was able to convince the high school principal to purchase the consumer education unit and was fortunate enough to borrow the game. She set aside a portion of each class period for trying out the unit and devoted two full class periods to the game. Then she gave her students a kind of take-home exam. They were to research and evaluate some products and judge and critique some ads. She also gave them a record sheet and asked them to keep track of their purchases and evaluate them for cost and quality using a procedure described in the unit. When the take-home exams and record sheets were turned in, Miss Logan studied them carefully. They showed that her students were demonstrating the skills of making critical judgments and evaluations, but that their own buying behavior did not reflect these skills. "I think next time I had better concentrate less on what to do and more on getting the students to do it," she said to herself.
>
> Miss Logan was functioning as a systems analyst without knowing it. She had established some objectives for herself and identified a subsystem that she hoped would meet these objectives. Her subsystem had two components: the unit and the game. As the teacher, she managed the system. She developed measures of the system's outcomes that she could then use to tell whether the system had met her objectives. When she saw that some objectives were not met, she decided to make certain changes.

The point to be made here is that measurement occurs in a context; measurement occurs with respect to something; measurement plays an educational role. **Those elements that connect measurement to the classroom system are called objectives.**

Another example may provide further clarification.

> Kitty, a fifth grader, was a poor student in math. She seemed to be falling further and further behind the class. Her teacher, Mr. Washington, tried giving her supplementary material, but it was ineffective in altering her performance. Finally, Mr. Washington said, "I had better look at math more systematically." He sat down one day and began mapping out all the things that students must learn before learning to add and subtract sequences of fractional expressions—a skill Kitty couldn't master. He ended up with a list of twelve items:

1. adding two dissimilar fractions
2. subtracting two dissimilar fractions
3. expressing mixed numbers as improper fractions
4. expressing improper fractions as mixed numbers
5. supplying fractional equivalents
6. identifying the lowest common denominator
7. identifying common multiples
8. adding two similar fractions
9. subtracting two similar fractions
10. identifying fractional equivalents of whole numbers
11. identifying multiples
12. dividing with a remainder

He then constructed a test which included items to measure each of the twelve competencies in his math system. After school one day he gave Kitty the test and then took it home and scored it. He discovered that Kitty did not know how to identify common multiples (for example, what number can divide into both 9 and 12 evenly? answer: 3). Kitty's problem in subtraction of fractions was actually based on her difficulties in understanding division. Because she could not identify common multiples, she had difficulty in finding the lowest common denominator of two fractions and hence adding or subtracting them. Mr. Washington had found the weak link in the system, the missing piece so to speak, and could then concentrate on teaching Kitty how to overcome this problem.

In the above example the teacher found it necessary to generate a list of objectives before he could use the techniques of measurement to identify the basis for a learning difficulty. Kitty's teacher could not measure her mastery of skills in mathematics until he could first specify what these skills should be. Again, objectives served as a link between the learning system and measurement of the characteristics and quality of that system.

This brings us to our next question: what are objectives?

WHAT ARE OBJECTIVES?

Many adjectives have been placed before the word *objectives* including instructional, behavioral, performance, measurable, expressive, terminal, and enabling. An **objective** will be defined here as **an intended outcome stated in such a way that its attainment (or lack of it) can be observed and measured.** We might broaden this definition by saying that an objective can be the statement of an intended or prescribed characteristic, although when used in relation to instruction those intended characteristics typically represent intended instructional outcomes. Gagné (1974) considers an instructional objective to be an expression of a learning outcome in terms of human performance including a specification of the situation in which it is to be observed. Others have referred to an objective as an attempt by the teacher to clarify or communicate the sought for changes in the learner, or a statement of what the learner is to be like when he has successfully completed a learning experience, or a description of a pattern of performance we want the learner to be able to demonstrate.

Objectives so defined may be reasonably called *instructional* since they represent the goals of instruction. (Moreover, such objectives can be labeled as measurable or behavioral—relatively interchangeable terms—since they specify outcomes in observable form.)[1] For the most part, tests that teachers construct will represent an attempt to assess the students' attainment of instructional objectives. Test objectives represent those performances or characteristics that a test has been designed to measure. When tests are used to evaluate the effects of instruction, test objectives will be represented by the instructional objectives for the units of instruction being evaluated.

Objectives have many values for the teacher as instructor, primary among them being to aid the teacher as tester. Objectives help you determine **what it is you want students to learn and, hence, what you want to measure,** and suggest further **how to measure what you want to measure, whether students have achieved what is intended, and in which areas your instruction has been successful or unsuccessful.**

In the area of teacher-built tests that are used primarily (but not exclusively) to measure achievement, objectives are a necessary starting point. Before preparing test items (in fact, usually before preparing instruction), you should prepare objectives. They help tell you what test questions or items to write and increase the likelihood that the items you write will represent the things you want to measure. It makes little sense to talk about teacher-built achievement tests without talking about instruction since the purpose of the testing is to measure the effects of instruction. **Objectives must serve to guide both instruction and the construction of achievement tests.**

Published tests have, in some cases, explicitly stated objectives and, if not these, a detailed content outline. These object ves can help teachers select and interpret published tests by examining them in relation to their own objectives. The teachers' own objectives are thus of assistance even in test selection.

PREPARING OBJECTIVES

When an objective is written in full or detailed form, it has three parts:

- the action or behavior that the learner or test taker is to perform
- the conditions or *givens* under which the action or behavior is to be performed for observation
- the criteria by which the action or behavior is to be judged

---

[1]It is perhaps more reasonable to say that the outcome will be "measurable" rather than "behavioral" since it may be difficult to think of the writing of test answers as a behavioral demonstration in the usual sense of the word.

Action Statements

Let us concentrate initially on the first component, the action or behavior to be performed since this is the critical element of the objective and for shorthand purposes may be used as the statement of an objective by itself.[2] The emphasis is on the word **action** or **behavior** since this tells us what to test for. The action or behavior is **a descriptive statement of intended student performance.** Because measurement requires an active response by the test taker, the statement should include an **action verb** to depict the appropriate behavior. For example, we can observe and measure whether a student can *identify, describe,* or *demonstrate* something; hence, the emphasis on action verbs. From these observations or measurements we can then infer whether he or she understands or appreciates the subject of study. Our measurements are the vehicle for this kind of inference.

Any verb that expresses action will suffice for writing an objective. Figure 2-2 provides a lengthy list of such verbs keyed to the taxonomy of the cognitive domain, which will be described later in this chapter. Note the large number of usable verbs.

A second, considerably shorter, list—with definitions and examples—is shown in Figure 2-3. A third, even shorter list, appears on page 19. This list—based on the second—provides five action verbs, one of which can be used for writing any objective. This list also includes a description of the activity used to measure the attainment of each type of action.

Figure 2-2
Action Verbs for Writing Objectives Based on the Taxonomy of the Cognitive Domain

> **Knowledge:** define, describe, identify, label, list, match, name, outline, select, state
>
> **Comprehension:** convert, defend, distinguish, estimate, explain, extend, generalize, give examples, infer, paraphrase, predict, rewrite, summarize
>
> **Application:** change, compute, demonstrate, discover, manipulate, modify, operate, predict, prepare, produce, relate, show, solve, use
>
> **Analysis:** break down, diagram, differentiate, discriminate, distinguish, identify, illustrate, infer, outline, point out, relate, select, separate, subdivide
>
> **Synthesis:** categorize, combine, compile, compose, create, design, devise, rewrite, summarize, tell, write
>
> **Evaluation:** appraise, compare, conclude, contrast, criticize, describe, discriminate, explain, justify, interpret, relate, summarize, support

---

[2]Note that the objectives at the start of each chapter in this book are so written, although it is advisable to write all three components until you have gained considerable experience in stating objectives. In all cases, for measurement purposes the second and third components must be at least implied.

Figure 2-3
Nine Action Verbs for Use in Writing Objectives*

DEFINITION OF ACTION WORDS

The action words that are used as operational guides in the construction of the instructional objectives are

1. **Identifying:** The individual selects (by pointing to, touching, or picking up) the correct object of a class name. For example, upon being asked, "Which animal is the frog?" when presented with a set of small animals, the child is expected to respond by picking up or clearly pointing to or touching the frog; if the child is asked to "pick up the red triangle" when presented with a set of paper cutouts representing different shapes, he is expected to pick up the red triangle. This class of performance also includes identifying object properties (such as rough, smooth, straight, curved) and, in addition, kinds of changes (such as an increase or decrease in size).
2. **Distinguishing (similarities and/or differences):** Distinguish between objects or events which are potentially confusable (square, rectangle) or when two contrasting identifications (such as right, left) are involved.
3. **Constructing:** Generating a construction or drawing which identifies a designated object or set of conditions. For example, beginning with a line segment, the request is made, "Complete this figure so that it represents a triangle."
4. **Naming/Listing:** Supplying the correct name or names (orally or in written form) for a class of objects or events. For example, "What is this three-dimensional object called?" Response: "A cone." Or, "list two commonly seen three-dimensional objects." Response: "An ice-cream cone, a block."
5. **Ordering:** Arranging two or more objects or events in proper order in accordance with a stated category. For example, "Arrange these moving objects in order of their speeds."
6. **Describing:** Generating and naming all of the necessary categories of objects, object properties, or event properties, that are relevant to the description of a designated situation. For example, "Describe this object," and the observer does not limit the categories which may be generated by mentioning them, as in the question, "Describe the color and shape of this object." The child's description is considered sufficiently complete when there is a probability of approximately one that any other individual is able to use it to identify the object or event.
7. **Stating:** Makes a verbal statement (not necessarily in technical terms) that conveys a rule or a principle, including the names of the proper classes of objects or events in their correct order. For example, "What is the test for determining whether this surface is flat?" The

---

*Adapted from B. W. Tuckman, *Evaluating Instructional Programs*, 2d. ed., (Boston, 1985), pp. 134–38, by permission of Allyn and Bacon.

Figure 2-3 (continued)

acceptable response requires the mention of the application of a straightedge, in various directions, to determine touching all along the edge for each position.

8. **Demonstrating:** Performing the operations necessary to the application of a rule or principle. For example: "Show how you would tell whether this surface is flat." The individual must use a straightedge to determine flatness by touching of the edge to the surface at all points.

9. **Explaining:** The child should be able to take two or more pieces of data and describe relationships between or among them. For example, he may describe the relationship between a pencil, a known object, and a pen, an object new to him.

Identify—given a stimulus array, the student can point to (by recognition) the specific stimulus required by instruction.

Distinguish—given two potentially confusable stimuli, the student can point to (by recognition) the one possessing the specific, pre-designated property.

Describe—given an object or concept name, the student can state (by recall) those characteristics of the concept or of the object in a manner sufficient to "describe" it in accordance with its defined properties.

Construct—given the name of a "manufacturable" object or concept and sufficient equipment for doing so, the student can produce the object or concept in a way consistent with its defined properties.

Demonstrate—given a problem or performance request and all the necessary elements for completing it, the student can carry out a procedure sufficient for attaining the required performance by virtue of its conformity to defined rules and resulting in the appropriate outcome.

The advantage of working with such a short glossary of verbs is that once the verb is chosen, the method of measurement follows automatically.

Now that the words to describe measurable action have been presented, it may also be helpful to present the words that describe inferences, hunches, and hopes rather than observable acts. Chief among these are

understand
know
appreciate
be aware of
be sensitive to

As instructional goals the above are vital, but as outcomes they cannot be directly measured. They must be inferred from some performance or behavioral act. For example, we may want students to understand that many people in the world live in conditions of poverty. We can ask them to *describe* such living conditions or to *demonstrate* through statistics the extent of poverty in the world, but we cannot ask them to *understand* it. If they can describe it or demonstrate it, we may infer that they understand it.

By their very nature, not all of our instructional objectives will be measurable. When unmeasurable objectives are important, they should be retained. However, where possible, objectives should be in observable terms (particularly if they are going to be of any assistance in measurement) even though they are based on or derived from more general goals like *understanding*.

Let us consider the action portion of objectives starting out with more general goals. Suppose a chemistry teacher would like students to *understand* Boyle's Law. One manifestation should be the ability to use the law. Hence, one objective may be students' ability to *demonstrate* a procedure for calculating the temperature (or pressure) of a gas. Suppose an elementary school teacher wanted his or her students to *understand* the transitive property of numbers and mathematical sentences. Students who know a procedure should be able to demonstrate it; hence, students should be able to *demonstrate* a procedure for writing a mathematical sentence that illustrates the transitive property. Suppose a music teacher wants students to *appreciate* Beethoven's Fifth Symphony. Students will *describe* their feelings toward the symphony in positive terms (presumably in order to give the teacher feedback as to their appreciation or lack of it). The American history teacher wants students to *be aware of* the causes of the Civil War. Since the history teacher is likely to measure this awareness by giving the students a list of statements and asking them to check the ones that represent causes of the war, we might say that he expects them to be able to *identify* statements that represent causes of the war. (Note that this objective, as many, can be made measurable by replacing the in-action verb—"be aware of"—with a suitable action verb, in this case, "identify.")

The high school English teacher teaches students to *know* how playwrights create characterizations. Those who know could be expected to be able to either *demonstrate* a process for arriving at a characterization or *describe* one character in writing. Meanwhile, the teacher of a new vocational program in data processing wants his or her students to *understand* the microcomputer. The teacher may choose to evidence whether they do or do not by their ability to (demonstrate a procedure for) operating a microcomputer. And finally, Langston Hughes' admonition to "dig all jive" would probably come out in "objective-talk" as being able to (demonstrate a procedure for) carrying out a conversation in at least two English "languages," (that is, speak in at least two English dialects).

Conditions and Criteria

For the teacher as instructor, the action statement by itself suffices as the objective. However, the teacher as measurer will find it important to state both the conditions (that is, when will the behavior occur) and the criteria (that is, how will the acceptability of the behavior be judged for the teacher's objectives).

The statement of conditions typically appears at the beginning of the objective, preceding the action statement, and begins with the word *given*. The statement of criteria typically appears at the end of the objective, following the action statement.

The above illustrations have been expanded to include a statement of conditions and criteria and appear below:

> Given the pressure and temperature of a gas at time *1*, and its pressure (or temperature) at time *2*, students can demonstrate a procedure for calculating its temperature (or pressure) at time *2*, accurately to one decimal place in two instances.

> Given pairs of related mathematical sentences in the form of $a = b$ and $b = c$, students can demonstrate a procedure for writing a third sentence that will illustrate the transitive property (if $a = b$ and $b = c$, then $a = c$) in each of three instances.

> Given an opportunity to hear Beethoven's Fifth Symphony and asked to write a composition about it, students can describe their feelings in positive terms, as evidenced by the appearance of at least two positive evaluative terms (for example, enjoy, pleasant, good) and no negative ones.

> Given a list of statements, students can identify those that represent basic causes of the Civil War by placing a check mark next to every one that had previously been designated as acceptable by the teacher.

> Given a play to read, students can demonstrate a process for creating a characterization, as evidenced by identifying all characters, describing each, and relating each to the play's plot and theme.
>
> *or*
>
> Given a play to read and instructions to characterize, students can describe one character in writing, that description to include the character's basic qualities as manifested in the play, his or her relation to other characters, and relation to the play's plot and theme.

> Given a sheet of data in proper form, the student can demonstrate a procedure for entering it onto a microcomputer diskette.

> Given ten phrases in "street talk," the student can state the equivalent or translated phrases in standard written English, being completely accurate (to the satisfaction of the teacher) on nine out of ten.

Even though you may state your own objectives in the abbreviated form of action statements, you will find yourself having to select or identify the conditions under which the action statement is to be measured and the criteria by which the action is to be evaluated.

Unit Objectives

The objectives that represent the end result of an instructional unit are often called **terminal objectives.** Over the course of a school year, a teacher may have twenty or so terminal objectives in a subject matter area. The teacher's testing program will reflect an attempt to determine whether these objectives have been met. There are also other kinds of objectives, called **enabling objectives,** that build upon one another like steps and lead to a terminal objective. Teachers who test for the attainment of enabling objectives during the course of each unit are in a position not only to estimate mastery of terminal objectives but to diagnose sources of failure where failure occurs. Thus, enabling objectives form the basis for **diagnostic testing,** that is, testing to diagnose or detect areas in which learning has not taken place.

Unit objectives, therefore, are comprised of both terminal objectives and enabling objectives. Course or curriculum objectives would be a set of terminal objectives. However, because it is often arbitrary where one segment of instruction begins and another ends, what are terminal objectives in one segment, like a unit, become enabling objectives for a larger segment, like a course.

A set of objectives for a mathematics unit on solving equations with one unknown is shown below.

Unit Terminal Objective

> Given applied math problems in verbal form, solve equations with one unknown contained within.

Unit Enabling Objectives

> Simplify an equation by adding and subtracting terms to both sides.
> Simplify an equation by multiplying and dividing both sides by terms.
> Clear an equation of fractions.
> Simplify an equation by adding and subtracting numbers to both sides.
> Simplify an equation by multiplying and dividing both sides by numbers.
> Supply product and quotient equivalents to products and quotients (terms).
> Identify needed operations in order.
> Add and subtract terms in sequence.
> Supply sum and difference equivalents to sums and difference (numbers) and terms.
> Supply product and quotient equivalents to products and quotients.
> Combine fractions with like denominators.
> Simplify fractional expressions.
> Identify procedural order (left, right, collect, divide).
> Recognize equivalent terms.
> Recognize equivalence of multiplication and division terms.
> Divide parenthetical terms.
> Factor.
> Identify the order of operations (the use of brackets).
> Identify the equivalence of $1x$ and x.
> Identify an equation (equal sign).
> Obtain products with zero.

EVALUATING OBJECTIVES

How can you, the teacher, tell whether you have written the right objectives? How can you tell that these are the outcomes you should be aiming at for your students? Kriege (1971, p. 142) suggests that the teacher judge objectives against the following ten criteria:

Written in terms of *student performance?*
Observable by one or more of the five senses?
Specific enough to be meaningful?
Valid in relation (that is, relevant) to the major objective or goal?
Measurable in terms of (1) level of performance and (2) conditions
    under which the performance is to take place?
Sequential in relation to prior and subsequent objectives?
Relevant to the student's experience?
Attainable within the time period allotted?
Challenging to each individual student?
Acceptable to the societies of which the student is a member?

Some of the above criteria refer only to the *form* or *structure* of an objective (for example, student performance; observable, specific, measurable) and can be applied quite simply. "Did I use an action verb?" "Did I describe conditions and criteria?" "Did I avoid vague, undefinable terms?"

Others of the above criteria refer to the *relation* of the objective to the curriculum and the learning situation (for example, valid, sequential, attainable). The three questions shown in Figure 2-4 may be used for validating an objective based on its place in the sequence, that is, its relation to other objectives. An objective may be invalid because it appears too late or too soon in the sequence or because the proper prerequisites fail to precede it. Often, we can tell a great deal about what objectives we need or do not need in terms of where they appear in the sequence. When we cannot make these decisions on a logical basis, we can make them after seeing how students perform on a test. If students uniformly fail an objective (like B in Figure 2-4) but uniformly pass the one it presumably feeds into (like A in Figure 2-4), then objective B has little validity. Failure to pass A after passing B and C often means that an objective is missing (or else that instruction on A itself was insufficient). Performance data can be used not only to validate an objective in terms of its relation to other objectives, but to test the attainability of an objective within an allotted period of time.

The remaining three criteria (relevance, challenge, and acceptability) refer to the *reaction* by various audiences to the objectives. These criteria are the most judgmental of the ten. To apply them, the teacher would have to gain the reaction of experts, students, and parents through meetings and discussion groups as well as by questionnaire. One of the positive features of objectives is that they make public scrutiny and public acceptability of the curriculum possible. Indeed, if instruction occurs without thought-out objectives, this kind of public acceptability cannot occur.

Figure 2-4
Validating an Objective in Terms of its Place in the Sequence

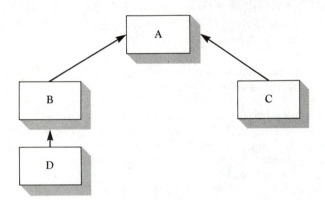

For example:

1. Does performance on given objectives (B & C) contribute to performance on a subsequent objective (A)?
2. Does performance on a given objective (B) depend on or require performance on an objective that precedes it (D)?
3. Is performance on a given objective (C) independent of performance on a parallel objective (B)?

All objectives can be evaluated as to form and structure. Enabling objectives in particular can be evaluated in terms of their relation to one another. Terminal objectives can be evaluated not only in their relation to other objectives but perhaps more importantly by the reaction they provoke from various audiences. Not only do students and parents represent potential sources of feedback—other teachers, subject matter experts, and curriculum designers as well can comment on the potential relevance, challenge, and acceptability in terms of students' patterns of development and career goals. The fact that objectives are tangible and visible (at least potentially so) makes them particularly suited to the process of public examination. Their relation to one another and potential for sequencing make them particularly useful for instructional purposes, and their form and structure make them useful for test design since they help the teacher determine what performances to measure for and the conditions and criteria that will be applied in the measurement situation.

THE WHAT AND WHY OF TAXONOMIES

A **taxonomy** is a device for classifying things in terms of certain of their characteristics; thus, it identifies the relationship of one thing to another in terms of these characteristics. As is generally known, taxonomies exist for classifying plants and animals and for classifying chemical elements.

What we are concerned about here are taxonomies of educational objec-tives, that is, of the goals of our educational system or parts of it. Bloom (1956) suggests that such taxonomies will help teachers (1) define nebulous terms such as *understand* so that they can communicate curricular and eval-uative information among themselves, (2) identify goals that they may want to include in their own curriculums, (3) identify directions in which they may want to extend their instructional activities, (4) plan learning expe-riences, and (5) prepare measuring devices. While we are primarily con-cerned here with the last of Bloom's points, it is unwise to isolate the measurement aspects of taxonomies from their other features.

Taxonomies are devices of human origin that not only help teachers label objectives in terms of one or more of their properties, but also give some idea of the sequences in which objectives may best occur, thus con-tributing to their validation.[3] This latter feature is based on the fact that many taxonomies attempt to be *hierarchical* (organized into levels or ranks). Let us illustrate these points with reference to a taxonomy of the cognitive domain (Bloom, 1956; usually called Bloom's Taxonomy) which is sum-marized in Figure 2-5.

Cognitive Taxonomy

Consider the elementary teacher who is interested in teaching students how to research a social studies topic. The objective might start out vaguely as something like "knowing where to go to get information about a topic." In essence, the teacher is interested in having students acquire knowledge; more specifically, it is knowledge about ways and means of dealing with specifics (rather than knowledge about the specifics themselves). That is, the teacher does not in this objective want the students to learn something about a topic such as "deserts" but to learn ways and means of finding out about that or other topics.

According to the taxonomy, knowledge of ways and means of dealing with specifics is of a higher order, that is, is more advanced or complex, than knowledge of specifics. Most specifically, the objective in question—knowing where to go to get information about a subject—falls into category 1.25: knowledge of methodology (the most advanced of the knowledge of ways and means categories). By referring to Figure 2-2 and looking under Knowledge, a teacher could find a set of action verbs that are useful for writing knowledge objectives. In this particular instance, the teacher could say, for example, that he or she wanted the students to be able to describe ways to get information about a social studies topic (deserts for example). Given this objective, the means for measuring it are fairly obvious—although there are undoubtedly a number of different test items that could be written for eliciting the desired behavior.

---

[3]It is important to emphasize that taxonomies are the product of human beings, not necessarily of nature. While they help us organize thoughts and observations, they must not be used as rigid strait jackets.

Figure 2-5
Taxonomy of the Cognitive Domain*

1.00 KNOWLEDGE
 1.10 of Specifics
  1.11 of terminology
  1.12 of specific facts

 1.20 of Ways and Means of Dealing with Specifics
  1.21 of conventions
  1.22 of trends and sequences
  1.23 of classifications and categories
  1.24 of criteria
  1.25 of methodology

 1.30 of the Universals and Abstractions in a Field
  1.31 of principles and generalizations
  1.32 of theories and structures

2.00 COMPREHENSION
 2.10 Translation
 2.20 Interpretation
 2.30 Extrapolation

3.00 APPLICATION

4.00 ANALYSIS
 4.10 of Elements
 4.20 of Relationships
 4.30 of Organizational Principles

5.00 SYNTHESIS
 5.10 Production of a Unique Communication
 5.20 Production of a Plan, or Proposed Set of Operations
 5.30 Derivation of a Set of Abstract Relations

6.00 EVALUATION
 6.10 Judgments in Terms of Internal Evidence
 6.20 Judgments in Terms of External Criteria

---

*Adapted from *TAXONOMY OF EDUCATIONAL OBJECTIVES: The Classification of Educational Goals: HANDBOOK I: COGNITIVE DOMAIN* by Benjamin S. Bloom et al. Copyright © 1956 by Longman Inc. Reprinted by permission of Longman Inc., New York.

Now that the teacher has dealt with the task of getting information, he or she will probably become concerned with having students understand the information they collect. This moves us into the second level of Bloom's Taxonomy, Comprehension. Perhaps the teacher's concern for comprehension will fall into the category, 2.20 Interpretation. Using an action verb from the list in Figure 2-2, he or she may formulate the objective to explain why the life styles of desert dwellers throughout the world take a similar form.

The teacher may feel that comprehension is not a sufficient place to stop and may go on to Application. He or she may want students to produce a model of a dwelling that they could use if they were going to spend their summer in the desert. From here the teacher may proceed to Analysis; for example, he or she could read students a short biographical sketch of a child in a desert tribe and then ask them to point out those aspects of desert life that have caused the child of the desert to be different from them. Moving on to Synthesis, the teacher may ask students to write a poem or an essay describing life on the desert and the feelings of the desert dwellers. Finally, in the category of Evaluation, students would be asked to contrast the things they like about their own life with the things they like about desert life.

Bloom's taxonomy can be helpful in developing tests to determine students' levels of cognitive skills. It can also help teachers gain more insight into their goals and into the relationship between their goals and instructional activities. Perhaps most importantly, the taxonomy enables teachers to better identify the level of their activities so that they can move to ever increasing levels of complexity. Rather than limiting objectives to the levels of knowledge and comprehension, teachers are encouraged to extend instruction into application, analysis, synthesis, and evaluation.

OBJECTIVES, TAXONOMIES, TESTING, AND THE TEACHER

Why should teachers be concerned with objectives and taxonomies? What does all this have to do with testing? These questions can perhaps be best answered by considering the systems model of the classroom given at the outset of this chapter. The classroom is a small system within which a teacher and a group of students operate. The mission of the system is that students learn and grow. The responsibility for this mission rests largely with the teacher. Thus, the essence of education is that the teacher arranges the conditions of learning (Gagné, 1985) including her own behavior so that students increasingly learn and develop. Mission attainment in any system is facilitated when the goals of the mission are spelled out; hence, objectives. Rather than merely representing an exercise in self-discipline, the writing or choosing of objectives provides the teacher with a set of goals or targets toward which to aim in his or her classroom. Whether the goals are formalized or not, most if not all teachers have them. Objectives are merely a way to make those goals more visible.

As we have seen, objectives help teachers evaluate the validity of their tests and test items. Objectives also help teachers know what to test for; they form the basis for the development of tests and test items. Objectives represent a definite point of reference in the classroom system both for instruction and testing. Since tests attempt to measure the attainment of the teacher's goals, and objectives are formal statements of goals, then objectives tell a teacher what to measure. The activities of the teacher with respect to goal setting, teaching, and testing are shown in Figure 2-6.

The primary purpose of classifying objectives is to gain additional insight about the levels of instruction and the relationship between instructional goals. But classified objectives also facilitate the preparation of test items. If one's instructional goal is knowledge acquisition, measuring for comprehension or synthesis would be invalid and unfair. If one's instructional goal is analysis, measuring simply for knowledge would be equally invalid. Not

Figure 2-6
Flow Chart of Teacher Activities in the Classroom System

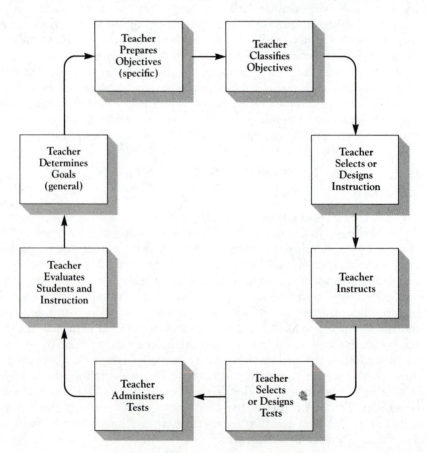

only do the taxonomies help you write items at the intended level, they also help you check on the validity of items for the intended purpose.

Proficiency Test

1. Define an objective and give three reasons why the classroom system needs objectives.
2. Think of a kitchen as a system. List four goals or objectives of that system.
3. State two activities of teachers for which objectives can serve as a guide.
4. If you were a student, what are two ways that knowledge of the teacher's objectives would be of help?
5. Which one of the following is part of an objective?
   a. knowledge to be understood
   b. appreciation to be felt
   c. action or behavior to be performed
   d. awareness or sensitivity to be developed
6. The conditions of an objective represent the standards by which performance on the objective is to be judged.
TRUE   FALSE
7. Write a full (three-part) objective for the goal, *to know the location of the longest river system in the United States.*
8. Write a full objective for the goal, *to be able to add two three-digit numbers.*
9. Which of the following is *not* a criterion of a good objective?
   a. measurable
   b. reliable
   c. specific
   d. challenging
10. In evaluating an objective, explain what is meant by the criterion *sequential* and how this criterion would be applied.
11. Into which one of the categories of the Taxonomy of the Cognitive Domain would the following activity be best classified: *producing a unique plan for enlisting community support?*
    a. comprehension
    b. application
    c. analysis
    d. synthesis
    e. evaluation

3

Basing Test Items on Objectives

OBJECTIVES

- Identify an appropriate test item for measuring a given objective.
- Identify two areas into which objectives can be usefully classified, namely: knowledge and comprehension and higher cognitive processes.
- Classify given test items into each of the two areas.
- Prepare objectives in shorthand form (that is, in action part only).
- Prepare a content outline for a given topic or objective as the first step in test construction.
- Prepare test-item specifications.

THE RELATIONSHIP BETWEEN OBJECTIVES AND TESTS

It has been emphasized before, and will be again throughout this section, that tests are constructed to measure whether objectives have been met. A test is defined as a sample of student performance on items that have been designed to measure preselected objectives. Even if objectives are not explicitly stated, tests still measure the performance of students. In order to insure that your tests and the performances they require are related to (that is, measure) the objectives you want them to measure, it is important to state them objectively, if only in "shorthand" form (that is, action portion only). The objectives, once stated, will help you determine the test items you need to construct to measure student mastery of those things you intend for students to master. The use of objectives in instruction or in communication of aims are also important purposes that justify their preparation.

Remember, also, that you must ask yourself the following questions in regard to each objective: (1) do I use it as a basis for instruction? (2) does it help me know what and how to teach so that it can be achieved? (3) does it help me construct tests to measure the attainment of my goals? (4) are students motivated to attain it? (5) does it take into account my instructional time and resources and the capabilities of the students? and (6) does it fit into a sequence?

You are now ready to begin learning how to construct your own tests, most of which will be used to measure achievement or mastery of the material you teach. Test construction includes three steps: (1) preparation of objectives, (2) preparation of test items, and (3) evaluation of test items. Each step is important; none should be omitted. The purpose of this chapter is to (1) illustrate the relationship between objectives and test items through the use of sample tests, (2) show how different domains or areas of objectives relate to test items, and (3) demonstrate how to complete the first step in test construction—the development of objectives—referred to here as a content outline.

Some Illustrations of Objectives and Tests

Miss Hart teaches math in the seventh grade. She had just finished a unit on sets and was ready to give her students a test to see how much they had learned. As a first step, she sat down and thought about what she had been trying to teach them. She went over her lesson plans and wrote the following objectives.[1]

1. Given a statement of the elements or nonelements of a set, use mathematical symbols to represent the statement.

---

[1]It would have been better pedagogy, of course, had Miss Hart written her objectives before instruction rather than after.

2. Given a set in roster form, use set-builder notation to represent the set.
3. Given terms used to describe sets and their relationship (that is, equal, empty, sub-, and proper), identify the correct definition of each.
4. Given two or more sets, identify those that are equal.
5. Given a set and the empty set, identify their relationship and distinguish between them.
6. Given two or more sets, identify those that are subsets of and those that are proper subsets of one of the given sets.
7. Given a set, state the number of elements in it.

After further consideration, she decided that objectives 1, 2, 6, and 7 were equally important and that they were more important than the others; that objectives 3 and 4 were of equal but intermediate importance; and that objective 5 was least important. The greater importance of objectives 1, 2, 6, and 7 is based on their greater complexity and the fact that they form the basis for subsequent performance. She then decided on ten exercises with a total value of twenty-eight points: five points to measure each of the objectives 1, 2, 6, and 7; three points to measure objectives 3 and 4 respectively; and two to measure objective 5. Her next task was to write the ten exercises. Because the objectives gave her a strong clue as to what each item should be like, writing the test was not difficult. Miss Hart's test is shown in Figure 3-1.

Figure 3-1
Miss Hart's Seventh Grade Math Test*

1. Use mathematical symbols to indicate the following:
   a. C is equal to the set whose elements are 5, 10, and 15.
   b. 5 is a member of set C.
   c. 7 is not an element of set C.
   d. The set of all elements x such that x is an even integer.
   e. The set of all elements y such that y is an odd number greater than 7.

   (Objective 1; 5 points)
2. Use set-builder notation to indicate each of the following sets:
   a. {1,2,3,4,5,6,7,8,9,10}
   b. {1,3,5,7,9}
   c. {4,6,8,10,12}
   d. {a,b,c,d,e,f,g}
   e. {s,t,u,v,w,x,y,z}

   (Objective 2; 5 points)

3. Connect each term at the left with the correct definition at the right.

   a. equal sets
   b. the empty set
   c. subset
   d. proper subset

   i. every element of the set is also an element of the other set
   ii. every element of the set is also an element of the other set and vice versa
   iii. every element of the set is also an element of the other set but the reverse is not true
   iv. the set contains no elements

   (Objective 3; 3 points)

4. Which of the sets listed below are equal?
   A = {1,3,5,7}
   B = {2,4,6,8}
   C = {x/x is an odd number and x is less than 9}
   D = {5,3,7,1}

   (Objective 4; 1½ points)

5. Which of the sets listed below are equal?
   A = {1,2,3,4}
   B = {5,6,7,8}
   C = {y/y is an even number and y is less than 9}
   D = {2,4,6,8}

   (Objective 4; 1½ points)

6. Given A = {a,b,c,d} and the empty set ø:
   a. Is every element in ø in A?
   b. Is every element in A in ø?
   c. Is ø a proper subset of A?

   (Objective 5; 1 point)

7. Explain the difference between ø and {ø}.

   (Objective 5; 1 point)

8. Which of the following sets are subsets of (a,b,7, Δ)?

   a. {a,□}
   b. {7}
   c. {5,7}
   d. {a,b,7,Δ}
   e. ø
   f. {ø}
   g. {Δ,a,7}
   h. {Δ,b,7,a}
   i. {a,b,ø}
   j. { }

   (Objective 6; 3 points)

9. Which of the sets in item 8 are proper subsets of the given set?

   (Objective 6; 2 points)

10. State the number of elements in each of the following sets.

    a. {7,a,□,ø}
    b. {a,□,ø}
    c. {□,ø}
    d. {ø}
    e. ø

    (Objective 7; 5 points)

Answers

(1) a. C = {5,10,15}; b. 5εC; c. 7εC; d. {x/x is an even integer}; e. {y/y is an odd number greater than 7}

Mrs. Morris teaches first grade. The greatest amount of her time is spent in teaching reading. A school-wide achievement test is administered once a year to assess children's overall reading performance, but in order to provide continuous monitoring of reading performance she finds it necessary to test about once every two weeks. Before beginning a unit that stressed reading comprehension, she listed for her own use the following aims for student accomplishment.

1. Given a picture, name its contents and describe the activity going on (as a way of explaining it).
2. Given a sequence of story facts, draw a conclusion based on it.
3. Given the names of characters in a story, list the characteristics they have in common.
4. Given two stories, list the characteristics on which their settings differ.
5. Given the behavior of characters in a story, distinguish between those behaviors that are realistic and those that represent fantasy.

Although the five objectives were only a portion of Mrs. Morris' goals, she felt that they were representative of the reading comprehension skills that her students should possess. At the completion of the unit she made up a short test based on the five objectives. It is shown in Figure 3-2.

Mr. Emerson teaches English to eleventh graders in a course primarily devoted to poetry. His objectives for the first half of the course are shown below.

1. Explain the meaning of a poem on the
   a. literal level in terms of what the poem actually describes,
   b. figurative level in terms of what the poem's underlying message is—using the poem's symbols for evidence, and
   c. personal level in terms of how you relate to the poem.
2. a. Identify the tone of a poem (attitude conveyed toward subject matter and audience), and

---

Answers (*continued*)

(2) a. {x/x is an integer greater than 0 and less than 11}
   b. {x/x is an odd integer less than 11}
   c. {x/x is an even integer greater than 2 and less than 14}
   d. {x/x is a letter of the alphabet coming before h}
   e. {x/x is a letter of the alphabet coming after r}
(3) a. ii; b. iv; c. i; d. iii
(4) A = C = D
(5) C = D
(6) a. yes; b. no; c. yes
(7) ø is a symbol used to indicate the empty set which contains no elements; {ø} indicates a set containing one element, the empty set.
(8) b, d, e, g, h, j
(9) b, e, g, j
(10) a. 4; b. 3; c. 2; d. 1; e. 0

  b. describe in a short essay the means by which the poem's tone is revealed.
3. Demonstrate understanding of a poem's diction:
  a. identify words that connote multiple associations, and
  b. describe in a short essay the value and effect of these words.
4. Demonstrate an understanding of the relationship between figurative language and meaning in poetry:
  a. identify figures of speech in poetry,
  b. describe the feelings and ideas contained in each, and
  c. describe in a short essay their importance to the meaning of the poem.
5. Demonstrate an understanding of the function of repetitive sound in poetry (meter or rhyme):
  a. identify regular and irregular patterns of meter and rhyme in a poem, and
  b. describe in a short essay the contributions of the regularities and irregularities to the poem's meaning.

Mr. Emerson's exam is shown in Figure 3-3.

Figure 3-2
Mrs. Morris' First Grade Reading Comprehension Test*

1. Who and what do you see in this picture? What is happening?

                 (objective 1)

---

*Adapted from Instructional Objectives Exchange, Reading K–3.

Figure 3-2 (continued)

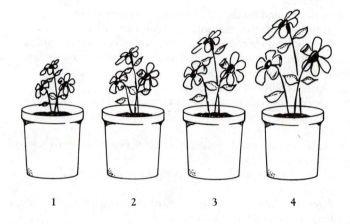

2. Why does picture 4 come after pictures 1, 2, and 3 and not before them or in the middle?

(objective 2)

3. You have read three stories: *Angus and the Ducks, Blueberries for Sal,* and *Michael Who Missed His Train.* In each story there were animals. Tell me three ways that the animals in each story were like one another.

(objective 3)

4. You have read the story, *City Streets and Country Roads,* about life in the country and life in the city. Tell me three ways that life in the city is different from life in the country.

(objective 4)

5. You have read the story, *The Three Bears.* Tell me three things that the bears in the story were doing that real live bears cannot do (like talking).

(objective 5)

Mrs. Dorfman teaches high school biology to a class made up of tenth and eleventh graders. She just finished a unit on reproduction that included the following objectives:

1. The student will be able to define and describe each of the following

---

Answers

1. A boy and a girl, two shovels, two pails, the ocean, a beach; they are building a sandcastle, using sand from the beach and water from the ocean. 2. Because the flowers are blooming a little more in each picture. 3. All have mothers, all can walk, all like to eat, all get into trouble, all like to play games. 4. Noisier, few trees, lots of houses, few animals, no farms, little grass. 5. Sleeping in beds, sitting on chairs, eating from bowls.

processes in terms of (I) when and (II) in what exact manner it occurs:
a. mitosis
b. meiosis (sexual reproduction)
c. asexual reproduction
d. natural selection
e. Mendelian heredity

2. The student will be able to describe and explain how each of the above six processes in its own way maintains the continuity of life, that is, makes it possible for certain forms of life to survive.
3. The student will be able to contrast the above six processes in terms of their
   a. simplicity–complexity,
   b. dependence on the environment,
   c. speed,
   d. predictability, and on any other dimensions that seem relevant, showing how each varies on each dimension.

Figure 3-3
Mr. Emerson's Eleventh Grade Poetry (English) Exam*

1. a. State briefly the literal level of the poem "Oh Who Is that Young Sinner" by A. E. Housman; that is, describe the story that the poem tells.
   b. "The color of his hair" is symbolic; explain what it symbolizes. What is the symbolic meaning of the poem?
   c. Briefly describe an instance in which you witnessed or experienced or heard of a person being discriminated against or put down for "the color of his/her hair" or skin.

   (objective 1)
2. What is the tone of the poem "In Just—" by e. e. cummings? How is the tone revealed?

   (objective 2)
3. Describe the connotations that the following words from "Richard Cory" by Edward Arlington Robinson have in common. What is their function in the poem?

   crown (line 3)   imperially (line 4)   arrayed (line 5)
   glittered (line 8)   King (line 9)

   (objective 3)
4. Name three figures of speech that are used in "Is Heaven a Physician?" by Emily Dickinson. What attitude is conveyed by each of these figures of speech?

   (objective 4)
5. Is the meter of the poem "Fife Tune" by John Manifold well-suited or poorly-suited to its meaning? (Justify your response with illustrations from the poem.)

   (objective 5)
   (Each item is worth 20 points)

---

*Adapted, Instructional Objectives Exchange, *English Literature 10–12.*

4. The student will be able to describe and present in an essay or poem
   personal feelings related to
   a. the transitoriness of "individual" life and
   b. the continuity of "class" life.

Mrs. Dorfman composed the test shown in Figure 3-4 below to determine
whether the students had learned the matter covered in the unit.

Tests Measure Objectives; Objectives Facilitate Test Construction

It can be seen from the preceding examples that teacher-built achievement
test items are written to reflect a set of objectives and that the existence of
objectives is an important asset in test construction. If one were to ask any
of the teachers in the illustrations what they thought their tests measure,
they would point out the relationship between their objectives and their
test items. Some teachers attempt to link goals and tests in a highly informal
and imprecise way, an approach that does not necessarily help them measure
what they want to measure. If you look closely at the objectives and test

Figure 3-4
Mrs. Dorfman's High School Biology Unit Test on Reproduction*

1. Show, *using pictures only and no words*, the process of
   a. mitosis
   b. meiosis
   (objective 1)
2. Imagine that you were a ball point pen. How do you think you might
   go through the process of asexual reproduction?
   (objective 1)
3. Imagine that you were a string bean. According to Mendelian heredity principles, how would you compare to your "mother" and
   "father"?
   (objective 1)
4. Suppose that you were a big, strong dinosaur. Explain how natural
   selection might have operated to put you out of existence.
   (objective 1, 2)
5. Describe two things that the processes of reproduction all have in
   common. Describe two things that the processes don't have in common (that is, in which they differ).
   (objective 3)
6. Write a short essay or poem on the difference between the "short"
   life of an organism and the "long" life of a "class." The essay or poem
   should suggest how you feel about this difference.
   (objective 4)

---

*Adapted from Instructional Objectives Exchange, *Biology 10–12*.

items in each of the four illustrations, you will be able to see their relationship with reasonable clarity.

Recall from Chapter Two that an objective is divided into conditions, behavior, and criteria. (Most of the objectives in the preceding illustrations have left the criteria unstated. In many instances, these criteria are implicit; for example, performing an operation or task correctly where correctness can be judged objectively.) The core of the objective is the behavior. Take the behavior, "identify an elephant." We would probably give a student a picture containing four or more animals and ask him or her to indicate which was an elephant since "pointing to" is the behavior called for by the action verb "identify." The mechanics of item writing will be discussed in the succeeding chapters, but the point here is that the objective accomplishes two purposes: **it reminds the teacher what he or she wants to measure** (or helps him or her to focus on it) and **it provides some guidance on how to measure** (provided that the teacher has built some information into the objective in the first place). Naturally, the more detailed the objective, the more information it provides for the "how to measure" question. Look closely at the objectives and corresponding items in the preceding examples and you will begin to appreciate the extent to which objectives facilitate item writing.

The examples are also intended to illustrate types of tests and test questions that involve paper and pencil to answer. Paper-and-pencil is the test medium in which most tests are written. (The medium of performance testing will be covered in a subsequent chapter.) We can distinguish between short-answer questions and essay questions, each representing a different question–answer format. Finally, we can roughly distinguish among the measurement of knowledge acquisition and comprehension and the measurement of the higher mental processes—application, analysis, synthesis, and evaluation—to use the terms from the taxonomy described in Chapter Two.

AREAS OF OBJECTIVES

Knowledge Acquisition and Comprehension

The most common use of tests in the classroom is measuring knowledge acquisition and comprehension. Basically, tests constructed for this purpose measure the degree to which students have acquired information and can understand what it means. If you reexamine Bloom's Taxonomy you will see that the first two levels are "knowledge" and "comprehension." These two levels refer to the acquisition, incorporation, and recall of factual information. The acquisition of knowledge and comprehension of facts are major goals in education, and considerable effort has been contributed to their measurement.

Two of the four tests presented as illustrations at the beginning of this chapter measure knowledge and comprehension. These are the ones in reading and math; the last two largely measure higher cognitive processes.

The most common and efficient measurement approach for measuring knowledge and comprehension is the short-answer item.[2] Although essay items may be used for this purpose, short-answer items are well suited to the measurement of fact understanding and recall and, of the two types, are the easier to score objectively.

Some examples of short-answer knowledge and comprehension items appear in Figure 3-5. These items range from those clearly measuring direct recall, such as the first, to those measuring some form of interpolation, such as the last. All attempt to measure what the student knows and can understand on the basis of his or her ability to identify the correct response choice. The particular types of short-answer items that may be used and their construction will be discussed in the next chapter.

Higher Cognitive Processes

In the domain of cognitive or mental processes, there are important educational goals that deal with more complex forms of mental activity than knowing or understanding facts. These higher cognitive processes can be thought of as *thinking* or *using knowledge* and have been labeled as applica-

Figure 3-5
Short-answer Items that Measure Knowledge Acquisition (Recall) and Comprehension*

1. About what proportion of the population of the United States is living on farms?
   a. 5%   b. 15%   c. 35%   d. 50%   e. 60%
2. The primary germ layer, from which the skeleton and muscles develop, is known as the
   a. ectoderm.   d. endoderm.
   b. neurocoele.   e. mesoderm.
   c. epithelium.
3. According to Daniel Webster, that which is most inseparable from "union" is
   a. "country."   c. "the North."
   b. "liberty."   d. "welfare."
4. If the volume of a given mass of gas is kept constant, the pressure may be diminished by
   a. reducing the temperature.   d. decreasing the density.

---

*Adapted with permission of Longman Inc., from B. S. Bloom, *Taxonomy of Educational Objectives: Cognitive Domain*, 1956.

---

[2] This is sometimes referred to as an *objective* or *objective-type* item, meaning that it is scored on a reasonably objective basis in contrast to the more subjective scoring of essay items. To avoid confusing the name of these items with the previously used term "objective," meaning goal or purpose, we will refer to these items throughout as short-answer (a reasonably descriptive term that distinguishes them from the essay type).

  b. raising the temperature.   e. increasing the density.
  c. adding the heat.
5. Which of the graphs below best represents the demand schedule of a
 commodity for which there is a perfectly inelastic demand?

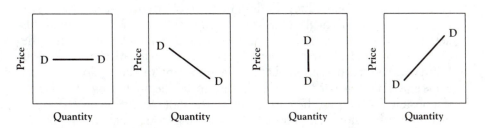

  Quantity   Quantity   Quantity   Quantity

6. "Milton! thou shouldst be living at this hour: England hath need of
 thee; she is a fen of stagnant waters."—Wordsworth
 The metaphor "she is a fen of stagnant waters," indicates that Wordsworth felt that England was
 a. largely swampy land.
 b. in a state of turmoil and unrest.
 c. making no progress.
 d. in a generally corrupt condition.
7. A scientist cultivated a large colony of disease-producing bacteria.
 From them, he extracted bacteria-free material referred to as substance X. A *large* dose of substance X was then injected into each
 animal of group A. These animals promptly developed some of the
 symptoms normally produced by infection by the bacteria in question. Then, into each animal of group B, the scientist made a series
 of injections of *small* doses of substance X. Animals in a third group,
 C, received no injections. Three weeks after this series of injections,
 and continuing for two years thereafter, group B could be made to
 develop the disease by injecting them with several thousand times
 the number of bacteria that was fatal to group C. Substance X acted
 upon the animals of group A as if it were a
 a. poison.
 b. destroyer of poison.
 c. stimulator of destroyer of poison.
 With reference to its effect upon the animals of group B, small doses
 of substance X appeared to act as
 a. a means of counteracting the effects of the disease-producing
  bacteria.
 b. a means of stimulating the production of the bacteria or of their
  poisonous products.
 c. if it were a poisonous product of the bacteria.

Answers
(1) a (2) e (3) b (4) a (5) c (6) d (7) a, a.

tion, analysis, synthesis, and evaluation by Bloom in his taxonomy of the cognitive domain.

It is far more difficult to measure improvement in these higher cognitive areas than in the preceding ones; the greater difficulty in measuring is probably what has accounted for the lesser degree of attention paid the higher cognitive areas. This neglect has manifested itself in the use of teacher-built achievement tests to measure knowledge and comprehension with the assessment of students' higher mental processes left to the teacher's judgment based on class participation. Difficulties inherent in the measurement of thinking skills have led some educators to condemn testing as a factor responsible for limiting the curriculum to the more mundane goal of information transmission. The limited use of testing in the higher parts of the cognitive domain is not an inherent failing in testing but one that has been prompted by the difficulty in measuring the use of the thinking process. By improving their test-construction skills, teachers will be able to feel more comfortable in aiming some objectives at the attainment of thinking skills, hence increasing the application of instruction to the development of thinking. The improvement of thinking may be ultimately facilitated rather than inhibited by the science and art of testing.

Sample paper-and-pencil test items for the higher cognitive processes appear in Figure 3-6. However, it must be pointed out that thinking skills need not necessarily be measured only by a paper-and-pencil test. They are often measured accurately by a test requiring an active, observable performance on the student's part. (Performance tests will be described in Chapter Six.) For illustration here, written items have been used. Note that the first item in Figure 3-6 requires that the student *apply* what he or she has learned in algebra and geometry to the solution of a real problem. The second involves the *analysis* of a position or opinion into those arguments that do and do not support it. The third requires that the student *synthesize* what he or she knows about desert life into the drawing of a suitable picture. The fourth calls for the *evaluation* of clothing materials in terms of criteria that the student must have already learned.

The higher mental processes are oriented more to the process by which an answer or solution is obtained than to the answer or solution itself. Consequently, test items that measure outcomes or responses based on these processes are usually more difficult to score since answers are not necessarily completely right or wrong; their degree of correctness is based on how they were obtained. The teacher, therefore, must have access to the solution process or the logic or justification behind it in addition to the solution itself. Perhaps it is this characteristic that accounts for the rarity of such tests and which requires that attention be paid not only to test item writing but to answer key or criterion writing as well.

DEVELOPING A CONTENT OUTLINE

The purpose of this chapter is to help you see the relationship between objectives and test items. Before test items are written, objectives should

Figure 3-6
Items that Measure Thinking Skills*

1. The length of a rectangular lot exceeds its breadth by 20 yards. If each dimension is increased by 20 yards the area of the lot will be doubled. Find the shorter dimension of the original lot. Show your work below.

   a. 20   c. 35   e. none of the above

   b. 30   d. 40

2. Resolved: *That the term of the president of the United States should be extended to six years.*

   Mark each statement (a–e) below

   A—if you feel that it could be meaningfully used by the affirmative side in a debate on the resolution.

   N—if you feel that it could be meaningfully used by the negative side.

   X—if you feel that it has no bearing on either side of the argument.

   (NOTE: You are not asked to judge the truth or falsity of the resolution or the statements.)

   a. Efficiency increases with experience.
   b. According to the principles upon which the United States was founded, the people should have a frequent check on the president.
   c. The party system has many disadvantages.
   d. During most of a presidential election year the economic life of the nation is depressed by the uncertainty of the outcome.
   e. The people should have the opportunity to keep a satisfactory president as long as they wish.

3. Draw a picture of a desert scene that shows different aspects of desert life and what the people who live there are like.

4. Jane is going to make a dress for school. The dress will receive heavy wear through most of the year, and will be laundered frequently. She has chosen dacron polyester over wool or cotton. Identify at least six criteria, such as convenience in washing and durability, that can be used for evaluating the chosen material, as well as the alternatives Jane considered. Indicate how your criteria apply to the three materials, and whether they lead you to make the same choice as Jane. Be as specific as possible in stating and applying criteria.

---

*Adapted with permission of Longman Inc., from B. S. Bloom, *Taxonomy of Educational Objectives: Cognitive Domain*, 1956.

Answers

(1) d. (2) a. A, b. N, c. X, d. A, e. X.

(3) Drawing should reflect awareness of topography, climate, dwelling places, dress, living habits, animal life, and so forth. (4) Response should use criteria such as the following to evaluate given materials: colorfastness, crease resistance, softness, durability.

be prepared. A shorthand list of objectives forms the basis for a **content outline**. Once the content outline is prepared, it can serve as the basis for determining what test items must be written. We shall talk here about the procedure for developing a content outline; the procedures for preparing test items will be presented in the next chapters. The examples given at the beginning of this chapter illustrate the kinds of tests that can result from content outlines based on objectives.

Some teachers develop lists of objectives to guide their development of lessons and others do not. Those that do not are encouraged to develop objectives at least as a basis for developing a content outline, that is a list of the concepts or tasks to be mastered in a shorthand form, rather than proceeding to write test items without any formal content structure. Where instructional objectives already exist, they should be summarized or listed in the shorthand form of a content outline.

In summary, then, a content outline is a list (in shorthand form) of concepts or tasks to be mastered. Sample content outlines for the subjects of reading and mathematics appear below. Note that each statement in the content outline represents a statement of an objective only in the form of the desired behavior or action. The statement of the conditions and the criteria have been left off, as they are typically in a content outline, for purposes of brevity.

Reading Content Outline

Recognizing the sound of final consonant digraphs
Recognizing the sound of initial consonant blends
Recognizing the sound of final consonant blends
Identifying vowels modified by r in words
Identifying vowel diphthongs in words
Classifying singular and possessive nouns
Classifying adjective endings
Classifying irregular verbs and verb endings, present tense
Classifying compound words
Classifying contractions
Identifying synonyms and antonyms
Identifying personal pronouns
Identifying words using context and configuration clues
Restating sequence of details
Inferring main idea

Mathematics Content Outline

Identifying place value (1s, 10s, 100s)
Adding columns of numbers without carrying
Recognizing applications of the associative principle
Subtracting two-digit numbers without borrowing
Recognizing applications of the distributive principle
Identifying common fractions

Identifying improper fractions
Identifying place value (1,000s, 10,000s)
Identifying decimal fraction values to (hundredths)
Reading and writing decimals
Converting decimals to fractions
Converting fractions to decimals
Adding two- and three-digit numbers with regrouping
Stating multiplication facts
Determining the product of two-digit numbers

Thus, test construction (to be described in the following chapters) begins as a first step with the preparation of a content outline (or list of objectives in brief form) that tells you what it is you want to measure. The following steps ordinarily occur in the preparation of a content outline.

1. Identify the segment of instruction for which testing will be done. Your test may be a unit test following completion of a unit, or it may cover a week of instruction, a half a year, a year or any other segment. Your test should be based on the chosen segment if it is to accurately reflect achievement in that segment.

2. Specify the concepts, ideas, or skills covered in the segment. What are the areas in the segment in which learning was to have taken place? These concepts, ideas, or skills to be learned should be stated in any form that has the most meaning to you. It is entirely likely that you have already stated these prior to offering instruction.

3. Restate the concepts, ideas, or skills in behavioral terms. What you will ultimately measure are performances that reflect the concepts, ideas, and skills to be learned. The preparation of test items is facilitated by the availability of objectives stated in behavioral or measurable terms. (For a review of these procedures, refer to Chapter Two.) To restate concepts, ideas, or skills in measurable terms requires that each statement include an action verb. (See Figures 2-2 and 2-3 for a list of action verbs.) Decide upon the appropriate action verb in each instance and restate the concept, idea, or skill accordingly. You need not include statements of conditions and criteria; these will be supplied, at least implicitly, when preparing the test items. However, it will simplify the subsequent development of test items and suggest certain content areas that will not prove measurable if conditions and criteria are at least considered.

4. Indicate any difference in relative emphasis of the various objectives. Each of the objectives in the outline may or may not be of equal emphasis. Where unequal emphases occur, objectives may be weighted using a system like the following: least emphasized objectives are weighted 1, the objectives of intermediate emphasis are weighted 2, and the most emphasized objectives weighted 3. Where all are of equal emphasis, weightings need not be added.

You are now ready to consider the conditions, actions, and criteria of measurement by preparing test-item specifications. You must write specifications for each and every objective in your content outline. Where objectives are equally weighted, the same number of items should be written for each objective. Where weightings occur, the number of items per objective must be proportional to the weighting of the objective. In other words, an objective with a weighting of 3 should have approximately three times as many items as one with a weighting of 1.

Using a content outline and test item specifications to construct a test are procedures aimed at insuring the validity of that test.

PREPARING TEST-ITEM SPECIFICATIONS

After you have written your objectives but before you write the test items, it is advisable to prepare test-item specifications. A simple way to carry out this intermediate step is to use index cards. At the top of the card, write the objective, and below the objective make a table consisting of three parts: the conditions, the action, and the criteria.

Some examples follow. Note that the specifications provide information about the range and kind of conditions that are suitable for measuring the objective, the specific action or performance required of the student, and the criteria for evaluation of the performance. The criteria represent *minimum acceptable performance requirements* and may define these requirements in terms of (1) time limits, (2) number of correct responses, (3) proportion of correct responses, (4) acceptable deviation from some standard, and (5) specific, desired performance, or any combination of these.

Example A

Objective: Given a map of New Jersey, the student will plot the natural and human-made boundaries, the capital and major cities.

Conditions	Action	Criteria
An outline map of New Jersey with water and human-made boundaries marked; and three dots, one in position of Trenton, one Newark, and one Atlantic City.	a. Label each body of water and human-made boundary that separates New Jersey from its neighbors. b. Each of these dots represents a city. Label each by name and indicate which is the capital.	Correct labeling of Delaware River, Delaware Bay, Arthur Kill, Upper New York Bay, Hudson River, and human-made boundary with New York State. Cities labeled correctly and Trenton marked as capital.

Example B

> *Objective:* Given a pair of numbers, the student will list their common factors and choose the greatest common factor.

Conditions	Action	Criteria
Two numbers between 2 and 100 that have no fewer than two and no more than four common factors other than one, for example, 24 and 8.	a. State all common factors. b. State the greatest common factor.	For example, states all common factors, 8, 4, and 2; designates largest, 8.

Example C

> *Objective:* Given a copy of a personal letter that has commas omitted, the student will demonstrate proper placement of all necessary commas.

Conditions	Action	Criteria
Personal letter of three or four paragraphs, including a heading, salutation, and closing. The body of the letter will contain compound sentences, introductory adverbial clauses, words in series, and at least one appositive.	Write in all necessary commas and no unnecessary ones.	Places commas in heading, after salutation and closing. Uses a comma to separate the two parts of a compound sentence, after the adverbial clause, before the word connecting the last two elements in a series of three or more, and to set off an appositive.

Example D

> *Objective:* Given the equipment and directions, the student will set up the equipment and conduct an electrical experiment in accordance with the instructions.

Conditions	Action	Criteria
All equipment and directions to do an unfamiliar experiment in electricity, for example, wiring a circuit to light a bulb. (Note, however, that the student should be familiar with the equipment and its use.)	Carry out the experiment in accordance with the directions to produce the results called for.	All equipment is used properly (safely and as called for in the directions). All procedures that are called for are followed. Experiment produces desired result, the bulb lights.

Writing specifications is an important step because it insures that the item will measure the objective and that the range of conditions suitable for the objective will not be exceeded. In preparing the specifications, do not repeat the wording of the objective; the point is to increase the level of detail preparatory to writing the items. At the same time, specifications should be broad enough to cover two items unless (as in Example A) one item would exhaust all possibilities. The final step is, of course, writing the items themselves and entering them on the back of the index card.

You now realize that you cannot just sit down and write test items "off the top of your head," so to speak. You must first identify or state the objectives that you want your test to measure and then organize these objectives into a content outline. It will also be useful to determine which objectives call for the demonstration of knowledge acquisition and comprehension and which call for the demonstration of higher cognitive processes. Finally, the items you write will be more likely to fit your objectives if you first prepare test-item specifications.

Objectives and test-item specifications are to the construction of a test what a blueprint is to the construction of a house. Now that you have your test "blueprint," you are ready to build a test that has a good chance of accomplishing the purposes for which you intend it. The next step is to learn the rules about writing the items themselves.

Proficiency Test

1. Listed on the left are three map-reading test items. Match each one with the shorthand form of the map-reading objective on the right that it measures. *

    a. To go from the post office   i. Use a given material to create

---
* These items and objectives were adapted from *Social Science (Geography) K–9*, distributed by the Instructional Objectives Exchange.

to the school (as shown on a map) would you go north then west or north then east?

b. On this map of the schoolroom, point out the fire alarm, piano, and chalkboard.

c. With a set of blocks, construct a model of the street on which your school is located and then position your school on it.

a representation of a specified area.

ii. Identify map symbols on an outline map.

iii. Use geographical directions to designate the route between given locations on a map.

iv. Identify objects that correspond to symbols on a map.

2. If you had the objective: *Describe the balance of power between the three branches of the United States government,* which one of the following items would best measure it?

a. The legislative power of the government is constituted in the _____.

b. Construct a chart that illustrates the balance of power.

c. What does the term *balance of power* mean and how is it carried out within the United States government?

d. In the United States system of balance of power, the judicial function is carried out by the Supreme Court.

TRUE   FALSE

3. For which one of the following areas is it possible to prepare test items with answers that are completely right or wrong?

a. values
b. higher cognitive processes
c. knowledge acquisition and comprehension
d. creative processes

4. a. In the classroom, tests are most often used to measure the area of higher cognitive processes.

TRUE   FALSE

b. To score an answer to an item that measures evaluation, the teacher needs access to the logic behind the answer.

TRUE   FALSE

5. Into which one of the areas (knowledge acquisition, comprehension, application, analysis, synthesis, or evaluation) would the test items a, b, and c in number 1 above be best classified?

6. Write an objective in shorthand form for the goal, to know who the United States senators are from your state.

7. Write a shorthand version of the following objective: *Given a familiar melody, the student will create an accompaniment for the melody, such accompaniment having the quality and mood of the melody, using the appropriate instruments.*

8. Given the shorthand form objective, *change a flat tire on a car*, prepare a content outline with at least three tasks.
9. Given the shorthand form objective, *define, describe, and compare facism and democracy*, prepare a content outline with at least three tasks.
10. Given the shorthand form objective, *add fractions with the same denominator*, prepare a table of test-item specifications.

4

Short-answer Items to Measure Knowledge and Comprehension

OBJECTIVES

- Identify six types of short-answer items: unstructured, completion, true–false, other two-choice, multiple choice, and matching.
- Identify and state rules and recommendations associated with the construction of each of the six item types.
- Construct sample items for a given objective using each of the six item types in accordance with the rules and recommendations.
- Distinguish between the different characteristics or features of the six item types and the testing situations in which each of the item types is best used.

TYPES OF SHORT-ANSWER ITEMS

This chapter deals with the measurement of knowledge acquisition and comprehension—areas of primary interest to the classroom teacher. The teacher typically monitors, by means of tests, the extent to which knowledge and the understanding of that knowledge have been transmitted to students. The majority (but not all) of a teacher's objectives probably fall into this area and thus it becomes an important area for testing. Such testing enables the teacher to evaluate students' learning progress, diagnose their weaknesses, and get some idea of the effectiveness of the instruction.

We will assume at this point that the teacher has completed the first three steps in test construction; that is, he or she has (1) specified the goals, (2) put them in the form of a content outline, and (3) written them as expanded objectives in the form of test-item specifications. In originally specifying his or her goals, the teacher should also have decided which objectives required knowledge acquisition and comprehension, which required thinking and problem-solving, and which involved behavior change. In this and the subsequent two chapters, the construction of test items—the next step in the process—will be covered. This chapter, in dealing with knowledge acquisition and comprehension, will focus exclusively on short-answer items, which are the type of items most commonly used for the measurement of these processes.

Short-answer items have either free or fixed choices. There are basically two free choice formats. One is the unstructured format, the other the fill-in or completion format. Fixed choice formats include true–false, other two-choice, multiple choice, and matching. Both free choice and fixed choice items have previously determined correct responses. However, in the free choice type, the student is not given choices from which to select the correct response as he or she is in the fixed choice type. In this chapter each type of short-answer item will be described and illustrated and some guidelines for the construction of each will be offered.

Short-answer items typically ask students to identify, distinguish, state, or name something. Such items may also, particularly in math, ask them to demonstrate something. In the free choice format, the measurement basically involves asking students a question that requires that they *state* or *name* the specific information or knowledge called for (that is, *recall* it), indicating acquisition of that knowledge. In the fixed choice formats, the measurement basically involves giving students two or more alternative responses and asking them to *identify* the correct one or *distinguish* between correct and incorrect ones (that is, to *recognize* the correct response). The act of identifying can be taken as an indication that the students have acquired the particular piece of information or knowledge called for in the item.

Keep in mind that objectives that call for students to identify, distinguish, state, or name something—and hence demonstrate knowledge acquisition or comprehension—are most readily measured by means of one of the various types of short-answer item formats that will be described on the following pages.

UNSTRUCTURED FORMAT

The unstructured short-answer format utilizes a question that can be answered by a word, phrase, or number. Some examples are given below.

Examples

- Who was the seventeenth president of the United States?
- What gland of the body secretes the hormone ACTH?
- What phrase did Hamlet use to describe Yorick?
- Which state in the United States produces more copper ore than any other?
- $\frac{1}{8} + \frac{1}{4} - \frac{1}{16} =$
- Who wrote the poem, "Ode on a Grecian Urn"?

Pros and Cons. The most attractive features of the unstructured format are that (1) it minimizes the likelihood of guessing, (2) the student is not given clues as, for example, in a multiple choice item, (3) it represents a reasonably easy type of item to write (the test maker does not have to think of alternative answers to present), and (4) it can be accommodated quite easily to the kind of item where a map, figure, or graph is given and the student must answer questions such as, "What is the name of the part labeled A?"

Most notable of the undesirable aspects of this format has to do with scoring (that is, keying and correcting). Some unstructured items invite any number of answers, many of which may resemble the correct one to some degree. Consider the item, "What chemical is often added to drinking water to help prevent tooth decay?" Students may answer fluorine, fluoride, sodium fluoride, stannous fluoride, fluride, among others. In scoring, the teacher will have to decide what the student had in mind. Mind-reading adds a difficult dimension to item scoring.

The unstructured response format works best for the **measurement of specific knowledge,** most commonly in math, science, and history.

Writing the Item. In writing an unstructured response item, the first point to keep in mind is **to write the item so that the correct response will require the fewest words possible.** Reducing response possibilities, which obviously simplifies the task of scoring, is often facilitated by **keeping the item itself brief and to the point,** and of such nature that **one response and only one will suffice as the correct response.** Scoring is further aided by

---

Answers
Andrew Johnson, pituitary, a fellow of infinite jest, Arizona, $\frac{5}{16}$, Keats.

supplying students with an answer blank identified by numbers with the items.

The items themselves should be **written in the simplest language possible** so that the act of understanding the item does not become a task in itself. Consider the two examples below written for the objective: distinguish between a ratio scale and interval scale in terms of the unique zero point feature of the former.

- A ratio scale has a principal feature that distinguishes it from an interval scale. What is that feature? _____
- What does a ratio scale have that an interval scale does not have? _____

Though the answer to both items would be "a zero point" the second item is simpler and clearer than the first and more clearly illustrates one major characteristic of an unstructured response item, namely that it is **written in question form** rather than statement form.

COMPLETION FORMAT

The completion or fill-in item format is also a free choice format in that the students must construct their own response rather than choose from among given choices. It differs from the unstructured item by requiring that they fill in or complete a sentence from which a word or phrase has been omitted.

Examples

- The man who discovered Florida while searching for the "fountain of youth" was _____.
- Boyle's Law states that pressure of a gas multiplied by its _____ is equal to a constant.
- "Give me liberty or give me _____" was the pronouncement of a famous American revolutionary.
- Among the hormones secreted by the pituitary gland, two are _____ and _____.
- A fixed zero point is the characteristic that distinguishes a _____ from an interval scale.
- _____ produces more copper ore than any other state in the Union.

Pros and Cons.   The completion format has many of the same advantages and disadvantages as the unstructured response format while being somewhat more difficult to write. Because the item must give sufficient clues so as not to be ambiguous but not so many as to be unchallenging, the wording of completion items is particularly critical. Completion items when

---

Answers
Ponce de Leon; volume; death; ACTH, pitocin, vasopressin, TSH; ratio; Arizona.

properly written are easier to score than unstructured ones but they do have the disadvantage of being quite constrained by their own grammar. However, by requiring that the students formulate their own answers, this type of item poses a challenge for them. Completion and unstructured items can both be included in the same test to offer the student a change of pace in situations where specific fact learning is to be tested.

Writing the Item. In writing completion items, the key is **to strike a balance between leaving out so much that the item becomes ambiguous and leaving out so little** (or otherwise providing so many clues) **that the item becomes too easy.** Consider the three examples below.

- The evolutionary theory of _____ is based on the principle that _____.
- The evolutionary theory of _____ is based on the principle that the fittest will survive.
- The evolutionary theory of Darwin is based on the principle that the _____ will survive.

The first example suggests a variety of answers. There the answer will depend on which theorist the student chooses for the first blank, thus making the item indefinite by inviting a wide range of possible responses. The third illustration provides a very strong clue; students are likely to remember the phrase *survival of the fittest* and quickly realize that the word *fittest* should be applied. The second item is best. Completion items should be used to measure simple factual recall and not to measure more complex thinking processes.

To write items that have neither too many nor too few clues, you should **try to avoid instances where the grammar of the sentence helps determine the answer.** Grammar is most often a problem with respect to the plural number and to the indefinite article (a, an).

- A subatomic particle having a negative unit charge and negligible mass is an _____.
- A subatomic particle having a negative unit charge and negligible mass is a (an) _____.

By using *a (an)* the second illustration avoids indicating to the student that the answer, *electron*, begins with a vowel.

The length of the blank space in a completion item also should not provide a clue to the length of the correct response. **Blanks of uniform length should be provided throughout the test.**

As a final point, **completion items should have a single correct answer, preferably a word or short phrase.** Those items that prompt students to give a range of responses are much more difficult to score than those that tend to elicit the same correct response from many students. It may be helpful to write an item originally as an unstructured item and then rewrite it as a completion item. Remember that completion items are only useful in measuring the acquisition of specific knowledge. Consider the following examples.

- Ebbinghaus, an Austrian psychologist, did experiments on human _____.
- Ebbinghaus, an Austrian psychologist, did experiments to discover the conditions under which human beings would _____ best.

Although both illustrations are aimed at eliciting the same general answer (in the first case, *memory*, and in the second, *remember*), a student might be tempted to write the word *beings* in answer to the first, an answer that would have to be considered acceptable. For either illustration, *learning* or *learn* might be chosen as answers but could legitimately be considered incorrect.

If you are having difficulty writing a completion item, consider the following two suggestions. The first is to include only a single blank in any item, thus avoiding the ambiguity that may occur with multiple completions. The second is to consider offering from two to four response choices— in effect making the item multiple choice. Consider the following:

- That branch of government charged with making the laws is the _____. (executive, legislative, judicial)
- Argon, neon, and xenon have something in common. They are all considered _____. (radiant metals, biological vapors, inert gases, rare earths)
- Boyle's Law states that the pressure of a gas multiplied by its _____ (volume, temperature, weight) is equal to a constant.

Substituting multiple choice items for completion items represents a reasonably effective strategy for limiting the ambiguity and scoring difficulty that often accompany completion items.

TRUE-FALSE (YES-NO) FORMAT

Some short-answer items provide two response choices. This differs from the unstructured or completion modes, which provide no response choice, and the multiple choice type, which provides three or more response choices. These two-choice items often include the options true-false or yes-no.

Examples

■ Australia, the island continent, was discovered by Columbus.	TRUE	FALSE
■ Most Australians live along the east coast of Australia.	TRUE	FALSE
■ Much of Australia is a cold desert.	TRUE	FALSE
■ Wheat is imported by Australia.	TRUE	FALSE
■ Sydney is the capital of Australia.	TRUE	FALSE
■ Uranium and bauxite have been found in Australia.	TRUE	FALSE

Answers
Legislative; inert gases; volume.

- Below is a list of plural animal words. Circle Yes for those that have
been done properly and No for those that have been done improperly.

oxes	YES	NO
deer	YES	NO
mouses	YES	NO
bear	YES	NO
monkeys	YES	NO

Pros and Cons.　One big advantage of true-false items is the fact that
they are perhaps the easiest type of item to write and can be answered quickly
by students. Their easiness to write is due to their simplicity—just a single
statement that is either accurate or inaccurate. Their easiness to answer is
due to the fact that the student need only read the statement and circle
true or false. But what about the false statements? Are we teaching students
information that is false by having them read these items? Another difficulty
is the significant amount of ambiguity that may be contained in these items.

- When a plane crashes exactly on the Cana-　　　　TRUE　FALSE
dian-American border, half of the survivors
are buried in each country.

How many of you read that item and answered it without realizing that it
contained the word *survivors,* and survivors are characteristically not buried.
Thus, the correct answer is *false.* Or,

- Early in his career, Will Rogers said, "I never　　　TRUE　FALSE
met a man I didn't like."

Did Will Rogers make that statement or did someone else? Was it exactly
what was said or has the statement been altered? If Will Rogers did say it,
did he say it early in his career? Here are three questions in one causing
ambiguity about what the student has or has not learned. Thus, although
true-false items are easy to write and quick to take, they may be ambiguous.

True-false items are best used for measuring the recognition of fact. Free
choice items deal with facts also but require the student to *recall* them. In
the true-false item the fact is given to the student in either accurate or
inaccurate form and he or she need only *recognize* it. True-false items are
considered to work well in the measurement of objectives that call for discrimination between absolutes, requiring the student to distinguish or discriminate between statements of correct and incorrect fact or interpretation.

Finally, there is the matter of guessing—perhaps the biggest weakness
in true-false items. When students guess, they have a fifty-fifty chance of
being right. Given all the clues in the item, they may be able to improve

Answers
F, T, F, F, F, T, N, Y, N, N, Y.

those odds. The purpose of a test is to measure what students are capable of, not how lucky they are. The large element of luck can usually only be controlled by using a great many items. Keep in mind, then, that good guessing can account for a considerable number of points on a true-false test, particularly for the brighter students whose adept use of clues leads them to make "educated guesses."[1]

Writing the Item. In writing true-false items be careful neither to give too many clues nor to build in tricks. One useful rule is to **avoid the use of absolute terms like "always" and "never."** First of all, absolute facts are hard to find, and secondly, you may fall into the habit of using absolutes to make items false—a habit students may come to recognize. Learn not to telegraph your intentions as does the fighter who touches his nose before throwing a punch or the pitcher who turns his glove before throwing a curve.

- The market value of gold always exceeds the market value of silver.   TRUE   FALSE
- The market value of gold exceeds the market value of silver.   TRUE   FALSE
- Today, the market value of gold exceeds the market value of silver.   TRUE   FALSE

The first illustration is too broad and sweeping while the second is ambiguous—not telling the time to which it refers. The third illustration is the most accurate of the three as a true statement because of its specificity. The first and second would not be recommended as either true or false items. The suitable false item then might be:

- Today, the market value of silver exceeds the market value of gold.   TRUE   FALSE

A helpful practice in writing true-false items is to **write only true items and then afterward turn about half of them around to make false items.** This system guarantees the items a certain degree of uniformity of form and structure and also produces a test on which half of the items are true and half are false (thus minimizing the effect of guessing). In turning items around, it is better to do so as in the above examples (that is, switching *gold* and *silver* to say that the "market value of silver exceeds gold") than by adding the word *not* (for example, "the market value of gold does not exceed the market value of silver"). Adding *not* does turn an item around (that is, switch it from a true to a false) but often also adds either a clue or an ambiguity.

---

[1]Such guesses can be a reflection of "test-wiseness" and not of knowledge in the specific area.

Also, **the items should be placed in a random order** with respect to one another[2] to avoid response patterns that serve as strong guessing clues.

To construct the test as clearly and unambiguously as possible **include only a single major point in each item,** that point being the relationship between two facts, and write the item so that it is the truth or falsity of that relationship that the student must judge. For example:

- Maid Marion, Little John, and Brother Tuck   TRUE   FALSE
  are all characters in *Robin Hood,*

is a bad item because its truth or falsity is not based on the relationship between characters and book but on the replacement of *Friar Tuck* with *Brother Tuck.* It would have been fairer to say

- Maid Marion, Little John, and Friar Tuck   TRUE   FALSE
  are all characters in *Ivanhoe,*

in which case it would have been the relationship between characters and book that was false.

An important basis for structuring an item is the objective that is being measured. If the objective were "to distinguish between the petal and the sepal of a flower," in terms of the former being part of the corolla, and the latter being part of the calyx, the following item might be written:

- The petals of a flower are parts of the flower's   TRUE   FALSE
  calyx.

TWO-CHOICE CLASSIFICATION FORMAT

There are a variety of two-choice formats other than true-false and yes-no. In most cases, these formats ask the student to apply classification to a set of stimuli, as shown in the examples below.

Examples

- Underline the words that could be used as verbs and draw a line through ones that could not.
  - a. eat   c. wrist   e. flew   g. myself
  - b. cat   d. knit   f. helps   h. were
- Use *a* or *an* before each word:
  - _____oak   _____hour
  - _____ear   _____mountain

---

[2]A table of random numbers such as appears in Tuckman (1987) is recommended for this purpose. Number your items in the order they are written; then choose a column in the table of random numbers and reorder the items. The resulting order will be suitably random.

_____uniform   _____orange
_____umbrella   _____letter
■ Teddy hasn't got (any/no) money.

Pros and Cons.   Two-choice formats such as those illustrated above provide teachers with an opportunity to use ingenuity in fitting test items to their specific needs, and also add a little variation to a test. These formats are less pat than the true-false format and may require less forcing and artificiality than multiple choices (meaning three or more choices). Moreover, the task of classification can normally be cast into at least two categories—the presence of a quality versus its absence. Thus, we have a European country versus a non-European country, gas versus a nongas, and so on. As you add classification categories, your item becomes a multiple choice item and eventually a matching item. However, the contrast between that which fits into a category and that which does not calls for the two-choice format.

■ Below are the names of eight cities in the United States. Mark a
check next to each city that is a state capital.
   a. Atlanta   e. Lansing
   b. Birmingham   f. Madison
   c. Chicago   g. New York
   d. Denver   h. Pittsburgh

Thus, a two-choice format most conveniently fits the task of a one-variable, two-level, classification.

As with all the other short-answer formats, the limitations of the two-choice format must be recognized. It works best for factual knowledge, is susceptible to guessing, and is invalidated by ambiguous items. However, it is easier to avoid ambiguity with this format than with the ones described thus far, and the guessing problem is often less severe since the students must react to stimuli presented in a series.

Writing the Item.   Remember that the two-choice format works well in a classification situation. **Make sure that the category to be used is clear and distinct from other potentially confusable categories.** Also, **make the stimuli to be classified clear instances or noninstances of that category.** Clarity is clearly illustrated in a field such as mathematics.

■ Circle those numbers that are prime.
   4, 5, 6, 7, 8, 9, 10, 11, 12

Answers
Underline a, d, e, f, h; all *an* except uniform, mountain, and letter; any; check a, d, e, f.

Ambiguity can arise when dealing in situations where right and wrong are more relative.

- Which of the following can be considered causes of the War between the States?

slavery	farm economics
states' rights	industrial vs. agrarian interests
personal conflicts	foreign interference

Some of the stimuli above are vague in their meaning (personal conflicts for example) while others seem to overlap. This criticism is not meant to suggest that the two-choice format should not be used in potentially confusing areas but that care must be taken to make each stimulus clear and understandable in its own right.

Those stimuli or instances that fit the given category are called *exemplars* of that category while those that do not fit are called *nonexemplars*. **There is no need to have the same number of exemplars as nonexemplars.** In fact, the numbers of each should vary each time the format is used to avoid giving an extra clue. Moreover, the order of each should be as random as possible so that each may fall at any point in the order and no pattern emerges.

It is often easiest to write an item of this type by **identifying the classification category first and then thinking of exemplars and nonexemplars.** For example, if your instructional objective deals with identifying ductless glands in the body, then *ductless glands* becomes the classification category. It becomes the explicit basis for choosing a stimulus as an exemplar or nonexemplar. Obviously, correct choices or exemplars would be the various ductless glands, such as the pituitary, thyroid, adrenal cortex, gonads, and so on. Then decide what category you want students to distinguish ductless glands from. Is this nonglands or duct glands or both? This decision will form the basis for the choice of nonexemplars. The item might come out as follows:

- Circle those parts of the body that are ductless glands.

pituitary	thyroid	kidney
thymus	parathyroid	adrenal cortex
liver	spleen	lymph nodes

Finally, item difficulty can be manipulated by the range of the nonexemplars based on the objective you are trying to measure. Remember that the exemplars or correct choices fit the given category, for instance *ductless glands* in the above example. The alternative to the given category can itself be a given specific category or can simply be the absence of a given category

---

Answers
5, 7, 11; all are correct except the last.

(depending on your objective). Thus, ductless glands can be contrasted with glands having ducts or with any part of the body that is not a ductless gland (glands vs. nonglands). When the categories are broader, the list of nonexemplars will also be broader and hence more difficult to deal with. Consider the following two examples.

- Which of the following are nineteenth century poets?

Keats	Hemingway
Frost	de Maupassant
Stevens	Wordsworth

- Which of the following are nineteenth century poets?

Keats	Whitman
Frost	Baudelaire
Stevens	Wordsworth

In the second example the stimuli have been limited to poets. The student must therefore only distinguish between nineteenth century poets and twentieth century poets. In the first example he or she must also distinguish between poets and nonpoets (novelists and short story writers). **Choices for categories and nonexemplars should be based on the distinctions that you are trying to teach students to make** (which in turn should be reflected in your objectives).

The two-choice format can be a useful and stimulating means of measuring knowledge acquisition. It challenges teachers to be reasonably creative in item writing (particularly in choosing nonexemplars) and particularly demands that teachers be aware of what they are trying to measure (that is, the objective).

MULTIPLE CHOICE FORMAT

Perhaps the most commonly used short-answer format is the multiple choice, although its ubiquity is probably more true in published than in teacher-built tests. A multiple choice item typically offers from three to five alternative answers of which one is correct; the rest are incorrect choices.[3]

Examples

- John, shy as he was of girls, still managed to marry one of the most desirable of them.

---

[3] These incorrect choices are sometimes called distractors.

Answers
Pituitary, thymus, thyroid, parathyroid, adrenal cortex; Keats, Baudelaire, Wordsworth.

Directions: Substitute *John's shyness* for *John, shy* and then rewrite the sentence, keeping its original meaning. Your correct rewritten sentence might contain which of the following?

    a. him being married to
    b. himself married to
    c. him from marrying
    d. was himself married to
    e. him to have married

- Which of the graphs could represent the velocity–time relationship of a box containing a weighted disk fastened solidly to it that is set in motion on a horizontal plane with no external friction between it and the plane?

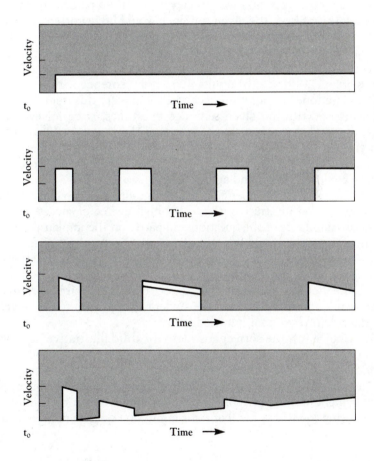

    e. None of the above.

- "In a flash it came upon me that *there* was the reason for advancing poverty with advancing wealth. With the growth of population, land grows in value, and the men who work it must pay more for the privilege. In allowing one man to own the land on which and from which other men live, we have made them his bondsmen in a degree which increases as material progress goes on. This is the subtle alchemy that in ways they do not realize is extracting from the masses in every civilized country the fruits of their weary toil."

The person most likely to have written these words is[4]
   a. John Jacob Astor
   b. William Jennings Bryan
   c. Thorstein Veblen
   d. Lincoln Steffens
   e. Henry George

Pros and Cons.   The correct answer to the first illustrative item, choice (c) (*him from marrying*) was chosen by about 60 percent of the test group. Using this phrase, the given sentence would be rewritten as follows: *John's shyness with girls did not prevent him from marrying one of the most desirable of them.* Choice (a) would result in a sentence that was grammatically incorrect. Choices (d) and (e) result in sentences that change the meaning of the original. Choice (b) results in a wordy sentence with a somewhat inappropriate tone. In order to successfully complete this item, a student would have to rewrite the given sentence five times, once for each alternative phrase, and then compare them to find the best one. Obviously, such an activity requires more than mere retention of facts; comprehension is clearly elicited. **Well-constructed multiple choice items have the potential to measure comprehension and application.**

Almost all the students in the test group gave the correct answer, (a), to the second illustrative item. This high degree of success is based partly on the simplicity of the question and partly on the implausibility of most of the choices, particularly (c) and (d). A shortcoming of multiple choice questions as used in achievement tests is that **the correct answer can sometimes be determined without any prior knowledge or instruction**—possibly because there are too many clues or too many implausible options or because an item tests the aptitude of the student to deal with it as a novel situation rather than testing for knowledge.

Choice (e), the correct answer to the third illustrative item, was chosen by only about a quarter of the test group, probably because the correct source of the given quote is the most unfamiliar person of the five given. However, **a certain degree of success on multiple choice items can be obtained through guessing.** Guessing can sometimes be minimized by a built-in penalty, such as scoring the test as number right minus one-quarter number wrong (when

---

[4]This and the preceding illustrative item are from *Multiple-choice Questions: A Close Look* (copyright © 1963 by Educational Testing Service. All rights reserved. Reproduced by permission).

Answers
c, a, e.

you have five answer choices and *four* are wrong) so that wrong answers lose points while omitted items do not.

Multiple choice items are unquestionably **easier to score and easier to analyze** in terms of patterns of incorrect responses[5]—which has undoubtedly reinforced their commercial use—than are other forms of objective items. They are, however, difficult items to write because **they demand plausible response options,** and **they usually require some preliminary testing, analysis, and refinement** in order to sharpen the contrast between the correct answer and incorrect choices. Both of these requirements have tended to limit their use by teachers, and, unfortunately when teachers have used them, the items often have not undergone the kind of scrutiny and refinement required for maximum effectiveness.

Writing the Item.   Perhaps the most critical part of the construction of a multiple choice item is the selection of the response alternatives—the correct answer and the incorrect choices. The difference in difficulty between writing any other type of objective item and writing a multiple choice item is the selection of incorrect choices. These wrong answers must be plausible to someone who does not know the answer, yet distinctly different from the correct answer. They should tap the kinds of errors that students are likely to make if they have incorrect knowledge or faulty comprehension. Obviously such care in writing items is a tall order. Item analysis, as will be illustrated in a subsequent chapter, can help considerably and the process can also be facilitated by keeping in mind the suggestions offered below.

1. **Consider the kinds of mistakes a student is likely to make and use them as a basis for writing the incorrect response choices.**

Not only should incorrect choices separate correct performance from incorrect performance, they should also help diagnose the kinds of incorrect notions that students have acquired. Wrong answers or distractors that tap common errors best accomplish these purposes; those that students never choose are useless and simply serve to reduce the number of effective or working response choices provided. For example

- The lowest common denominator of $\frac{1}{2}$, $\frac{1}{4}$, and $\frac{1}{6}$ is

  good   a. 6   **poor**   a. 4
  b. 24   b. 5
  c. 12   c. 12
  d. 8   d. 2

The choices to the left are better because all four choices represent a common denominator for at least two of the fractions, and two choices represent

---

[5] Analyzing patterns of incorrect responses as a way of understanding the nature of students' difficulty can only be done if the response choices are initially constructed to provide for this feature.

a common denominator for all three. The wrong choices on the right are too obviously wrong. (The correct choice is c.)

2. Construct incorrect choices that are, in fact, incorrect.

It is equally undesirable for all or nearly all students to select a particular wrong answer as it is for no one to choose it. If an incorrect choice is over-chosen that means it is probably too close to being correct itself or that the entire item or one or more answer/choices are ambiguous. When this occurs, either the particular incorrect choice or the whole item must be rewritten. Consider the following examples.

poor ▪ *Twenty Thousand Leagues under the Sea* is considered to be
      a. an adventure story.
      b. a science-fiction story.
      c. an historical novel.
      d. an autobiography.

better ▪ *Twenty Thousand Leagues under the Sea* is considered to be
      a. an adventure story.
      b. a tragedy.
      c. an historical novel.
      d. an autobiography.

In the "poor" example, while (a) is the correct answer, (b) might also be considered accurate by modern-day students. In the "better" example, choice (b) is changed to *a tragedy*.

3. Construct incorrect answers that are comparable in length, com-plexity, and grammatical form to the correct answer.

It is important to avoid giving clues in the construction of response alter-natives. The purpose of an item is to measure what a student knows and understands and not how clever a test taker he or she is. Some students have a tendency to choose the longer, more complex, or grammatically different form as the correct one. Equally long and complex alternatives of comparable structure neutralize this tendency. Consider the examples below.

poor ▪ When we say that a court possesses appellate jurisdiction
      we mean that it
      a. must have a jury.
      b. has the power or authority to review and decide
         appeals.
      c. can conduct the original trial.
      d. can declare laws unconstitutional.

better ▪ When we say that a court possesses appellate jurisdiction,
      we mean that it
      a. must have a jury.

    b. can review the decisions of other courts.
    c. can conduct the original trial.
    d. can declare laws unconstitutional.

Choice (b), the correct one, is longer and more complex than the other choices in the first example and also contains the word *appeals* that can be connected with the word *appellate* in the question. These clues have been eliminated in the second example.

    4. **Write the questions and choices in language that your students can understand.**

Construct a reading test only if that is your purpose. Do not introduce the various forms of bias described in Chapter Seven by writing items that measure general intelligence, test-wiseness, reading comprehension, or knowledge based on a selective interest. Consider the examples below.

poor   ■ Which of the following is a statement of the Yerkes-Dodson Law?
        a. The rate of acquisition of habit strength is a nonlinear decreasing function of delay of reinforcement.
        b. The relation between intensity of noxious stimulation and acquisition of habit strength is U-shaped.
        c. The relation between stimulus intensity and maximum mean physiologic response is positive and linear.
        d. The response extinction rate is more rapid following ratio scheduling than following interval scheduling.

better   ■ Which of the following is a statement of the Yerkes-Dodson Law?
        a. Learning occurs more slowly when rewards are delayed than when they are immediate.
        b. Learning is greatest when pain or stress is intermediate rather than absent or intense.
        c. The more intense a stimulus, the greater the bodily response.
        d. Forgetting or unlearning occurs more quickly when previous rewards have occurred regularly rather than intermittently.

In both examples (b) is the correct answer, but in the first the excessive use of complex jargon clouds the purpose of the item. Good measurement is not pedantic. Its purpose is to measure objectives of instruction rather than vocabulary.

    5. **State your items so that there can be only one interpretation of their meaning.**

It is important to be specific, as the examples below illustrate.[6]

poor   ■ The shortest day of the year is in
   a. March.
   b. June.
   c. September.
   d. December.

better   ■ The shortest day of the year in the Northern Hemisphere is in
   a. March.
   b. June.
   c. September.
   d. December.

By indicating Northern Hemisphere, the second question quite clearly requires (d) as the correct response.

6.   **In constructing response choices, avoid the use of such words as "always," "never," and "all" whenever possible.**

The above kind of extreme words are *specific determiners.* Their use often increases the likelihood of correct guessing by disqualifying an otherwise plausible choice. Test-wise students in particular have learned that things rarely occur either *always* or *never* and that many test builders are using these words to try to throw them off the track. In fact, their use serves as a clue to avoid choices that contain them.

poor   ■ The theme of Wordsworth's poem, "Composed upon Westminster Bridge," is
   a. a city is always most beautiful in the morning.
   b. the countryside is more beautiful than the city.
   c. the city shares in the natural beauty of all created things.
   d. the city is never an attractive sight.
   e. all the people of the city believe in its natural beauty.

better   ■ The theme of Wordsworth's poem, "Composed upon Westminster Bridge," is
   a. a city is more beautiful in the morning than at night.
   b. the countryside is more beautiful than the city.
   c. the city shares in the natural beauty of created things.
   d. the city is not an attractive sight.
   e. the people of the city believe in its natural beauty.

The presence of *always, all,* and *never* in a distractor often serves to make the choice obviously wrong, thereby reducing its value as a plausible dis-

---

[6]Taken from *Making the Classroom Test. A Guide for Teachers* (copyright © 1959 by Educational Testing Service. All rights reserved. Reproduced by permission).

tractor. In the "better" example, these words have been eliminated from both the distractors and from (c), the correct response.

7. **Do not provide extra clues to the correct answer within the item statement itself.**

The items below illustrate this point.

poor
■ The Missouri city most often referred to as the "Gateway to the West" is
   a. Topeka.
   b. Kansas City.
   c. Chicago.
   d. St. Louis.
   e. Des Moines.

better
■ The city most often referred to as the "Gateway to the West" is
   a. Topeka.
   b. Kansas City.
   c. Chicago.
   d. St. Louis.
   e. Des Moines.

The poor example provides the clue—*a Missouri city*. In the better example, only the "Gateway" city, *St. Louis,* is asked about.

8. **Do not test more than one point in a single item (except as noted in point 9).**

If there are two points you want to test, use two items. Testing for multiple points in a single item makes an item confusing because the student does not know which point to answer.

poor
■ The principal value of a daily program of exercises is to
   a. eat less.
   b. develop musculature.
   c. increase intelligence.
   d. keep fit.
   e. use up extra time.

better
■ The principal value of a daily program of exercises is to
   a. eat less.
   b. develop musculature.
   c. increase intelligence.
   d. help make friends.
   e. use up extra time.

In the "poor" example, either (b) *develop musculature* or (d) *keep fit* can be considered the correct answer. Two acceptable answers make it impossible to key the item. The item is improved by replacing one of the acceptable choices, (d) *keep fit,* with a clearly unacceptable one, *help make friends.*

9. **However, multiple points can be made in a single item, where appropriate, by providing choices that specifically include two or more of the choices already given.**

The so-called multiple multiple choice item uses options such as "both a and b," "all of the above," "none of the above," "both b and c." The following is an example.

- ■ The principal value of a daily program of exercises is to
  a. maintain optimum weight.
  b. develop musculature.
  c. keep fit.
  d. improve self-image.
  e. all of the above.

Here, the correct answer, (e), includes all the other choices as well. There is no reason to avoid multiple or combination answers as long as they are clearly indicated, unambiguous, and where all or more than one choice is correct. However, 'the repeated use of combination answers as incorrect answers but not as correct answers (or vice versa) quickly leads the student to be clued in to their relevance or irrelevance.

10. **After the test items are written, vary the location of the correct choice (between the options a to d or e) on as random a basis as possible.**

It is only natural for test takers to seek whatever clues a test might offer. A response pattern is one such clue. They might note that (e) had not occurred in ten items and use that as a basis for guessing (e) on the eleventh item. By being as random as possible in choosing the location or letter designation of the correct choice, you render this kind of pattern studying a superstitious behavior.

11. **Be careful not to let one question on your test reveal the answer to another or depend on the answer of another.**

This is not an uncommon pitfall. To avoid it, read your test over, looking for instances of clues from one item to another. For example:

- ■ *Rien* means
  a. nothing.
  b. something.
  c. laughing.
  d. otherwise.
  e. then.

■ *Rien n'est parfait* means
   a. all's well that ends well.
   b. nothing is perfect.
   c. reading is fun.
   d. everything is lost.
   e. ice cream is good.

When a student sees two such questions on the same test, he or she can use one to figure out the answer to the other. In these examples, he or she could observe the word *rien* in each to get answers (a) and (b) respectively.

12. **Response alternatives should be short, unique from one another, and not specifically clued by the question.**

The "poor" example for item 3 concerning appellate courts illustrates a question cluing the correct response by means of the connection between the words *appeal* and *appellate*. The "better" example overcomes this deficiency by substituting *decisions* for *appeals*. Following is an example of answer choices that overlap in their degree of correctness.

poor   ■ An isosceles right triangle contains
                a. a pair of equal sides.
                b. three equal sides.
                c. a 90° angle.
                d. a pair of equal sides and a 90° angle.
                e. three equal sides and a 90° angle.

better   ■ To be labeled an isosceles right triangle, a triangle must contain
                a. a pair of equal sides.
                b. three equal sides.
                c. a 90° angle.
                d. a pair of equal sides and a 90° angle.
                e. three equal sides and a 90° angle.

In the "poor" example, (a), (c), and (d) are all correct. This overlap is eliminated by changing the question or stem. The use of the word *must* in the "better" example provides the specificity that enables the student to discriminate between partially correct (a and c) and completely correct (d) choices.

MATCHING FORMAT

Matching items require that the student deal with multiple questions or stems and multiple responses at the same time. Primarily this type of test is used to determine whether the student can distinguish between similar ideas or facts. Matching items are typically considered to be the most difficult type of short-answer item to construct.

Examples

- 1. was the "father of our country."
  2. was son of a president.
  3. was the first secretary of the treasury.
  4. killed a cabinet member in a duel.
  5. wrote the Declaration of Independence.
  6. chaired the Constitutional Convention.
  7. won the Battle of New Orleans.
  8. regretted having only one life to give his country.

  a. Aaron Burr
  b. Nathan Hale
  c. James Madison
  d. Andrew Jackson
  e. John Quincy Adams
  f. Alexander Hamilton
  g. George Washington
  h. James Monroe
  i. John Adams
  j. Thomas Jefferson

- 1. The argument
  2. The opposing argument
  3. The resolving argument

  a. synthesis
  b. prethesis
  c. thesis
  d. antithesis

Pros and Cons.   Matching items are fun to take because they are like puzzles, and the student has the task of putting the pieces together. They also **enable the teacher to cover a lot of ground in a single item.** In essence they are many items rolled up into one and therefore represent a certain degree of efficiency. A third big plus is that matching items **require students to distinguish or discriminate between things.**

Matching items also have shortcomings, principal among which is that **they are difficult and time-consuming to write well** because writing one matching "exercise" (as they might more appropriately be called than "items") is like writing a half a dozen of another type of short-answer item. They are also hard to write because all the "pieces" must fit together, yet each must be clearly distinguishable from every other. It may also be pointed out that matching exercises **cannot be used for eliciting all types of information.** There are certain situations, particularly those involving lists of potentially confusable things, where matching exercises work well and other situations, involving individual pieces of information, where they do not work as well. Finally, matching exercises **have a tendency to provide clues within the items themselves.** Like all puzzles, guides exist to help fit pieces together and every time a correct fit is made, fewer pieces remain and are, therefore, easier to fit. Students usually first match the stems and responses they know go together (assuming no option can be reused), thus immediately reducing the difficulty of the remaining matching tasks because the number of available responses has been reduced. Then, too, stems often contain clues as to the correct response (for example, the shortest response fitting the shortest stem). Effective writing of matching exercises can minimize these problems.

Answers
(1) g, (2) e, (3) f, (4) a, (5) j, (6) c, (7) d, (8) b; (1) c, (2) d, (3) a.

Writing the Item.   The first rule for writing a matching exercise is that **each item must deal with common elements of a single category** (all leaders; all parts of a flower). Because cluing is a principal area of difficulty in a matching exercise, the second rule for writing this type of exercise has to be **avoid cluing where possible.** (This, in fact, is a rule for writing any type of test item, particularly those where response options are given.) Some suggestions are **keep the responses short, make the responses distinct and nonoverlapping, and provide plausible incorrect responses that do not match with any stem.** These extra incorrect response choices will prevent answers from becoming obvious toward the end of the question.

Another very important suggestion is to **select stems and responses that focus on those things between which the student is required to distinguish.** Consider the examples below, in which students are asked to match items in the right-hand column with items in the left-hand column.

poor	■	1. ubiquitous	a. harmful
		2. enigmatic	b. equivalent to
		3. deleterious	c. widespread
		4. tantamount to	d. purposeful
			e. puzzling
better	■	1. prosthetic	a. predictive
		2. pathetic	b. itinerant
		3. prophetic	c. artificial
		4. peripatetic	d. abundant
			e. pitiable

In the "poor" example the stem words bear little relation to one another; hence, little or no discrimination is required. Secondly, stem 4 and response (b) are clued to one another by the additional word *to*. Finally, the one incorrect option is just a random choice and does not relate to the list other than by virtue of being an adjective. In the "better" example, the words all are potentially confusable (at least in appearance), which may affect their discriminability in meaning (since associations tend to become blurred in memory). No clues are inadvertently provided and the distractor is a synonym for *prolific*, another *look-alike* word to those provided.

In fairness to the student it is imperative that you **include all the necessary information within the matching exercise.** Matching exercises, by virtue of their size and complexity, can contain an entire situation with which a student must deal and can be used to measure sequencing, classifying, and analyzing. Consider the following example.[7]

---

[7]Taken from *Making the Classroom Test. A Guide for Teachers* (copyright © 1959 by Educational Testing Service. All rights reserved. Reproduced by permission).

Answers
To both exercises: (1) c, (2) e, (3) a, (4) b.

■ Read the statements below, carefully paying attention to their relation to one another. Then next to each statement mark a, b, c, or d, as indicated.

  a. If the statement contains the central idea around which most of the statements can be regrouped.
  b. If the statement contains a main supporting idea of the central idea.
  c. If the statement contains an illustrative fact or detailed statement related to a main supporting idea.
  d. If the statement contains an idea or ideas which are irrelevant.

  1. The Roman roads connected all parts of the Empire with Rome.
  2. The Roman roads were so well built that some of them remain today.
  3. One of the greatest achievements of the Romans was their extensive and durable system of roads.
  4. Wealthy travelers in Roman times used horse-drawn coaches.
  5. Along Roman roads caravans would bring to Rome luxuries from Alexandria and the East.
  6. In present-day Italy some of the roads are original Roman roads.

Responses should quite clearly relate to a particular stem. When matching items focus on facts, they are much more likely to satisfy this requirement than when they involve interpretation such as is the case in the preceding example; however while the recall of "hard facts" is less ambiguous, it is also less challenging than the more complex process of interpretation.

Matching exercises—like all objective items—**should not contain systematic response patterns.** Do not trust your own ability to scramble the order from one matching item to another. You are more systematic than you may think. Use a table of random numbers (as suggested earlier) or number slips in a hat or a pair of dice.

Finally, **do not mix stems and options in a matching question.** An option may fit many stems (George Washington in the first example on matching was many things besides the "father of our country," but the only person referred to as the "father of our country" was George Washington). Keep the stems on the left and the response options on the right with the stem normally being the longer and more specific of the two.

Generally in matching exercises, options (that is, responses) are used only once and that is a good strategy to follow *except* in those instances where you want to make an item particularly difficult or to elicit a pattern or classification (as in the preceding illustration).

The *don'ts* of item writing for each of the five formats are summarized in Figure 4-1.

Answers
(1) b, (2) b, (3) a, (4) d, (5) c, (6) c.

Figure 4-1
The *Don'ts* of Item Writing

FILL-IN ITEM

1. Don't leave out so much as to create ambiguity.
2. Don't leave out so little as to provide clues.
3. Don't let sentence grammar serve as a clue.
4. Don't let the length of the blank space serve as a clue.
5. Don't have more than one correct answer.
6. Don't require that the student write too much.
7. Don't have more than one blank per item.

TRUE-FALSE ITEM

1. Don't use absolute terms like *always* and *never*.
2. Don't write only trues or only falses.
3. Don't put all the trues or all the falses together.
4. Don't measure more than one idea per item.

TWO-CHOICE ITEM

1. Don't use potentially confusable classification categories.
2. Don't use stimuli to be classified that fit more than one of the categories.
3. Don't always use the same number of exemplars and nonexemplars.
4. Don't write the exemplars and nonexemplars until you have identified the classification category.
5. Don't choose categories or nonexemplars that do not fit the distinctions you are trying to teach your students.

MULTIPLE CHOICE ITEM

1. Don't choose *distractors* (that is, incorrect choices) that do not fit the kinds of mistakes students are likely to make.
2. Don't choose distractors that are actually correct or plausible answers.
3. Don't make distractors stand out from the correct answer either by length or grammar.
4. Don't use language your students won't understand.
5. Don't use statements that have multiple meanings.
6. Don't use absolute terms such as *always, never,* and *all.*
7. Don't build clues into the item statement.
8. Don't test more than one point per item.
9. Don't always assign the correct choice the same letter.
10. Don't let one item clue the answer to another.
11. Don't write long answer choices.
12. Don't write overlapping answer choices.

MATCHING ITEM

1. Don't include elements of more than one category.
2. Don't build clues into your response choice.

Figure 4-1 (continued)

3. Don't write long responses.
4. Don't write overlapping responses.
5. Don't write implausible responses.
6. Don't write responses that distinguish between points other than the one being measured by the item.
7. Don't write items that require information not contained within them.
8. Don't build in systematic response patterns.
9. Don't mix stems and options.

CHOOSING AMONG SHORT-ANSWER FORMATS

The six types of short-answer items are summarized on a comparative basis in Figure 4-2. While each has certain unique features that make it useful for specific testing needs, there are occasions when the types can be used interchangeably. In deciding which type of test to use consider item writing difficulty, item scoring difficulty, and specific measurement purposes (objectives). Tests that are used extensively or repeatedly generally utilize multiple choice questions because repeated use justifies their difficulty in preparation while their ease in scoring and wide range (to measure knowledge acquisition, comprehension, and occasionally more complex processes) clearly recommend them. They also lend themselves better to item analysis and hence can be refined and improved.

For the one-time/one-class test, unstructured and completion items might be recommended because of their ease of construction and because scoring may not be a major problem with a small group. These item types seem to work better with elementary school children who have not developed the test-taking sophistication of their older counterparts. For older students, these free choice item types may yield too great a range of responses. (Some teachers may prefer to avoid altogether the arguments that can ensue from scoring free choice items and thus use more structured formats with any age students.)

True-false items can be used under a wide range of circumstances as a substitute for either multiple choice or free choice items although good "false" items can be very difficult to write. This difficulty plus the great susceptibility of true-false items to guessing, makes them one of the less generally useful short-answer types.

Matching items are time consuming to score particularly on a large-scale basis. They are best used on an occasional basis for variation. In certain situations, however, matching items are the best format to measure recognition of knowledge or comprehension.

Other two-choice item types most readily measure the student's ability to classify and are quite useful in the same context as the free choice types. They lend themselves quite well to worksheets as a way of aiding students in learning classification tasks (within the instructional process). These points are summarized in Figure 4-2.

Figure 4-2
An Overview of Types of Short-answer Items

Type	Format	Sample Item	Difficulty in Writing	Difficulty in Scoring	Measure of	Recommended Use
Unstructured	Free Choice	What form of economic system is most often instituted in African and Asian countries following independence?	Easiest 6	Can be difficult	Recall of knowledge	One-time/ one-class testing
Completion (Fill-in)	Free Choice	The form of economic system most often instituted in African and Asian countries following independence is _____ .	5	Can be difficult	Recall of knowledge	One-time/ one-class testing
True-False (Yes-No)	Fixed Choice	The form of economic system most often instituted in African and Asian countries following independence is socialism. True False	3	Easy	Recognition of knowledge	Multi-group/ repeated testing
Other Two-choice	Fixed Choice	Circle those African and Asian countries that have introduced socialism upon achieving independence: India, Ghana, Zaïre, China, Somaliland, Libya, Djibouti	4	Easy for small groups but more difficult for larger ones	Classification of facts	One-time/ one-class testing
Multiple Choice	Fixed Choice	Upon achieving independence, the majority of Asian and African countries turned economically to a. capitalism. b. laissez-faire. c. socialism. d. mercantilism.	2	Easy	Recognition of knowledge or comprehension (or occasionally of higher levels)	Multi-group/ repeated testing

Figure 4-2 (continued)

| Matching | Fixed Choice | Match the countries to the economic systems.
1. Capitalism
2. Communism
3. Socialism
4. Isolationism
    a. South Africa
    b. Sri Lanka
    c. Ghana
    d. Madagascar | Most difficult
1 | Easy for small groups but more difficult for larger ones | Recognition of knowledge or comprehension | Change of pace |

Proficiency Test

1. a. In a free choice format, students are asked to _____
   (*state, identify, evaluate*) the correct response.
   b. In a fixed choice format, students are asked to _____
   (*state, identify, evaluate*) the correct response.
2. Match each item on the left with its type of item from the list on the right.

   a. The capital of Maine is
      1. Bangor.
      2. Portland.
      3. Augusta.
      4. Bath.

       i. other two-choice
       ii. unstructured
       iii. multiple choice
       iv. completion

   b. The capital of Maine is _____.
   c. What is the capital of Maine?
3. Which one of the following is *not* a recommendation to follow in writing multiple choice items?
   a. Vary the location of the correct choice.
   b. Make sure that incorrect choices are implausible.
   c. Avoid letting the item clue the correct choice.
   d. Make correct and incorrect choices about the same length.
   e. Make sure that incorrect choices are completely wrong.
4. Indicate whether each of the following statements is true or false.
   a. Completion items should have a single correct answer, preferably a word or short phrase.
   b. Answers to earlier items should help clue students to answers for succeeding items.
   c. In writing true-false items, one useful rule is to include absolute terms like *always* and *never*.
5. Given the objective, *name the first three presidents of the United States in the proper sequence,* write an unstructured, a completion, a true-false, an other two-choice, a multiple choice, and a matching item, to measure this objective.

6. Given the objective, *add two 1-digit numbers,* write one of each type of short-answer item to measure it.
7. Which one of the types of items listed below is the easiest to score?
   a. completion   d. unstructured
   b. matching   e. other two-choice
   c. true-false
8. Which one of the types of items listed below is most frequently used for repeated testings with large groups?
   a. multiple choice
   b. other two-choice
   c. completion
   d. matching
   e. unstructured

5

Essay-type Items to Measure Thinking Processes

OBJECTIVES

- Describe the meaning of four thinking processes, namely: application, analysis, synthesis, and evaluation.
- Identify the component parts of essay-type items written to measure each of the four thinking processes.
- Construct essay-type items to measure the student's ability to use each of the four thinking processes individually and in combination.
- Name and describe the criteria and procedures for reliably scoring an essay item response.

THE USE OF ESSAY-TYPE ITEMS

In the preceding chapter we focused on the use of short-answer items to measure knowledge acquisition and comprehension. However, we are often as concerned with the ability of students to *think about* and *use* what they know as we are with their simply knowing it. In these instances, types of items are needed that allow greater latitude in the form of the response; the response cannot be restricted to a word or phrase. **Essay items provide test takers with the opportunity to structure and compose their own responses within relatively broad limits.** Essay tests enable them to demonstrate their ability to apply knowledge and to analyze, to synthesize, and to evaluate new information in the light of their knowledge. Avoid using essay items when your *only* purpose is to have the students demonstrate that they have acquired certain knowledge.

The process of scoring essay tests is characteristically a more difficult one than the process of constructing the item, one reason being that the answer to the item will usually be many times longer than the item itself. Considerable space in this chapter will be devoted to the scoring of essay items.

Again, as in the preceding chapter, we will assume that objectives have already been prepared and a content outline developed and that you are ready to sit down and construct and subsequently score essay tests. Essay items will be subdivided, for presentation purposes only, into those that measure (1) application, (2) analysis, (3) synthesis, and (4) evaluation. (Note that the types of essay questions used for these four purposes are similar; the subdivision is primarily for organizational purposes.)

We will now consider procedures for constructing essay items that can be used for the four different purposes listed above.

ITEMS TO MEASURE APPLICATION

Application refers to the use of knowledge in the solution of problems. As set forth by Bloom (1956), application involves

> . . . the use of abstractions in particular and concrete situations. The abstractions may be in the form of general ideas, rules of procedures, or generalized methods. The abstractions may also be technical principles, ideas, and theories which must be remembered and applied. (p. 205)

Examples[1]

- You are in charge of planning meals and ordering food at a small summer camp. There are one hundred campers—boys aged twelve to fifteen years—and a staff of fifteen adults. You must be concerned both

---

[1]A number of examples in this chapter have been adapted with permission from the David McKay Company, Inc., from Bloom (1956).

with cost and nutritional value since these will be the criteria for judging your menus. Write out menus for five days of breakfasts, lunches, and suppers and explain why you made the choices you did.

■ When a geyser begins to erupt, hot water overflows at the orifice and this is followed by a rush of steam, mingled with hot water. Explain how the first overflow of hot water aids in the production of steam. Show how the principle of the geyser is used in the production of energy (that is, how it applies to one or more of the energy-producing techniques described in class).

■ You have just bought a thermometer to measure the temperature in your house and the strip of metal that contains the degree markings has been left off. How would you go about making a set of degree markings so that you could read the temperature using your thermometer? (Do not use more than one side of a page to write your answer.)

Writing the Item.   An essay item intended to measure application must require that the student use knowledge that has been acquired (probably in school) to describe a way of dealing with a concrete situation. Thus the first rule in the measurement of application is that **the item must present a concrete situation**—one that can somehow be included in the reality of the students being tested and one to which they can relate. The second rule in the measurement of application is that **the item must require that some action be taken or choice be made in the situation in order to accomplish a given task.** The third rule is that **the action or choice should be based on knowledge that has been transmitted.** (However, the specific problem itself that measures the application of previously acquired knowledge must be new and unfamiliar to the student.)

The relationship between the required solution and school-based knowledge may be a close one or one that is not so obvious. The likelihood that application will occur increases as the relationship between the task and what has been learned increases. **The teacher can increase the likelihood that application will occur by increasing the salience of the relationship between the knowledge and the task.** For example, the item might be, "To arrive at a solution, apply the knowledge you have gained in the unit on interest rates." Such a direct instruction establishes the degree of application of school knowledge as a criterion for evaluating performance and is likely to increase the degree of application. The salience of the relationship between acquired knowledge and the task solution can also be increased in more subtle ways within the problem statement itself—often by the inclusion of cue words. In the first example above the term *nutritional value* may provide a strong cue to the materials that formed the basis for the preceding weeks of instruction. Thus, application can be prompted by directly instructing the students to do it (that is, explicitly making it a performance criterion), or by cuing them toward it by the inclusion of terms dealt with in classwork.

Essay questions are not to be thought of as being entirely without structure. **The greater the clarity and detail provided, the more likely the item is to measure what you intend it to.** In the application item, clarity and detail must be sufficiently present in the two major parts—**the statement**

of the situation and **the statement of the problem** or choice—to enable all students to work within a common, understandable context. The less the detail, the greater is the required interpretation simply to understand what is required, a situation that produces a greater range of responses and makes scoring difficult.

In addition to the *situation* and *problem* parts, there is also a part of essay items to measure application called *response instructions*, which represents an attempt to structure responses to some degree. Response instructions include such things as minimum or maximum lengths, specific points to be covered or performances required, such as explaining a solution in addition to describing it or stating the number of suggested solutions required; and various *criteria* for evaluating performance such as organization of material, neatness, and spelling.

Very often in writing an essay item to measure application, one thinks first of the problem and then builds a situation around it. This approach is most common since our objectives usually contain problem statements. Typically, response instructions are added last. Suppose, for example, that your objective dealt with writing skills. First try to think of a practical demonstration of writing skills, for example, writing a letter to apply for a job. Now create the appropriate situation and compose the item.

- You are interested in a summer job and have learned of one as a camp counselor that interests you. Write a letter in proper form to the director of the camp describing yourself and why you want the job. You will be graded on the basis of how clear, interesting, and well-written your letter is, on its neatness, form, and spelling, and how convincing you are.

It is important to realize that measuring application is in a gray area between multiple choice items and essay items. To choose between the multiple choice format and essay format, consider the basic requirements of your objective.

ITEMS TO MEASURE ANALYSIS

According to Bloom (1956),

> Analysis emphasizes the breakdown of the material into its constituent parts and detection of the relationships of the parts and of the way they are organized. It may also be directed at the techniques and devices used to convey the meaning or to establish the conclusion of a communication. (p. 144)

Typically, analysis is undertaken to identify the elements or parts of concepts or objects, relationships between the parts, or organizational principles among the parts. Once these elements or principles have been identified through analysis, the same problem presented again will only require recall of facts. Thus, analysis requires the student to be accomplishing the process on the specific problem for the *first* time; accordingly, none of the sample essay questions below should have been discussed in class before the test.

Examples

- Galileo was interested in investigating the problem of acceleration of freely falling bodies but had no means of measuring the very short intervals of time over which acceleration occurred. Instead he studied the problem by rolling balls down very small planes inclined at increasing angles, and used the data to extrapolate for the case of free fall. Implicit in the extrapolation was a number of assumptions. Identify two, explain why they were necessary, and comment on their validity.
- Identify four reasons why Hamlet did not kill King Claudius until the end of the play despite his commitment to do so at the beginning. Describe how you determined what these reasons were.
- You have just seen a movie about the United Nations. What are some of the reasons that the U.N. was founded in the first place? Can you think of any other organization in your community that attempts to contribute to the betterment of humanity? What are some of its activities?
- You have just heard a story about a girl who was severely and unfairly punished. Describe some of the feelings that such punishment might have aroused in her. Can you think of times in your own life when you had these feelings? Describe one such time.

Writing the Item.   Similar to application items, **analysis items typically include a *situation* or *setting* and *response instructions.* Unlike application items, analysis items do not contain *problem* parts.** The situation is one with which the student presumably is familiar and that contains elements, relationships, or organizational principles which can be analyzed. Such items often ask the student to make comparisons and contrast, as seen in the example below.

- Consider the ways A. S. Neil and B. F. Skinner might teach a child to swim. In what ways would their techniques be different? In what ways the same? How can you tell?

As in the case of application items, the clearer and more detailed the description of the situation, the less the variability in response and the easier the scoring. Of course, detail can be carried to the point where so few different answers might result that it would be more like a free choice, short-answer item.

The response instructions in analysis items usually call for the student to *identify* certain elements, relationships, or organizational principles. However, the mere act of identifying or listing is basically short-answer performance of the type called for by unstructured or free choice items. To utilize the vehicle of the essay item, it is useful to ask the student to *describe* the basis by which the analysis was accomplished. Another invitation to expand upon an identification is to ask the student to *compare* or *contrast.* (This instruction may also yield evaluation or application. Since the distinction between essay item types in this chapter is made primarily for instructional purposes, there is no reason why multiple objectives and hence multiple thought processes cannot be measured by a single essay item. Most of the examples in this chapter are limited to single processes only for the sake of avoiding instructional confusion.)

Analysis items can be used very effectively in conjunction with students' intellectual, emotional, and aesthetic experiences and provide a basis for determining whether the student can analyze component ideas and feelings contained in and provoked by the experience. This ability to analyze or differentiate the component parts of an experience is an important prerequisite for producing unique thoughts and solutions and hence is worthy of measurement.

While Bloom suggests the use of multiple choice short-answer items for measuring analysis, the essay approach is recommended here for teachers who want to build their own tests. It is extremely difficult to write plausible distractors for multiple choice analysis items since to do this one must first analyze a situation thoroughly and know many of the pitfalls and cul-de-sacs of faulty thinking. Then, item testing must be done to check out one's choices of right and wrong answers. All of this preparation represents considerable impracticality for the working classroom teacher who will find the use of essay items in this instance an expedient despite the difficulty of scoring them. As was mentioned in the last chapter, the multiple choice item is the raw material for the often used test and is characteristically most effectively employed in published tests.[2]

ITEMS TO MEASURE SYNTHESIS

In describing synthesis, Bloom writes:

> Synthesis is here defined as the putting together of elements so as to form a whole. . . . This is the category in the cognitive domain which most clearly provides for creative behavior on the part of the learner. However, it should be emphasized that this is not completely free creative expression since generally the student is expected to work within the limits set by particular problems, materials, or some theoretical and methodological framework. (p. 162)

Bloom (1956) subdivides synthesis into the production of a unique communication (like a story), a plan or proposed set of operations (like a machine), and a set of abstract relations (like a theory).

Examples

- Add a second verse of four lines to the verse written as follows.

---

[2]However, for those cases where you prefer to use multiple choice exercises to measure analysis, it is recommended that you construct them as free choice items initially and use the incorrect responses to collect plausible distractors.

Men cannot swim
As fishes do
They only slave
A hard way through.

- Draw and describe a design for a mechanical lung. Label all parts in the drawing and explain how the mechanical lung would work and how it would be made.[3]
- Develop and describe a new plan for succession to the vice-presidency of the United States in the event the Vice-President leaves his or her position. Give the reasons behind your choice. (Do not simply describe the current constitutional procedures for vice-presidential succession.)
- Suppose you have been put in charge of raising money to build a clinic aimed at providing health services for the poor people in your community. Plan and describe a promotion campaign for soliciting donations.

Writing the Item.   Bloom (1956) warns us against limiting the creativity required in synthesis items by making instructions and situations too detailed.

> If the effort is to be rather creative, the student should also have considerable freedom of activity—freedom to determine his own purposes, freedom to determine the materials or other elements that go into the final product, and freedom to determine the specifications which the synthesis should meet. (p. 173)

As in items measuring application, items measuring synthesis present a problem to be solved. The difference lies in the fact that the application problem requires the direct use of knowledge already acquired while the synthesis problem requires that the students go beyond their existing knowledge to the creation of new and, if possible, unique thoughts and productions. (These new thoughts and productions based on the synthesis of learned information need not be new for society but they should be new for the students formulating them.) Thus, **the problem statement** in an essay item intended to measure synthesis **should be outside of the range of the familiar or the practical and require the production of a novel solution.** Writing a creative piece, formulating a theory, designing a novel piece of equipment, and proposing a new procedure are among the problem statements of synthesis items.

Moreover, **the particular problem itself must also be novel for students.** That is, they should have neither seen the exact problem or a close parallel

---

[3]This biology item is predicated on the students having just completed units on the lungs and the design of a mechanical heart. Here, they are called upon to synthesize the information on function and structure of the lungs with information on mechanical organ substitution. The idea of a mechanical lung would not have been discussed in class.

nor had direct experience with the specific solution through instruction (although the knowledge to be synthesized must have already been acquired). Since synthesis represents or requires original thinking, problems to measure it must be completely *original* from the students' frame of reference.

Bloom (1956) is also concerned about response instructions in essay items for measuring synthesis. With regard to the variable of time, he writes the following:

> Many synthesis tasks require far more time than an hour or two; the product is likely to emerge only after the student spends considerable time familiarizing himself with the task, exploring different approaches, interpreting and analyzing relevant materials, and trying out various schemes or organization. (p. 173)

It may well be that the procedures a teacher uses for measuring synthesis should themselves have a creative quality. A take-home exam, for example, may provide more of the conditions described above than would a conventional classroom test. Perhaps students should be encouraged to seek inputs from other sources that can be synthesized into their solutions. In some cases the teacher might provide resource material that can contribute to the synthesis task.

It is important to keep in mind the thought that **synthesis should be measured under conditions favorable to creative work** and that testing is usually done under conditions that are perhaps antithetical to creative work. Response instructions should be designed to break the mold of the conventional test and put the student more at ease. Untimed tests, instructions reinforcing the idea that creativity or novelty or originality is to be strived for, a statement that there are no "right" or "wrong" answers are appropriate kinds of instruction for items aimed at measuring synthesis.

ITEMS TO MEASURE EVALUATION

Of evaluation, Bloom (1956) writes:

> Evaluation is defined as the making of judgments about the value, for some purpose, of ideas, works, solutions, methods, material, etc. It involves the use of criteria as well as standards for appraising the extent to which particulars are accurate, effective, economical or satisfying. (p. 185)

Bloom further distinguishes between evaluations based on internal standards such as consistency, logical accuracy, and the absence of internal flaws (more subjective criteria), and evaluations based on external standards such as efficiency, economy, utility of means for ends, and standards of excellence.

Examples

- Write an essay of 250–500 words, evaluating the following poem. The evaluation should include, for example, the poem's structure, meter, organization, form, meaning, and symbolism. Your principles of evaluation should be made clear—although they need not be elaborately described or defended.[4] Take time to organize your essay carefully. Save time for revisions and proofreading so that the essay as it appears in your examination booklet represents your best intention. It is suggested that you give twenty minutes to planning, eighty to writing, and twenty to revising your essay. *Please try to write legibly* (although handwriting will not be counted against you).

> Since there's no help, come let us kiss and part;
> Nay, I have done, you get no more of me,
> And I am glad, yea glad with all my heart
> That thus so cleanly I myself can free;
> Shake hands forever, cancel all our vows,
> And when we meet at any time again,
> Be it not seen in either of our brows
> That we one jot of former love retain.
> Now at the last gasp of love's latest breath,
> When, his pulse failing, passion speechless lies,
> When faith is kneeling by his bed of death,
> And innocence is closing up his eyes,
> Now if thou wouldst, when all have given him over,
> From death to life thou mightst him yet recover.[5]

- An important function of the United Nations is to help settle disputes among nations. Describe how one such dispute was handled successfully, pointing out how the settlement illustrates a general strength of the United Nations. Your essay should be about 300–400 words in length (two to three pages in longhand).[6]

- Above is a diagram of an electrical circuit in the starting mechanism of a machine. [In the actual problem a diagram is supplied.] Do you think the circuit is sufficient to start the machine? [The specifications of the machine are also provided.] Write a short report stating your evaluation of the capacity of the given circuit to start the given machine. Be as specific as possible in your evaluation and provide as much evidence or support for your evaluation as possible. Keep your report to within two pages.

Writing the Item.   Evaluation items contain two parts: **that which is to be evaluated,** and **response instructions.** Response instructions also include information about the criteria that are to be used in the evaluation.

---

[4] The requirement for evaluation in terms of formal characteristics involves analysis in addition to evaluation.
[5] The poem was written by Michael Drayton (1563–1631).
[6] Adapted from *Making the Classroom Test. A Guide for Teachers* (copyright © 1959 by Educational Testing Service. All rights reserved. Reproduced by permission). To do an adequate evaluation, it will be necessary for the student also to analyze.

The student must be given something to evaluate. As illustrated in the examples, that "something" may range from a poem to an organization to an electrical circuit. Anything that is subject to rational examination can be submitted to evaluation. Thus, evaluation items can range widely across subject-matter areas.

Students must also have available to them a criterion or criteria on which their evaluations are to be based. Will the "something" work? Is it successful in keeping the peace? Does it conform to the acceptable internal structure? Have its effects been positive? These are some of the criterion questions that can be asked. Beyond this, additional and more detailed criteria must be supplied by the students themselves. Students may be expected to supply the specific evaluative criteria as well as to use them in evaluating that which is given. In some cases these criteria may be objective and universal; in other cases they may be more individual in quality. Usually, there are some of each—some criteria that the student has learned and others that he or she has invented.

Finally, there may be in evaluation items, as there are in all the essay items, specific response instructions about length, detail, and so on. Admonitions for detail or for defending one's point of view are perhaps most frequent in evaluation items since evaluation is intended to solicit judgments and it is the use of argumentation and justifiable supporting evidence that distinguishes between whimsical opinion and responsible judgment. (If only an opinion were necessary, the short-answer format could be used.) It is in defending and supporting an evaluative position that students demonstrate the breadth and depth of their thinking relative to the teacher's objectives and criteria.

Thus, an essay item intended to measure evaluation provides the student with something to be evaluated, a general criterion for evaluating it (at the minimum, and occasionally more specific criteria as well), and general response instructions with a usual admonition to provide detailed support for one's evaluative position or judgment.

An important difference between essay items and the short-answer items described in the previous chapter is that essay items produce responses that may be quite noncomparable and thus difficult to score. (Short-answer items, of course, produce more directly comparable responses particularly in the case of fixed-choice items.) In order to further the likelihood of comparable essays (not equivalent essays but ones that can be *compared*), the types of judgments or evaluations required must be set forth in the item. It is hoped that such detail will eliminate the tendency for some students, when asked to evaluate the poem in the first example, to write, "I liked this poem because . . . ."

A last point in understanding the use of essays for measuring higher cognitive processes is an important one. These processes build on, and thus include, the "lower" ones of knowledge and comprehension. Where the underlying processes are deficient, the higher-order ones cannot be expected to operate to their maximum level of capability.

ITEMS TO MEASURE COMBINATIONS OF PROCESSES

At times a teacher will have objectives that require a student to demonstrate more than one process in dealing with a problem situation. For example, an essay item might require that a student use synthesis to generate a problem solution and then critically evaluate his or her own solution (for example, construct a solution to a problem in social management and then evaluate that solution according to given criteria). Another possibility is for a student to have to analyze a performance and then to evaluate it. For example, the first two sample assignments under evaluation (pages 87–88) require both analysis and evaluation, in the first example of a poem, and in the second example of the operation of the United Nations.

As the following examples show, by combining processes, a single essay item can be used to measure the attainment of two or three objectives.

Examples

- Look at the poster at the front of the classroom. (Posters could deal with any one of a number of subjects; for example, a fund drive, a clean-up campaign, a political campaign, alcoholism.) (1) Describe what you think the artist was trying to say and how he or she made use of form, texture, color, etc., to say it. Try to be brief and to the point. (2) How successful would you say the artist was in getting the point across? On what do you base your opinion? (3) How would you change the poster to better make the point you think the artist was trying to make?
- Write a one-page composition describing the kind of work your mother or father does for a living. Discuss all the different aspects of the job. For example, does he or she wear a uniform, a suit? Does he or she work indoors or outdoors? Does the job require physical strength? Does it require an ability to deal with details? Does it offer opportunity for advancement? Then, evaluate each part of the description you have given in terms of how well that aspect of the job would fit your idea of the perfect job for you. Defend your judgments.
- Describe ten possible uses for a horseshoe magnet. Then consider each use you have named and decide whether there would be a better way to accomplish that particular purpose. If so, describe the better way.

Writing the Item.   Analysis, synthesis, and evaluation can all be combined in a single, multiple-part item as illustrated by the first example. Giving students an object, an organization, an occurrence, and asking them to *analyze* its parts or workings is the first step. *Evaluating* the parts or workings is the second step and redesigning or improving upon it through *synthesis* is the third step. The major shortcoming of this combination approach is that each part is contingent on the preceding parts: a failure in analysis will serve to affect the subsequent evaluation and the subsequent synthesis. However, since evaluation and synthesis items often leave the responsibility for prerequisite analysis to the students (at least implicitly), the combination item has the advantage of requiring explicit analysis before evaluation and synthesis in order to open up the total thinking process.

It would be wise for a teacher to contrast performances of synthesis and evaluation items: (1) those that make no mention of analysis and thereby leave its requirement implicit; (2) those that explicitly require analysis first (that is, combination items); and (3) those that provide the students with the analysis so they do not have to do it themselves.

The second example illustrates the combination of analysis and evaluation. Again the prototype is for the students to analyze a given situation, phenomenon, or object and then evaluate its components against a set of criteria. Often the students themselves must determine the criteria: in this illustration, the various aspects of a particular job in terms of the students' own job ideals.

The third example combines synthesis (or possibly application—depending on how creative the solutions are) with evaluation. The value of this particular combination is that it provides students with the opportunity for creativity but influences that creativity to be functional by virtue of the requirement for self-evaluation. However, it must be made clear to students if they are to generate their own criteria for evaluation, as in the item on the horseshoe magnet. (In some items, the criteria for evaluation are provided.) Also, the teacher must recognize the fact that when students generate their own evaluative criteria their essay responses will not be comparable in terms of content. In such instances the teacher must be prepared to react primarily to the process illustrated by the response (as we shall see below) rather than to the content alone.

CRITERIA FOR SCORING ESSAY ITEMS

In essence, scoring an essay item confronts the teacher with the task of evaluation, a process that requires criteria. It is important that these criteria be predetermined and if possible prespecified as part of your objectives. (Criteria can form the basis for constructing a model response at least in outline form.) Following is a discussion of various criteria as they apply to scoring.

Content Criterion

Although the reason for using essay items is not to elicit facts as much as to measure the thinking process, within an essay a considerable amount of information is likely to be presented. The content criterion deals only with the presence of knowledge and its accuracy and not with its application, analysis, synthesis, or evaluation. All you are trying to judge is whether the content that the student provides leads you to conclude that he or she is knowledgeable in the area of the essay. Since knowledge is the underpinning for thinking and problem-solving skills, some knowledge will be needed as a prerequisite to solving the problem. In essence the content criterion reflects the prerequisite knowledge that the student has acquired in a particular area.

Organization Criteria

Organization and other writing skills are important components of essay performance and of many other sorts of academic performance as well. If they become criteria for essay response scoring, their importance is likely to become more formally recognized by students.

What do you look for as evidence of organization? Initially look to see if the problem has been set up or introduced. When recommendations are made, they should be accompanied by supporting evidence. It should be possible for the reader to tell which statements are the recommendations and which supporting statements go with which recommendations. The traditional organization of an essay includes three parts: an introduction, a body, and a conclusion.

An essay response is not intended to be merely thinking out loud, for such a procedure tends to result in rambling. Students should be encouraged to prepare outlines for their responses before writing. A strategy of organization for communicating thoughts reflects a logical mind; thus the kinds of progressions and sequences that are the vehicles of organization should be looked for and evaluated by the scorer of essay questions. Response instructions should alert students that these various aspects of essay organization will be evaluated.

Process Criteria

Since the major purpose of essay-type items is to measure application, analysis, synthesis, and evaluation skills, or some combination of them, the most important criteria for scoring are those that reflect the adequacy with which these processes were carried out. Each of these processes results in a **solution** or **recommendation** (often with details of its implementation) and **reasons for justifying or supporting that solution or recommendation.** Hence, essay response scoring must evaluate the adequacy of the solution and the adequacy of the reasons behind it.

In essence the scoring of process must focus on the problem-solving behavior that the response is intended to represent. Let us consider problem-solving behavior to include the five steps shown below.

1. Define the problem.
2. Generate alternative solutions.
3. Weigh alternative solutions and choose among them.
4. Implement the choice.
5. Evaluate the outcome.

It should be possible to find evidences of some or all of the steps in every essay response, depending on the nature of the task to be done. In general, the first three steps should always be present, and, if the first step has clearly been provided in the item itself, the second and third step should be a minimum performance requirement. Within the second and third step, it may be that only a single solution need be generated (step 2) and that its defense or support would constitute the weighing process. (The teacher would have to predetermine the minimum number of solutions necessary and may or may not communicate this number to the students.)

The evaluation of a problem solution and reasons to support it can be made on the basis of (1) accuracy or reasonableness in terms of external criteria, (2) completeness and consistency in terms of internal criteria, and (3) originality or creativity. *Accuracy* or *reasonableness* refers to the extent to which the proposed solution is judged to be workable, that is, to yield a satisfactory outcome. Will the proposed application work? Have the correct analytical dimensions been identified? Is the synthesized product appropriate? Has the given object been correctly evaluated? Since there are rarely absolute and objectively correct answers to essay items, the decision of solution accuracy is one based on the judgment of the scorer.

Beyond these kinds of suggested criteria, only procedural recommendations can be made for scoring. In the final analysis, scoring decisions are judgmental. The teacher must formulate in his or her own mind those solutions that he or she deems accurate but still must be prepared to consider open-mindedly unanticipated solutions. Criteria of reasonableness and accuracy should also be applied to the reasons cited in support of the solution. Again, judgment must be used in weighting these arguments.

The question of *completeness* and *internal consistency* refers primarily to the extent to which the supporting material is appropriate for and fits the proposed solution, and the degree to which it suffices in dealing with the problem posed. Obviously, partial and incomplete responses will not receive as high scores as complete ones. Obviously, too, the teacher must have a preconceived idea of what constitutes the complete answer to use as a basis for judgment.

Originality and *creativity* both in proposed solutions and in arguments to support them are important components in an unstructured testing format such as the essay. Again, the judgment of the scorer is called upon to recognize the unexpected and to credit it.

Criteria and the Student

It is important to recognize that essay items are intended to measure discreet objectives that have been prespecified in a content outline and that students should be informed of these objectives so that they may engage in goal-oriented learning. Objectives, as you may recall, include mention of criteria. Consider the following one.

- Given an impressionist poem, the student will be able to evaluate the effectiveness of its symbolism and defend that evaluation in an accurate, complete, and creative manner.

The point here is that the students should know the criteria that will be applied to the evaluation of essay responses so that they may goal-direct their behavior toward those criteria as part of the learning experience. Rather than being a private and mysterious set of judgments, the bases for scoring essay responses, that is, the criteria, should become themselves a subject for learning. Moreover, performance feedback to students should contain more than a grade. Students can learn from performance if they are shown how their behavior fit the criteria, and, more importantly, how it did not. The result will undoubtedly be an increased tendency by students to generate essay responses that can be judged successful in terms of scoring criteria.

Three Kinds of Scoring

There are three kinds of scoring that can be used for assigning grades to essay responses. These are point scoring, rank scoring, and grade scoring.

Point Scoring.   A point-scoring scale is made up of a series of numerical scores that can be considered to be equidistant. A useful one for scoring is the one to ten scale shown below.

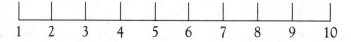

Note that the distance between numbers is a constant. There is nothing magic about the number ten; it is simply a convenient scale to work with. In using it the teacher would first of all identify all of his or her criteria as shown in Figure 5-1 and his or her weightings for each. As shown in Figure 5-1, process criteria taken together have a weighting of thirty as compared to ten for each of the other two criteria, content and organization. These weightings of course are only for illustrative purposes. You may set any weightings you please as you decide the relative importance of each of the criteria. (For fairness, the scoring system should be explained to students before they write their essays.)

After the scoring sheet has been made up, a useful second step in scoring the essay is to write an outline of the correct essay response in terms of the categories of the scoring sheet (content points, organization points, and the various process points). Your outlined answer should reflect the aspects the student must mention and evaluate in each category in order to earn *full credit.* The value of outlining these aspects is that it gives you a standard model of acceptability against which each student's essay response can be compared.

Now you are ready to read each essay response. The following rules must be established.

1. Hide the name of the student who wrote the essay; read every essay *blind*;
2. Read each essay once (Judge A), shuffle the order and hide your first scores, and read each essay again (or have a second person read them—Judge B);[7]
3. After you read an essay, use your best judgment (and your outline or model answer) to assign it a numerical score of 1 to 10 (10 being the highest or best) on each criterion.

The importance of *blind* scoring is to avoid introducing a bias based on expectations for student performance. Some teachers have a tendency to evaluate the work of the better students higher (or sometimes harder) because they come to view them as more likely to produce. The double reading is done in an effort to establish scoring reliability (discussed in the next section) in order to overcome some of the subjectivity of essay response scoring. The interval 1–10 scale is then applied as a best judgment within the structure of the scoring sheet. Note that the scoring sheet forces the teacher to make eight judgments, rather than to allow the entire scoring outcome to be based on a single judgment. The scores from the two judgments or two judges are now averaged, the averages summed to give a total score, and the total score converted into a percentage score by dividing into it the maximum possible score and multiplying by 100.

It seems like a lot of work, and it is! But is is important to guard against subjecting students to the tyranny of a subjective, undisciplined scoring system. The use of a proper scoring system and an outline or model response plus the use of detailed feedback (give the student back a copy of his or her scoring sheet including detailed comments) makes the essay item a constructive and authentic part of the schooling process.

Rank Scoring.   The rank-scoring scale simply substitutes overall rankings of the total essay response for scores on each criterion. (Rather than assigning performance on each criterion a score between 1 and 10, the ordinal procedure involves evaluation of total worth of responses on a comparative or relative basis.) First, all responses to an essay item are read through quickly, and then, upon a second, more intensive reading, are placed in a sequence or order from best to worst—considering all the scoring criteria together. The best essay response would then end up on top of the pile, the second best would be second on the pile, the third best, third, and so on until the worst essay response which would end up at the bottom of

---

[7]Or, if two sets of judgments are impossible because of time, at least read every fourth or fifth essay (chosen at random) a second time.

the pile. You then make a note on a separate sheet of paper of the order or ranking and then reread and rerank the responses or have them read and ranked by another person. All judgments should be made blind, that is, without an awareness of who wrote the response. Each essay would then receive the average of the two ranks. The last step is to convert ranks to grades which can be done by assigning the top so many percent an A, the next so many percent a B, and so on.

Grade Scoring.   If you wish to end up with five grades or categories of scores such as A, B, C, D, E or outstanding, good, acceptable, marginal, and unacceptable, you would read each essay response and then assign it to one of the five categories. (You may first choose to read all the essay responses to give yourself an idea of their relative quality and then read them again and assign each to the category judged to be of best fit.) Like the ordinal approach, the nominal approach is a global one in which criteria are applied in total as a basis for judging performance rather than discreetly and independently as is true in the interval approach. As with the other approaches, judgments should be made blind and either done twice or once each by two readers. In each case the judgment is a categorical one—deciding which of the five categories each essay response belongs in—relative *not* to one another but to the scoring criteria that have been established.

Summary.   The point scoring system represents more work than the rank or grade systems but it is also more systematic, more objective, and more closely related to the kinds of criteria of mastery normally specified in instructional objectives. It is recommended that teachers use the point method in the expectation that its use will improve their scoring consistency.

INTER-RATER RELIABILITY

The general concept of *test* reliability will be covered in Chapter Eight. Here we are dealing with that aspect of reliability known as *inter-rater reliability* or *inter-judge agreement*. The teacher as an essay response scorer is an imperfect measuring instrument, subject—as any human being is—to fatigue, biases, expectations, and other sources of influence. However, because the teacher is functioning as a measuring instrument steps must be taken to insure the greatest degree of objectivity (or consistency or accuracy) or reliability. To this end, multiple judgments are recommended. A second independent judgment will compensate for some of the subjectivity in the first judgment. This second judgment can be made by the same teacher who made the first or by another person. Using the average or mean of the two judgments increases the reliability of the scores.

It is possible to compute the degree of inter-rater reliability by determining the degree of correspondence or overlap between the two sets of scores.[8] What is recommended is that (1) each essay be scored twice by the teacher or once each by two teachers, (2) each set of judgments or scorings be as independent of the other as possible, (3) teachers work on the blind, that is, not know whose response they are scoring or what score it has already received, and (4) separate judgments be made for each criterion as illustrated in Figure 5-1.

Sometimes reading essay questions twice becomes a prohibitive task, and it is not always possible to find a second reader. When such is the case, randomly select one-fifth to one-quarter of the essays for a second reading to help make some judgment about your scoring reliability.

Two sample essay items, the responses, and the teacher's notations and scoring appear in Figure 5-2. Figure 5-3 contains the teacher's objectives and criteria along with the scoring rules. By giving back the student his or her essay with the teacher's markings on it (that is, check marks, underlinings, item scores) along with a copy of the information shown in

Figure 5-1
A Sample Essay Response Scoring Sheet

Student _____   Test _____
Date _____   Item _____

Criterion	Weight	Points Possible	(Judge A) Points Obtained	(Judge B) Points Obtained	(Average) Points Obtained
Content	1	10			
Organization	1	10			
Process					
Solution					
Accuracy	½	5			
Consistency	½	5			
Originality	½	5			
Argument					
Accuracy	½	5			
Consistency	½	5			
Originality	½	5			

Total Points Possible = 50
Total (Average) Points Obtained =

$$\text{Percent Score} = \frac{\text{Total Points Obtained}}{\text{Total Points Possible}} \times 100 =$$

Comments:

---

[8]Technically, this may be accomplished by computing a correlation coefficient between the two sets of scores but for practical purposes it can be judged by eye.

Figure 5-3, the student will have sufficient feedback to be able to identify the nature of the information required and of the errors made.

A Final Point.   We have now covered the two most common types of classroom test items, short-answer and essay. Reasons for use of essay items should not be that they are the easier to write of the two types and fewer of them need to be written. Essay items should be chosen when and if the objectives to be measured call for the types of processes best measured by essay items, and then only if the teacher is serious enough about objectivity and consistency to use the kind of scoring outline, form, categories, and procedure described and illustrated in this chapter.

Figure 5-2
Two Sample Essay Items from a Tenth Grade Anthropology Course and the Actual Responses of a Student*

1. Name and describe five of the most important features of human beings that make them very adaptable to different environments. (5 pts.)
2. Briefly describe the everyday life of a typical man of the Australopithecus genus. (5 pts.)

Men and women have been pretty generalized, so they can adapt to almost any environment here on earth. The ✓ most important feature is their <u>brain</u>. Because of our brain we are capable of developing instruments to help us cope with our environment. We are both ✓ vegetarians or ~~carnibars~~ carnivores. Therefore, the type of food in our environment doesn't necessarily bother us. We can swim but also dwell on land. We can ✓ <u>survive in the cold</u> with technology, etc., but can <u>withstand the heat</u>. ③ We pretty much can survive through any environmental change. Our

---

*The markings are those of the teacher.

brain, leg and arm muscles pretty much help to generalize us.

The everyday life of Australopithecine was based around his searching for food and shelter. He probably woke

✓✓ *up went out hunted or gathered his food, slept a little maybe spent*

✓ *some hours drawing in the ground or counting his toes, and then*

⑤ *probably went to sleep again. He*

✓ *didn't need to do much of anything else. Therefore slept and ate*

✓ *like all wild animals.*

Figure 5-3
The Teacher's Objectives (Including Criteria) and Scoring Rules for the Two Essay Questions Shown in Figure 5-2

Question 1: Objective—The student will be able to name and describe at
(analysis)   least five important features that contribute to human adaptability to environment, drawn from among the following:

- brain—leads to tools, shelter, creativity, and so on
- stereoscopic vision—helps us see clearly
- eat meat or vegetables—helps us live more completely off the land
- delineate hand control—to make things
- warm-bloodedness—live in wide range of temperatures, climates, and humidities—lets us tolerate land and water
- social cooperativeness—helping one another to survive
- long period of caring for young—increases likelihood of survival

Scoring rule—One point will be awarded for each of the above points covered up to five.

Figure 5-3 (continued)

Question 2: Objective—The student will be able to describe (drawing from his or her own imagination) the daily life of a typical man of the genus Australopithecus, his or her descriptions dealing with the areas of

- getting food
- sleeping
- culture

  and emphasizing the

- routineness of life
- animal-like existence
- primitiveness of culture.

Scoring rule—For each of the above points mentioned by the student in creating the description, one point will be awarded up to five.

Proficiency Test

1. The left-hand column lists the four thinking processes measured by essay items. Match each of these items with its particular characteristic listed in the right-hand column.

   a. application
   b. analysis
   c. synthesis
   d. evaluation

   i. puts elements together to form a whole
   ii. applies criteria to judge an idea, a work, a solution, a method, or a material
   iii. measures knowledge acquisition and comprehension
   iv. uses abstractions to solve concrete problems
   v. breaks down material into constituent parts and determines the relationship of the parts

2. Essay items to measure the higher cognitive processes should present situations that are novel for the student.
   TRUE   FALSE
3. Construct an essay item to test whether the student can *apply* knowledge gained from a unit on economic theories to a specific situation.
4. Construct an essay item to test whether the student can *analyze* four potentially confusable animals (birds, plants) to show what characteristics they have in common and others in which they differ.
5. Construct an essay item to test whether the student can, through *synthesis*, describe a procedure for making a useful object out of materials not normally used for that purpose.
6. Construct an essay item to test whether the student can *evaluate* a solution to a political problem.

7. You are about to score essay question responses for your class. List criteria that you would use for scoring.

8. Check each statement below that represents a recommendation for reliable scoring of essays.

   a. read as quickly as possible
   b. use a scoring sheet
   c. score separately by categories
   d. read no more than half the essay at one time
   e. score blind
   f. score twice
   g. read between the lines
   h. construct a sample response

Checklists and Scales to Measure Performance and Behavior

OBJECTIVES

- State criteria for choosing to do performance testing.
- Specify desired performance outcomes and testing situations for performance testing.
- Prepare a performance checklist containing process and product criteria.
- Specify and describe classroom behaviors to be evaluated.
- Prepare a behavior rating scale.
- State uses for behavior measurement in the classroom.

WHY MEASURE PERFORMANCE AND BEHAVIOR?

Although some people see the teacher's role in measurement limited to paper-and-pencil testing administered on a group basis, teachers frequently say that they do not rely on such tests alone as the basis for student assessment. In addition, they observe students' performance and behavior on a day-to-day basis and use these observations as part of their student assessments; indeed in certain situations such evidences may be more real than paper-and-pencil test performance for both the teacher and students.

Thus, the need arises to provide teachers with ways of measuring that can be applied to a specific performance or to ongoing behavior so that this real and relevant evidence of student capabilities can be utilized. Such measurement must be designed without totally compromising the standards on which good measurement is based, namely that the measurement procedure be content valid and reliable (see the next two chapters). The procedures described in this chapter are aimed at making the assessment of **performance** and **behavior** possible within the limits of these criteria.

MEASURING PERFORMANCE

The typical situation for the measurement of performance is an individualized testing setting in which a student is given a task, that task being to solve a problem, to identify a malfunction, to make a decision, or to implement a decision or solution. Typically, performances are associated with either solutions (that, in some cases, are products) or implementations or both. While the student is operating in a hands-on manner to achieve a solution or implementation, he or she is observed by one or more judges who use a checklist to record or evaluate each step in the performance. In a school setting, of course, the teacher would be the sole judge. (The student may or may not be aware that the performance is being observed, but usually he or she is.)

Measuring Skills and Competencies

To measure skills and competencies a student is asked to solve a problem and/or perform a task. For example: (1) Where is the malfunction in the system? (2) Get all the washers on a peg in decreasing order of size without ever putting a larger washer on top of a smaller one. (3) Of this series of cards, which one has been preselected as the correct one? (4) What would be the fastest and safest way to get across the island shown on the map assuming that there were eight of you and two were so injured that they had to be carried? (5) Act out a skit that illustrates the reason why Francis Scott Key wrote the "Star Spangled Banner." In each instance the individual student or group of students is asked to perform in order to produce a solution. Evaluation focuses on the procedures or steps undertaken to achieve the solution as well as on the quality of the solution.[1] Let us consider some specific illustrations in more detail.

Some Illustrations.   Our first example provides a checklist for measuring a diving performance.

> Have you ever attended a diving, gymnastics, or figure skating competition or seen one on television? They constitute performance tests. Have you noticed how, after a performance, judges hold up cards with numbers on them (7, 7½, 8, and so forth) to indicate their evaluation of the performance? We can presume that the judges are all using a similar checklist, based on their expertise and judgment, although the checklist is often unwritten. Here is an example of what a checklist for the triple somersault dive might look like:
>
> Performance checklist: completing a triple somersault dive from a three meter board (tuck position).
>
> _____ a. shows balance in approaching jump
> _____ b. jumps evenly, erectly, and high
> _____ c. goes smoothly into tuck position (that is, initial entry into tuck position describes an arc)
> _____ d. completes three complete somersaults
> _____ e. doesn't roll while somersaulting
> _____ f. comes out of tuck position in three motions
> _____ g. is out of tuck position before entering water
> _____ h. body is straight in entering water
> _____ i. entering splash is small and quiet
> _____ j. entire motion from start to finish is smooth
> _____   Overall performance on a 0–10 scale

Note that there are ten criteria. If each criterion that was met with minimal acceptance were scored ½ point, each criterion met "perfectly" scored 1, with a 0 for each failed, the addition of points would represent a final judgment.

The second illustration deals with the measurement of performance in electronics by the United States Army in the training of signalmen. Students were given a piece of electronics equipment with a fault or malfunction programmed in. Equipment to locate the fault was available. The test administrator evaluated not only whether the fault was located but how the student went about locating the fault—particularly in terms of his use of test equipment and troubleshooting procedures. A sample administrator's instruction sheet for the test appears in Figure 6-1.

Good examples of performance tests can also be drawn from science and mathematics. A sample performance test in science dealing with units of

---

[1]When the performance being judged is a group performance, each student is usually given whatever evaluation the group receives, unless individual contributions can be separated, in which case each student is evaluated individually.

Figure 6-1
Instructions for Administering a Performance Test in Electronics

STRATEGIC MICROWAVE RADIO REPAIR COURSE PHASE VIII
ADMINISTRATOR'S INSTRUCTION SHEET

Purpose:
To measure the student's ability to: (1) select and operate test equipment
associated with the AN/FRC-109 receiver; (2) develop and apply a logical
procedure in locating malfunctions in the AN/FRC-109 receiver.

Equipment:
The AN/FRC-109 receiver training facility and Simpson 260 VOM, Hi-
Band test set, Frequency Selective Voltmeter Sierra 128A, Oscilloscope
Tektronix Type 561A, Oscillator H/P 651B, Miscellaneous matching
transformers, Aids-Block Diagrams, level diagrams.

Procedure:
1. All equipment will be warmed up and in proper operating condition
    before the test is administered. A problem will be inserted into two
    different radio receivers at the same time.
2. The testing procedure will be described to the students.
    a. All test equipment necessary will be at the test position. You will
        be required to select and then calibrate the proper test equipment
        to be used.
    b. There will be one fault in each of two receiver racks. You will be
        required to locate the fault in each rack using the correct trouble-
        shooting procedure.
    c. The time limit for each problem is six minutes.
    d. You will be graded on the following items: (1) selection, calibra-
        tion, and application of test equipment; (2) procedure used in
        locating the faults; (3) localization of the faults.
    e. If you have any questions, ask them before you begin one prob-
        lem; talking will not be permitted during the test.

Scoring:
The test administrator will assign scores in accordance with the following:

1. Completing correctly problem 1	5 points
2. Completing correctly problem 2	5 points
3. Selection and use of test equipment	5 points
4. Troubleshooting procedure	5 points
	Total Points	20 points

force appears in Figure 6-2. In this test intended for fourth graders, the
student is given a spring scale, weights of known force, and graph paper,
and is asked to calibrate the spring. He or she is then asked to determine
the magnitude of an unknown force using the calibration developed in the
first test exercise. Note that the performance test includes (1) a list of the

Figure 6-2
A Performance Test in Science for Fourth Graders*

UNITS OF FORCE

(Objective 1)   1–3

Provide the child with four containers, each of which weighs one newton; a spring that he has not seen before mounted on a tripod (for example, Macalester Tripod Spring with centimeter tape on plastic cylinder); a pencil and some graph paper. Tell him, "Each one of these containers weighs one newton. Use them and the graph paper to calibrate the spring so that you can use the stretch of the spring to measure forces." One check should be given in the acceptable column for task one if the child plots one point correctly, one check in the acceptable column for task two if he plots two points correctly, and one check in the acceptable column for task three if he plots three or more points correctly.

(Objective 2)   4.

Using your hand, pull on the spring until it is stretched to some length within the range of calibration. Tell him, "Measure the force that I am exerting on the spring with my hand. Draw an arrow on your graph to show me where you are reading the force, and tell what the reading is." One check should be given in the acceptable column for task four if the child indicates the correct point on the graph with an arrow and states the measure of the force in newtons. If he merely gives a value (say 3.5), it is allowable to prompt with the question "3.5 what?" Allow an error of 0.2 newtons.

---

*Adapted. From *Part E* of *Science—A Process Approach*, Copyright © 1968, by American Association for the Advancement of Science, published by Ginn and Company (Xerox Corporation).

materials required, (2) instructions for the test administrator in terms of both what to do and what to say, and (3) scoring instructions, including a description of acceptable performance.

Figure 6-3 is a teacher-built performance test in mathematics on the fifth grade level. (One could argue that all testing in mathematics is performance testing since math-related behavior is essentially of a problem-solving nature. Even where multiple choice items are used in math, essentially problem-solving behavior must occur to make a correct choice. The most useful distinction may be that in performance testing, as opposed to short-answer testing, the tester gains access to the problem-solving process as well as or in addition to the problem solution.) In this test, the student is asked to measure an angle, label others, and make a determination of an angle that would be produced by reflected light.

In English an example of a performance test would be an assignment for high school seniors to write a letter to the Acme Employment Agency, 100 Main Street, Centerville, N.Y. 10345 to try to obtain a job for the following year. The students are told that the letter should include a descrip-

Figure 6-3
A Sample Performance Test in Mathematics for Fifth Graders

Use your protractor to measure this angle: <a = _____ °

(2 points)

Imagine the ray of light hitting the mirror as shown. Draw a line showing the path of the ray of light reflected by the mirror at the correct angle.

(2 points)

Label the *angle of incidence* with the letter a.   (1 point)
Label the *angle of reflection* with the letter b.   (1 point)

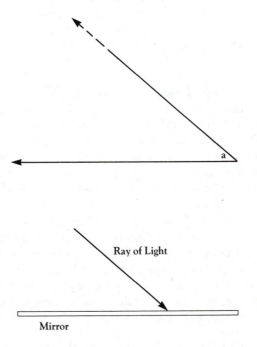

Ray of Light

Mirror

tion of their background and capabilities and the kinds of jobs they would be interested in. They are also told that the form of their letter (proper business form), spelling, punctuation, and neatness will be evaluated as well as content. There is a time limit of thirty minutes.

The above performance test illustrates the less-than-exact line that separates the different kinds of tests. This test seems much like an essay test primarily because the materials are paper and pencil or typewriter. The major distinction between an essay test and a performance test is that the end result of a performance test is an actual product rather than a set of thoughts or ideas. You might say that performances have a functional quality in that their outcome usually has some potential use for the performer. Beyond this, these distinctions may have their primary value in teaching and learning about test construction rather than in the construction of tests themselves.

DECIDING ON A PERFORMANCE TEST

Essential Considerations (criteria)

A performance test is usually given on an individual basis; therefore it is a time-consuming form of testing. Before engaging in performance testing, the teacher should examine these criteria:

Real Performance Requires a Hands-on Situation.   Certain performances can occur only if the student can handle actual materials or equipment. In such cases, abstracting the performance on a paper-and-pencil basis will rob it of its essential validity, that is, you will be measuring something other than your objective. Where an objective requires a hands-on demonstration or construction, performance testing is required (including performances for which paper and pencil are the equipment, as in letter writing).

Access to the Solution Process Is Essential.   Group paper-and-pencil testing often prohibits the teacher from having access to the process or procedure by which the outcome or product was arrived at. In order to see how a student solves a problem or makes a product or implements a solution, the teacher must observe the performance of that student. If the process is itself as worthy of measurement and evaluation as the product, then a performance test is needed to allow the teacher to witness and judge the process.

The Final Outcome or Product Has a Material Form.   Often we try to get students to produce decisions or ideas. These can usually be measured by paper-and-pencil tests, but the situation is completely different if the final outcome of the test has a material form. Asking a student how to make something is not always a valid substitute for having him or her make it. If your purpose is to measure both knowledge of process and skill in performance, a performance test is needed.

You Are Trying to Assess Psychomotor Learning (that is, Skills).   While cognition (what you know) and affect (what you feel) can often be measured by paper-and-pencil tests, skill acquisition cannot. To demonstrate skills, a student must physically do them. Hence, a performance test is required.

You Are Trying to Assess Individual Effectiveness in a Group Setting.   Where the purpose of the test is to measure one person's effect on another (for example, leadership skills), actual performance testing is needed. (You have to observe the person in a leadership situation that you may have contrived in order to see how effectively he or she could help the group solve a problem.) A person might be able to solve a problem individually or to describe in writing the desired behavior but be incapable of actually working in a group. Performance tests require the test taker to demonstrate performance rather than describe it.

You Are Trying to Measure Understanding by its Application. You can use a performance test to measure understanding but only in terms of the concrete application of that understanding. The outcome is still a concrete product but its construction may well be a reflection of certain cognitive processes. (Habitual performances like riding a bike soon become automatic, and no longer reflect cognition.)

CONSTRUCTING A PERFORMANCE TEST

A performance test, as we have seen, is a test initiated by the teacher and involves the student in a performance under a controlled set of conditions. It is usually given on an individual or one-to-one basis although it is possible sometimes to utilize group administration for part or all of it, and some testing—leadership skills, for example—requires group administration. Typically performance testing involves both a product and a process—the process being the manner by which the product was produced or arrived at. It does, in all instances then, deal with the ability of the student to do something rather than simply to know something, identify something, or describe something, and it usually involves the use of materials or equipment. What is important to emphasize is that this kind of test is not simply an informal, casual, or happenstance appraisal of actions. It is a test that is planned, designed, and carried out to sample a person's ability to use a process and produce a product under a *given* set of conditions.

The rules to follow in constructing a performance test are listed and explained below.

Specifying Desired Performance Outcomes. The first step in constructing a performance test is to specify desired performance objectives. Since performance objectives state actions by the learner under given conditions (and ultimately include criteria for evaluation), they represent a set of desired performance outcomes. For performance test purposes, teachers should focus on those objectives that use such verbs as *demonstrate* and *construct* because these verbs specify hands-on performance (that is, demonstrations and constructions); if such objectives do not exist, the teacher should write them. Below are examples of performance objectives.

- Demonstrate a procedure for measuring the volume of a liquid.
- Demonstrate a procedure for bisecting an angle.
- Construct a poem that describes personal feelings about some aspect or aspects of nature.
- Demonstrate a procedure for tuning a car.
- Demonstrate a procedure for conducting an interview.
- Construct a model of an American Indian village.
- Demonstrate the ability to take shorthand at the rate of twenty-five words per minute.
- Construct a cubic meter out of cardboard.
- Demonstrate a procedure for staining pine.
- Construct a display for teaching about different leaves and their characteristics.

Specifying the Test Situation.   A test situation is a set of givens with which the student attempts to produce the desired performance. It is the conditions of the objective or what the student must be given in order to perform the objective. (Recall that conditions, performance, and criteria were described in Chapter Two as the components of an objective.) While a performance test can be a sampling of ongoing behavior, it usually is an examination of a *prespecified* performance using a set of givens and following a set of instructions. Hence both conditions and instructions must be specified. Consider the examples below.

- Demonstrate the use of a balance for weighing objects of unknown weight.
  Givens: a balance, a metal cylindrical prism of unknown weight, and a set of known weights as follows: ten 1 milligram weights, nine 100 milligram weights, five 1 gram weights, and three 5 gram weights.
  Instructions: Here is an object of unknown weight, a balance, and a set of weights. Use the balance to determine the weight of the unknown to within one milligram. You will have five minutes to do this.

- Construct a rock display.
  Givens: information in advance so that you can bring all the material you need (including rocks that you have gathered) to class. The minimum number and the types of rocks that are needed are included in the advance information.
  Instructions: Make a rock display that is clear and interesting and that contains at least seven rocks with some of each type that we learned about. The rocks should be mounted so that the display can be stood up on a table in the classroom. You will get up to 10 points for the accuracy of your display, up to 10 points for its completeness, and up to 10 points for its attractiveness of presentation.

- Install an electrical outlet in an open wall.
  Givens: access to a standard set of tools and wire, an outlet fixture, a mounting box, an open wall, an accessible live power source.
  Instructions: Here is an outlet fixture and box. Install the outlet on one of these studs and connect it to the classroom power source so that it can be used.

The instructions should be very clear, whether they are written or oral. The givens should be sufficient for successful task completion although all need not be specifically supplied by the teacher; the student may be required to supply some. When part of the requirements is to choose or to find necessary tools, materials (such as the rocks in the example), or information, the teacher should insure that these are uniformly accessible to the students. The teacher is not interested in measuring the adequacy of the conditions—they should be adequate; he or she is interested in measuring the skills of the student. A test that is inadequate in its givens or instructions will not measure a student's skills with any validity. Proper test construction includes suitable preparation of givens and instructions.

Specifying Process (or Procedure) and Product Criteria. Performance tests give the teacher access to the product and potential access to the process or procedure undertaken to attain that product, but obviously access to the process, when it occurs, is very temporary.[2] Once the procedure is complete, the observer no longer has access to it unless it was filmed or videotaped or unless the student is asked to do it again. Consequently, the teacher must prepare a set of criteria in advance to apply to the process or procedure. Criteria are necessary, too, to try to make the judgments as objective as possible, for the performance test—like the essay test—has a certain amount of subjectivity built into it. The teacher is the judge. On what basis does a teacher decide what steps the student should take and whether these steps are done correctly? To answer this question, he or she must list the necessary steps in the procedure. The occurrence of these steps then constitutes a criterion for evaluating performance. Consider the following criteria for demonstrating the use of a balance, constructing a rock display, and installing an electrical outlet.

- Demonstrate the use of a balance for weighing objects of unknown weight.
  a. Place object of unknown weight on one tray of balance.
  b. Place objects of known weight on the other tray.
  c. Add or subtract known weights when underbalance or overbalance occurs.
  d. Use lesser weights as balance is approached.
  e. Try a minimum number of different weight combinations to achieve balance within additions and subtractions, always bringing the scale closer to balance (rather than combining weights on a hit-or-miss basis).
  f. Add the weights that produce balance to determine the weight of the unknown.

- Construct a rock display.
  a. Collect different kinds of rocks to include at least three of the igneous class, three sedimentary, and one metamorphic. (These proportions are based on the general availability of these three types of rocks.)
  b. Clean and polish rocks.
  c. Mount attractively.
  d. Label (including name, class, and where found).

- Install an electrical outlet in an open wall.
  a. Select proper tools.
  b. Determine and prepare amount of material needed (wire for example).

---

[2] Also, when the process occurs in the student's mind the teacher will be limited to only those aspects that can be verbalized or acted out.

    c. Decide whether or not (and when) to cut power.
    d. Mount box on stud.
    e. Connect wires with proper polarization to fixture.
    f. Install fixture in box (and put on cover if needed).
    g. Connect to power source.
    h. Test to see if it works.[3]

    Recall that an objective includes a statement of criteria for evaluating either the process or the product or both. In essence this third step is simply an elaboration of the criteria that will be used to evaluate the performance. These criteria should be spelled out in sufficient detail so that the teacher can adequately evaluate the performance in as systematic a way as possible. They should also be presented to the students, either as part of the test or during the instruction related to the task. Detailed criteria reduce the subjectivity of the judgment.

Preparing the Performance Checklist.   The performance test is made up of a set of instructions and givens that are presented to the student, and a performance checklist that is used by the teacher or judge. The performance checklist is just a format for listing the criteria that were developed in the preceding section. If a criterion on the list is met, it is checked; if it is not met, it is not checked. Consider the examples below.

- Performance checklist: Bisecting an angle.
  - _____a. compass is used
  - _____b. point placed on vertex; arc is made between sides
  - _____c. point placed on each intersection between arc in (b) and side; equal arcs are made
  - _____d. line is drawn from vertex to intersection between arcs in (c)
  - _____e. two resulting angles are equal when checked with protractor
  - _____ Overall quality of performance on a 0–5 scale

- Performance checklist: Drawing a realistic nature scene.
  - _____a. a sketch (outline or layout or some sort of plan) is made first
  - _____b. materials are used properly
  - _____c. drawing is completed neatly
  - _____d. elements of nature can be seen in the drawing
  - _____e. colors are realistic
  - _____ Overall quality of drawing on a 0–5 scale

---

[3]In skill performances, the steps are usually more accurately described as procedures rather than processes. That is, the steps represent what one must do to produce the product rather than necessarily revealing what one must _know_ (other than knowing the procedures).

The performance checklist reflects both the steps undertaken in arriving at the product and the quality or acceptability of the product itself. It is a set of instructions and procedures by the teacher to himself or herself in terms of what to look for in evaluating a performance. It also provides a basis for giving students useful performance feedback and attempts to make the evaluation of performance as objective and quantitative as possible.

Obviously, not all performances are equally susceptible to this treatment and hence all performance checklists are not equally detailed. The checklist is a way for the teacher to take those criteria that are in his or her head and to externalize and systematize them by writing them down. The performance checklist can be considered the scoring key for a performance test. The criteria listed as a to e form the basis for the overall evaluation of the performance shown at the bottom of the checklist.

SCORING THE PERFORMANCE TEST

The final exam in paratrooper training is a test jump. Trainees are taken up in a plane wearing parachutes they have packed themselves and jump from a height of 8,000 to 10,000 feet. The next day is graduation. Any trainee who shows up for graduation receives a diploma.

Unfortunately, there are few such performance tests where the criteria for success can be so objectively applied. In other words, there are usually no absolute rules for teachers to use in scoring a performance test. By considering their own requirements (that is, the requirements as set forth in their objective), the relative importance of the different criteria in an absolute sense, and the extent to which they can differentiate degrees of performance, teachers can build their own appropriate scoring procedures. However, some guidelines may be helpful and are offered below.

It is not necessarily true that all criteria must be checked for the total performance to be judged acceptable or that 50 percent or some other arbitrary number must be checked. (However, if some arbitrary number is demanded, 70 or 80 percent is probably the most reasonable.) Examine your checklist and ask yourself questions such as: Are all of the components in the checklist equally important? Are some absolutely essential for acceptable performance? What degree of success constitutes mastery? Your answers to these questions will lead you to decide whether you want to use a weighting system or to follow the somewhat arbitrary *80 percent success = acceptable proficiency* rule. Or you may simply want to assign an overall rating to the performance based on the checklist entries and record this rating as an indication of the student's degree of proficiency or quality of performance. Consider the checklist on the following page.

Suppose that you felt that each criterion was equally important but that you wanted to reflect the degree of performance. You might give a student one check for a category if the performance was minimally acceptable. (A student who, for example, got up on the second try might get one check

■ Performance checklist: Doing a handstand.

_____a. student sets up on first try
_____b. student is perfectly upright
_____c. student stays up for at least fifteen seconds
_____d. student lands on feet
_____e. student exhibits grace and coordination
_____   Overall quality of performance on a 0–15 scale (or a 0–5 scale)

on criterion a.) Clearly acceptable performance (such as getting up on the first try—wavering—but staying up) might earn two checks while outstanding performance (getting right up the first time) might earn three checks. The student's score for the total performance of doing a handstand then would be the number of checks he or she earned ranging from zero to fifteen. Teachers desiring a simpler scoring procedure could give one check or no checks and require four checks out of five as an indication of acceptable performance. A third possibility would be to consider criterion c to be most essential and to require that it be met as a requirement of mastery with three out of the remaining four needed in addition as a basis for "passing."

MEASURING BEHAVIOR

How do students behave in class? Do they exhibit tendencies to work willingly and capably with others toward the achievement of a common goal or would they be more likely characterized as nonconstructive in the area of interpersonal relations? Are they the kind of students who work beyond required goals or ones who can barely keep up with the class? Are they on time or usually late? Is assigned work completed on time or is it consistently late? Do the students continue to perform and work well with others in a high stress situation or do they seem to lose composure? These are some of the things that teachers look at and consider important in their assessments of the *personal attributes* of students.

Why Measure Behavior?

We have talked about measuring what students know, how they think, and how they perform. Clearly, all of these are important goals in education. Now we are talking about their class behavior (which, in turn, forms the basis for judging their personal attributes). Are classroom behaviors and personal attributes also relevant and important educational goals? Should teachers be concerned about them? The answer must surely be *yes*. Part of an education is developing the kinds of personal attributes that enable one to behave in a constructive manner—not in an automatic, robot-like way but in a way that reflects concern and consideration for others, self-discipline, cooperativeness, drive, and other qualities generally considered desirable. Part of the learning task involves developing constructive behavior patterns (and the underlying personal attributes) both for the present and the future.

Do teachers currently evaluate student behavior and the personal attributes that this behavior reflects? Again, the answer is *yes*. In some form or another teachers observe, record, and often report student behavior, and judge personal attributes. In doing so, they are at least implicitly acknowledging performance objectives such as:

- The student will demonstrate **self-control** by attending to an activity without constant supervision.
- The student will demonstrate the **ability to work constructively** with classmates and share things with them.
- The student will demonstrate the **tendency to do the work** that is expected of him or her in the time available.
- The student will demonstrate **maturity** through socially acceptable behavior and not engage in fights, shouting matches or other forms of acting out.

If such behaviors are to be developed, then there is value in determining whether and to what degree they are being formed. In other words, if we are interested in enhancing or changing the personal attributes of students and the behaviors they prompt, it makes sense to measure them.

Do We Test Behavior?

The key to the question, "Do we test behavior?" is the word *test*. If you were asked, "Do you observe behavior?" you would quickly answer *yes*. When you are asked, "Do you or should you test behavior?" you may not be sure of what to answer. Clearly, you would not be inclined to test behavior in the sense in which the word *test* is commonly used. You would not be inclined to construct a specific test situation into which students would be placed and their behavior observed. In this kind of formal test situation, moreover, students would be likely to perform at their maximum, that is, manifest their "best" behavior, because of their high motivational state. If your interest is to measure "typical" behavior, you would not want to create an obvious test situation that might alter the "typicalness" of behavior. However, you might leave the classroom on purpose to see if students would control themselves, or give an independent study assignment to see if students could generate self-initiative. For the most part though, behavior is an ongoing stream without the clear starting and ending points that characterize a test.

There is an important sense, however, in which we do want to "test" behavior and that is the sense in which a test is systematic and reasonably objective. We need a vehicle for describing typical behavior (and not the usual test vehicle that measures intended performance) so that we can refer to it, report upon it, study its improvement, and determine the effects of specific experiences on it. Thus, we need a methodology and more particularly instruments for measuring behavior that will have some of the characteristics of a test though not necessarily all of them. We will be specifically concerned with a system for describing behavior that can be used with consistency and some degree of objectivity. For this purpose, we will find that scales or checklists are most suitable.

Examples

Some examples follow which illustrate ways of measuring behavior. These are instruments that have been used before (but are not for sale in the usual sense of published tests). They are presented here to serve as a guide for teachers in constructing their own instruments to measure the behavior of students (and students' personal attributes) both individually and collectively and as guides for using those that may be required by their school.

The first sample behavior measure appears in Figure 6-4. It is called the **Maturity Index** and represents an attempt to quantify student behavior on six dimensions. Teachers are given further guidance on the meaning of the numerical ratings that are assigned to each dimension. While this example illustrates a system-wide procedure, it represents the kind of behavior ratings that teachers can develop on their own. Notice that this measure summarizes all results.

The second example appears in Figure 6-5. Unfortunately, some of the labels used to describe student "behavior" in this measure (interesting, appealing, needing approval) sound more like indications of teacher attitudes toward a student than the way he or she is seen to behave. In order to use the instrument as a behavioral measure, specific instructions would need to be given to teachers to make the meaning of the terms clear. They should be instructed to respond to observable indications of behavior (and underlying personal attributes) rather than manifestations of attitudes toward particular students. For example, "curious" behavior might be described in the instructions as trying to find out how things work, asking frequent questions, looking up information, taking objects apart, and generally taking an active role in the learning and exploring process.

The third example appears in Figure 6-6. It is called the **Student Self-discipline Scale** and can be used for describing the behavior of individual students or of a class of students. It is a series of descriptions of student behaviors in the task area (for example, moved to a new task without teacher intervention) and in the social area (for example, did not treat others violently). It represents both the forces urging the student to perform (for example, carried a task beyond its given requirements) and those restraining him or her from performing improperly (for example, "behaved" for an adult other than the teacher). This kind of instrument can be profitably used by either the teacher or an observer to describe student behavior (either individually or collectively) in terms of self-discipline or self-controlled activity.

Figure 6-4
Sample Maturity Index

<table>
<tr><td colspan="7" align="center">**Trenton, N.J., Public Schools**
Maturity Index</td></tr>
<tr><td colspan="7">Name . . . .</td></tr>
<tr><td colspan="7">   Last   First   Initial   H.R.   Adv. Gr.</td></tr>
<tr><td colspan="7">Address . . . . Date of Birth . . . . Date . . . .</td></tr>
<tr><td>Teacher's
Signature</td><td>Reliability</td><td>Work
Habits</td><td>Self
Control</td><td>Initiative</td><td>Sensitivity</td><td>Punctuality</td></tr>
<tr><td>. . . . .
. . . .
. . . .
Home Room
Teacher: . . . .
Pupil's
Estimate . . . .</td><td>. . . . .
. . . .
. . . .

. . . .

. . . .</td><td>. . . . . .
. . . . . .
. . . . . .

</td><td>. . . . .
. . . .
. . . .

. . . .

. . . .</td><td>. . . . .
. . . .
. . . .

. . . .

. . . .</td><td>. . . . .
. . . .
. . . .

. . . .

. . . .</td><td>. . . . .
. . . .
. . . .

. . . .

. . . .</td></tr>
<tr><td colspan="7" align="center">The rating guide appears below</td></tr>
</table>

Indicate the degree to which this student measures up to the goals described below.*

                4—Exceptional
                3—Above average
                2—Average
                1—Below Average

Reliability   —Does he work willingly and capably with others toward the achievement
                    of a common goal? Is he truthful, honest, dependable, conscientious? Does
                    he assume responsibility for his actions?
Initiation   —Does he work beyond required goals? Does student assume leadership? Is
                    he creative, original, exploring?
Work Habits—Does the student complete assigned work?
Self Control —Does student remain emotionally poised and physically restrained under
                    stress?
Sensitivity —Is student sensitive enough to be thoughtful about his attitudes and
                    responses? Is he considerate of the rights of others?
Punctuality —Is student on time?

---

*All results are summarized. A cluster of good ratings will offset one poor rating.

CONSTRUCTING A BEHAVIOR RATING SCALE

The construction of a behavior rating scale, that is, a measure of the quality or style of ongoing behavior, involves three steps: (1) specifying the behaviors to be evaluated, (2) describing these behaviors, and (3) designing the specific scale or yardstick.

Specifying the Behaviors to Be Evaluated.   What behaviors will you choose to evaluate? This will depend on those that you deem important and

Figure 6-5
A Classroom Behavior Rating Scale to Measure Student Behaviors

Name of Child _____

Name of Teacher _____

1. To what extent can the child's behavior be described as CURIOUS?

   NOT AT ALL   1 2 3 4 5 6 7 8 9   EXTREMELY
   CURIOUS   CURIOUS

2. To what extent can the child's behavior be described as INTERESTING?

   NOT AT ALL   1 2 3 4 5 6 7 8 9   EXTREMELY
   INTERESTING   INTERESTING

3. To what extent can the child's behavior be expected to lead to FUTURE SUCCESS?

   NO
   EXPECTATIONS   EXTREME
   OF FUTURE   1 2 3 4 5 6 7 8 9   EXPECTATION
   SUCCESS   OF FUTURE
                                               SUCCESS

4. To what extent can the child's behavior be described as ADJUSTED?

   NOT AT ALL   1 2 3 4 5 6 7 8 9   EXTREMELY
   ADJUSTED   ADJUSTED

5. To what extent can the child's behavior be described as APPEALING?

   NOT AT ALL   1 2 3 4 5 6 7 8 9   EXTREMELY
   APPEALING   APPEALING

6. To what extent can the child's behavior be described as HAPPY?

   NOT AT ALL   1 2 3 4 5 6 7 8 9   EXTREMELY
   HAPPY   HAPPY

7. To what extent can the child's behavior be described as AFFECTIONATE?

   NOT AT ALL   1 2 3 4 5 6 7 8 9   EXTREMELY
   AFFECTIONATE   AFFECTIONATE

8. To what extent can the child's behavior be described as HOSTILE?

   NOT AT ALL   1 2 3 4 5 6 7 8 9   EXTREMELY
   HOSTILE   HOSTILE

9. To what extent does the child behave in such a way to indicate that he (she) NEEDS APPROVAL?

   NO
   INDICATION   EXTREME
   OF NEEDING   1 2 3 4 5 6 7 8 9   INDICATION
   APPROVAL   OF NEEDING
                                               APPROVAL

Figure 6-6
Student Self-discipline Scale*

STUDENT:	Degree of Occurrence								
	ABSENT								PRESENT
Moved to new task as required without teacher intervention	1	2	3	4	5	6	7	8	9
Worked on a task without the teacher's presence	1	2	3	4	5	6	7	8	9
Engaged in task behavior without the teacher's prompting or maintaining it	1	2	3	4	5	6	7	8	9
Carried a task beyond its given requirements	1	2	3	4	5	6	7	8	9
Made accurate evaluation of the quality and completeness of his/her work	1	2	3	4	5	6	7	8	9
Used or assisted classmate(s) as a source of information about doing or correcting his/her work	1	2	3	4	5	6	7	8	9
Used interest center as integral part of work activity	1	2	3	4	5	6	7	8	9
Organized his/her work schedule such that teacher's task requirements are met	1	2	3	4	5	6	7	8	9
Initiated teacher information-giving behavior as resource for on-going activity	1	2	3	4	5	6	7	8	9
Did not treat others violently	1	2	3	4	5	6	7	8	9
Did not attempt to interfere with another's activity	1	2	3	4	5	6	7	8	9
Did not press for the teacher's attention and affection	1	2	3	4	5	6	7	8	9
Maintained work areas	1	2	3	4	5	6	7	8	9
"Behaved" for an adult other than the teacher	1	2	3	4	5	6	7	8	9
When asked by peers, contributed effort or material to their activity	1	2	3	4	5	6	7	8	9

*From B. W. Tuckman, *Evaluating Instructional Programs*, 2d ed., (Boston, 1985), pp. 240–41, by permission of Allyn and Bacon.

relevant primarily in terms of the underlying personal attributes you are trying to enhance. In essence, whether you have formalized them or not, you have objectives regarding student behavior and personal attributes. These probably involve such things as self-control, self-direction, adjustment, and the like. You may have some highly specific behavior goals in areas where you are consciously and systematically trying to affect student behavior. The first step in constructing a behavior scale is to make a list of the behaviors you want to evaluate.

Let us say for illustrative purposes that your list appears as follows:

The student will
1. complete his or her work.
2. cooperate with the teacher.
3. work harmoniously with classmates.
4. exhibit an interest in learning.
5. utilize the resources of the classroom and school.

6. be neat and organized.
7. participate freely in the classroom process.

No one can make up a complete list for every teacher. Each teacher has his or her own specific objectives when it comes to classroom behavior although there is probably a common pool from which teachers can draw. Feel free to borrow bits and pieces from the various sources you come in contact with in constructing your own list. The above list emphasizes minimal rule-following (completing work, cooperation, neatness, organization) and involvement (learning interest, resource use, classroom participation).

Describing the Behaviors.   The behaviors to be evaluated must be more than named. They must also be described as operationalized so that they can be judged with reasonable objectivity, reliability, and consistency. (The determination of reliability will be discussed in Chapter Eight.) Some behaviors will be easier to describe than others but all must be described at some level. These descriptions constitute the criteria with which to evaluate.

Let us continue with our six sample behaviors and attempt to describe each.

1. **Completion of work:** (a) classwork is completed on time, (b) homework is handed in when due, (c) classroom performance indicates that assignments have been done, (d) things once begun are finished in the form required.
2. **Cooperation:** (a) helps teacher when asked (and often when not asked), (b) maintains proper classroom decorum, (c) helps classmates, (d) shares with classmates.
3. **Interest in learning:** (a) exhibits knowledge not acquired in school, (b) exhibits curiosity about new things to be learned, (c) pays attention to information being presented, (d) tries to learn about the why and how of things rather than just accepting them.
4. **Use of resources:** (a) uses specific resources when instructed to do so, (b) uses specific resources on own initiative, (c) uses resources (including people) outside of the classroom, (d) uses resources to best advantage (for example, in library consults card catalogue).
5. **Neatness and organization:** (a) keeps desk and work area organized and neat when not in use (stores things neatly), (b) keeps self neat, (c) helps keep classroom neat, (d) organizes work and materials in a systematic way.
6. **Participation:** (a) asks questions in class, (b) answers questions posed by teacher, (c) volunteers for activities, (d) contributes materials and information to the class and classroom.

Although the above criteria still involve to some extent a teacher's subjective reactions, they do provide specific cues for the teacher to use in making judgments. Four points of reference provide greater help in structuring a judgment than a single one.

If your value for each of the behaviors is not the same, weight them to reflect their differential importance. Suppose, for example, you think that sample behavior (three) is the most important behavior in the list and sample behavior (five) the least important. To reflect this you could assign behavior (three) a weight of 2 and behavior (five) a weight of ½. All other behaviors would have a weight of 1. Of course, if you had no interest in the total score but simply in recording each individual behavior, weighting would be unnecessary since weighting is used to reflect *relative* importance.

Designing the Scale.   As we have seen before, a scale is a numbered continuum where each number represents the degree of a particular quality such as acceptance or rejection, presence or absence. Scales may have as few as three points or as many as one hundred. The most common rating scales are three-, five-, seven-, and nine-point scales. More scale points introduce greater variations while fewer points limit the possibilities of response. The odd number of scale points has the advantage of providing a middle point to reflect an undecided or down-the-middle judgment and the disadvantage of allowing raters to avoid making a clear-cut choice.

For illustrative purposes let us cast our six behaviors into five-point rating scales.

STUDENT COMPLETES WORK

1	2	3	4	5
never	rarely	occasionally	frequently	always

STUDENT COOPERATES WITH TEACHER AND CLASSMATES

1	2	3	4	5
never	rarely	occasionally	frequently	always

STUDENT EXHIBITS AN INTEREST IN LEARNING

1	2	3	4	5
never	rarely	occasionally	frequently	always

STUDENT UTILIZES EDUCATIONAL RESOURCES

1	2	3	4	5
never	rarely	occasionally	frequently	always

STUDENT IS NEAT AND ORGANIZED

1	2	3	4	5
never	rarely	occasionally	frequently	always

STUDENT PARTICIPATES IN CLASSROOM ACTIVITIES

1	2	3	4	5
never	rarely	occasionally	frequently	always

The five-point scale is a convenient size, and frequency ratings are reasonably easy to structure. Armed with such an instrument, teachers can include the realm of classroom behavior as part of their total evaluation of students and of their own educational effectiveness.

USING A BEHAVIOR RATING SCALE

Here are some examples of the use of a behavior rating scale.

Including classroom behavior as part of the overall basis for student evaluation.   We grade students on what they know and how they perform. If we want to include students' behavior as part of our evaluation of them, we must measure it.

Diagnosing and documenting behavioral difficulties.   Some students present what has been referred to as "behavioral problems." Such students often require special services and parental consultation. Behavioral measurement helps in the diagnosis and documentation of such cases. However, we must be careful not to create a stigma for a student that will influence the expectations of that student's future teachers and hence their treatment of him or her.

Altering, improving, and enhancing particular behaviors.   Changing and enhancing certain behaviors and inhibiting others is part of growing up. Teachers often attempt to take some responsibility for this process. In order to give feedback and to try different programs and interventions with different students, the teacher must keep track of and monitor behavior. Hence, the measuring instrument.

Teacher self- and program evaluation.   Teachers may be trying certain strategies, such as the open classroom approach, that aim to change the behavior of students (and teachers) in certain specific ways. To determine whether these interventions are producing the desired effect, evidence about student behavior is needed—evidence not focused on individual students but on the overall behavior of the class as a reflection of the outcome of the teacher's approach. An illustrative scale to gather such evidence is shown in Figure 6-7. In this case the observations are made by a department head or principal rather than by the teacher.

Figure 6-7
Sample Classroom Observation Scale to Measure Implementation of Learning Unit Plan and General Teaching Effectiveness

	Degree of Occurrence				
Classroom Climate	ABSENT				PRESENT

Students

1. maintain a conversational noise level	1	2	3	4	5
2. move freely and purposefully about the classroom	1	2	3	4	5
3. involve themselves in creative activities to capitalize on their talent and/or interest	1	2	3	4	5
4. interact with one another in meaningful ways	1	2	3	4	5
5. seek help from teacher when in need of assistance	1	2	3	4	5
			Subtotal _____		

Motivation

Students

1. are aware of learning unit goals as they apply to themselves	1	2	3	4	5
2. establish some of their own priorities and objectives	1	2	3	4	5
3. make choices and select from among options and alternatives relative to unit objectives	1	2	3	4	5
4. work at their own pace within approximate time intervals	1	2	3	4	5
5. self-assess and record their work and progress per objective	1	2	3	4	5
6. move from one learning activity to another with minimum teacher intervention	1	2	3	4	5
			Subtotal _____		

Interaction

Teacher

1. asks provocative questions that lead students to participate in class	1	2	3	4	5
2. accepts, clarifies, and supports students' feelings and ideas	1	2	3	4	5
3. provides for student interaction in a variety of positive ways	1	2	3	4	5
4. gives students direction and provides structure as needed	1	2	3	4	5
5. uses varied grouping patterns to achieve learning objectives	1	2	3	4	5
6. moves from student to student and from group to group	1	2	3	4	5
			Subtotal _____		

Specific Teaching Variables

Teacher

1. engages in continuous evaluation of students' progress on objectives	1	2	3	4	5
2. confers with students on goals and use of materials	1	2	3	4	5
3. prescribes learning procedures on the basis of individual student diagnosis	1	2	3	4	5
4. focuses instructional content on the objectives of the unit	1	2	3	4	5
5. implements instructional strategies geared to the objectives of the unit	1	2	3	4	5
6. makes available a variety of instructional media and materials to facilitate individualized learning	1	2	3	4	5
7. provides instructional sequences to fit different learning styles and rates	1	2	3	4	5
8. evaluates each student relative to unit objectives	1	2	3	4	5
			Subtotal _____		

Some Suggestions

When the scale is used by an outside observer, it is best to do it when the class is in session. Although the scale is best used by the teacher when he or she is not directly engaged in the instructional process, he or she may want to jot down critical incidents as they occur. To increase the objectivity of the entire process, the teacher should try to focus on actual observed behaviors.

To increase the reliability of judgments, particularly when they are made of individual students, the judgments should be made twice, each time independently. Making two judgments helps the teacher become more aware of his or her own internal judgment process; this awareness can then be applied to overcome bias and to increase consistency. When outside observers are employed, observations should be made by two persons, observing independently but at the same time. (The discussion of reliability will be continued in Chapter Eight.)

The most important quality required for rating the behavior of people is objectivity. Sufficient work in the development of the scale, adequate understanding of the meaning of scale terms, and time and patience in practicing with the scale (trying it out, for example) will help the teacher develop techniques for rating behavior objectively.

Proficiency Test

1. State three criteria teachers should examine and consider before engaging in performance testing.
2. State two objectives that you would use a performance test to measure and give the reason why you would use a performance test in these cases.
3. You are interested in testing to find out whether students know how to construct an equilateral triangle. Specify the *test situation* and *desired performance outcome*.
4. Prepare a *checklist* that can be used to evaluate student performance in constructing an equilateral right triangle.
5. You have just finished teaching a unit on space relations and want to find out whether students can visualize a spatial arrangement such as a floor plan. Specify a *test situation* and *desired performance outcome*.
6. Prepare a *checklist* that can be used to evaluate student performance in drawing a floor plan.
7. You are interested in measuring the extent to which each student in class is motivated to learn. Specify the behavior to be measured and describe it by listing four observable criteria for its detection.
8. Prepare a behavior rating scale that can be used to measure the extent to which a student is motivated to learn.
9. You want to measure the extent to which a teacher is prepared to

teach a lesson. Specify the behavior to be measured and describe it by listing four observable criteria.

10. Prepare a behavior rating scale that can be used to measure the extent to which a teacher is prepared to teach a lesson.

11. You are at a faculty meeting that is devoted to the construction of educational goals and objectives. Cite one argument you might use in favor of the rating of student behavior.

12. Your school is experimenting with a program in which students engage in discussions of values relative to the issues and problems that they are facing. How might the measurement of student behavior be used in conjunction with such a program?

Content Validity

OBJECTIVES

- Define content validity, a criterion of achievement tests, as the consistency between test items and objectives.
- Describe and illustrate the use of a content map for building content validity into an achievement test.
- List and apply checklist procedures for evaluating the content validity of a test by determining its overall fit to objectives, correspondence to intended behavior, correspondence to conditions, and correspondence to criteria.
- Define domain-referencing and its use as a means of increasing a test's content validity.
- Identify and list factors based on instructional and student characteristics (rather than objectives) that can make test items invalid, namely: testing what was never taught, response sets, and cultural bias.

WHY EVALUATE A TEST?

A test is a device for sampling behavior or performance related to the skills, competencies, attitudes, or other characteristics of people. It is in essence a performance sample constructed by the test maker to be representative of a student's proficiency or character and whose results have some credibility. Just as we evaluate the appropriateness of instruction based on objectives, we can evaluate the content validity of tests based on objectives. The parallels between the two types of evaluation are strong.

Suppose you were a student in a college course called introduction to psychology and your instructor gave you the examination shown in Figure 7-1. When this exam was given to the faculty and graduate students of a psychology department (a total of forty people) the following results were obtained.

No. Correct	Frequency (No. of People)
0	5
1	9
2	12
3	7
4	4
5	3
6	0
7	0
8	0
9	0
10	0

Most of the faculty and graduate students were able to get only two of the ten items right; none got more than half right. If 65 percent correct had been set as the passing grade (that is, 6.5 right out of 10), the entire faculty and graduate student group who took the test would have failed, even though it was in their area of expertise! Is this, then, a suitable test for measuring a student's competence in introductory psychology? No! Why not? Because it is too hard? Is it too hard because no one could answer more than half of the questions? This is not the reason for it being too hard; this is the *evidence* for it being too hard. The *reason* for it being too hard is that people who are subject-matter specialists did not have the information required to answer the questions. If subject-matter specialists are unfamiliar with this information, it is unlikely that an introductory psychology course would cover it. In other words, we need to *evaluate* a test and we need *criteria* for evaluating the quality of that test. Without test evaluation in terms of criteria, we might be building or selecting tests that have nothing to do with what we want to measure and therefore are likely to be too hard or too easy.

Figure 7-1
An Example of an Invalid Test

Introduction to Psychology   Spring 1985
    830:121
                            FINAL EXAM

1. The Whorfian hypothesis suggests that
    a. the implicit, unverbalized values of a culture affect the behavior
       of its members.
    b. the structure of perception and thought is dictated by the struc-
       ture of the language one speaks.
    c. a part of speech is defined by the role the word plays in a sen-
       tence rather than by what it stands for.
    d. the agreement between cultures about the meaning of words is
       high.
2. The Zeigarnick effect specifies a superior retention of incompleted
   over completed tasks in the ratio of
    a. 3 to 1.   c. 2 to 1.
    b. 2.5 to 1.   d. 1.5 to 1.
3. A transactional view of perception is most clearly associated with
   the work of
    a. Ames.   c. E. Gibson.
    b. J. J. Gibson.   d. Riggs.
4. Nafe's model of thermal sensitivity of the skin is usually referred to
   as the
    a. concentration theory.   c. local generator theory.
    b. gradient theory.   d. vascular theory.
5. The Freudian concept of *reversal of affect* is most clearly illustrated
   in the case of
    a. The Wolf Man.   c. Dora.
    b. Little Hans.   d. Leonardo da Vinci.
6. The earliest piece of psychological laboratory research on memory
   was conducted by
    a. Ebbinghaus.   c. William James.
    b. Hering.   d. Wundt.
7. In establishing test validity, the *standard error of estimate* is found by
   which of the following formulas?

   a. $\sigma_y^2 \sqrt{1 - r_{xy}^2}$ c. $n\sigma_y \sqrt{1 - r_{xy}^2}$

   b. $2\dfrac{(1 - \sigma_x^2 + \sigma_y^2)}{\sigma_+^2}$ d. $\sigma_y \sqrt{1 - r_{xy}^2}$

8. The *comparison level* as a concept influencing choice of social behavior has been defined as a standard for evaluating the rewards and
   costs of a given relationship based on the model value of all the
   outcomes known to the person. This definition was stated by
    a. Thibaut and Kelley.   c. Jones and deCharms.
    b. Homans.   d. Heider.

9. A positive conditioned stimulus is firmly established in a dog by means of the usual repetitions with reinforcement. A new stimulus is now occasionally added, and whenever the combination is applied, which may be at intervals sometimes extending to hours or even days, it is never accompanied by the unconditioned stimulus. In this manner the combination is gradually rendered ineffective, so that the conditioned stimulus when applied in combination with the additional stimulus loses its positive effect, although when applied singly and with constant reinforcement it retains its full powers. Pavlov named this phenomenon

   a. external inhibition.　　　　　c. experimental extinction.

   b. conditioned inhibition.　　　d. deconditioning.

10. Piaget has labeled the process by which the young infant makes interesting spectacles last as

   a. reproductive assimilation.　　c. generalizing assimilation.

   b. recognitory assimilation.　　　d. accommodation.

APPLYING THE CRITERIA OF A GOOD TEST

The preceding chapters of this book were devoted to test construction. Once you have constructed your own measuring instrument, you are confronted by the practical problem of evaluating and, if necessary, revising it. This chapter and the next will provide a set of guidelines for assessing the adequacy or suitability of a test in terms of the criteria of **content validity** and **reliability**.

Before the testing criteria can be applied, two practical assumptions must be met:

- You, as a teacher, are interested in and willing to take the time to evaluate and improve your tests.
- Once you have given a test, you are willing to consider the results not only as a way of evaluating your students but also as a way of evaluating your test.

A TEST SHOULD HAVE CONTENT VALIDITY

A test is of no use if it does not measure what we want it to measure. If we call what a test is supposed to measure its *objectives* and what it does measure its *outcomes,* then **one criterion of a good test is that it measures outcomes that are consistent with its objectives.** A test that measures what we intend

---

Answers

(1) b, (2) c, (3) a, (4) d, (5) c, (6) b, (7) d, (8) a, (9) b, (10) c.

it to measure has a special kind of suitability that we will refer to as *content validity*.

If a test lacks a purpose or objective, it will be impossible to assess its content validity, that is, to evaluate it on this particular criterion. The purpose of a test is to measure some characteristic of people: what they have learned, what they are like, what they like, and so on. The first thing we try to find out about a test (if we are considering selecting it) or should specify about a test (if we are about to construct it) is what its objectives are, that is, what we intend it to measure. Once we have decided what a test is intended to measure, we can determine whether it measures what we want it to, that is, whether it has content validity.

We should say two more important things about the concept of content validity. First of all, it is applied primarily to the evaluation of achievement or gains resulting from instruction. It represents an important way to judge achievement tests but it is not as helpful in judging predictive or psychological tests such as intelligence tests or personality tests. Second, content validity is usually not given much coverage because of its limited value for evaluating psychological tests. However, because of its value for evaluating the kinds of tests most typically used by teachers, it is distinctively labeled here and given a full chapter.

The various questions for applying the content validity criterion are listed below.

Is My Test CONTENT VALID?

1. Does it fit my objectives:
   a. Are there at least two items for each and every objective and zero items that fit no objectives?
   b. Do the number of items per objective accurately reflect the relative importance of each objective?
2. Does it reflect the action verbs:
   a. Does each item for a given objective measure the action called for by the verb in that objective?
   b. Have I used the item format most appropriate for each action?
3. Does it utilize the conditions:
   a. Does each item for a given objective employ the statement of givens or conditions set forth in that objective?
4. Does it employ the criteria:
   a. Is the scoring of each item for a given objective based on the criteria stated in that objective?

The Importance of Objectives

Having spent a large portion of preceding chapters dealing with objectives, it will now be seen again how the specification of objectives is important for test construction. If a test's content validity is based on the extent to which it measures its own objectives, we must first specify the objectives of the test. If a test fails to measure some of its objectives or measures things that are not part of its objectives then its value will be limited.

Remember that content validity **represents the extent to which the test content is representative of the content or skills** (objectives) **that it is intended to sample.** If a teacher gives a test after two weeks of instruction, then the content validity of that test will be based on the extent to which the test items represent or reflect the material that was covered (and hence that students were expected to learn) during those two weeks. Content validity is like a *mapping* or matching of what is being measured to what is intended to have been learned (and hence presumably taught) in order to see if what is being measured is what was taught. Content validity has its time reference in the past, that is, it refers to what *was* intended, and can be applied particularly to achievement tests.

For purposes of illustration, let us take a unit of instruction and prepare such a map. The map must tell us what was covered—that is, a **list of objectives** (sometimes referred to as a **content outline**) and to what degree each part was covered—that is, how much time was devoted to each part (presumably, though not necessarily, a partial indication of importance). Figure 7-2 shows a **content map** for a unit in fourth grade social studies, this particular unit dealing with the deserts of Africa. The unit contains seven objectives that have been listed down the left column. Units of importance (a judgment by the teacher of the relative importance of each objective) have been listed across the top.

The test for this unit has been constructed so that a student can obtain a number of points for performing each objective to the degree indicated by its units of importance. Thus, the test not only represents each of the objectives (no more, no less), but also represents each in proportion to its importance or emphasis. Importance is reflected in test points either by having more items or by having more complex items for which more than a point may be obtained.[1] Importance, thus, is represented by the number of performances required for each objective.

The more accurately a test's content and coverage reflect its content map (made up of objectives and their relative importance), the more content valid a test. If you build your content map before you teach your unit or construct your test, and then teach your unit and construct your test based on your content map, the content validity of your test will be high (given properly written items). If your test items are written to be good reflectors of your objectives, a test based on these objectives should attain as high a level of content validity as can be expected.

---

[1]Scoring may be done by item or by objective. The number of items per objective reflects not only the importance but also the complexity of the objective: the more complex the objective, the more items required to measure it.

Figure 7-2
Content Map for a Unit and Test on the Deserts of Africa (Social Studies, Fourth Grade)

Objectives for Unit on Deserts of Africa Given a map of North Africa students can:		Units of Importance*					
		1	2	3	4	5	6
1	Mark in the location of the three major deserts	◉	◉				
2	Recall and write in the names of these deserts	◉					
3	Identify indigenous plant life	◉					
4	Identify indigenous animal life	◉	◉				
5	Describe how humans satisfy their basic needs there	◉	◉	◉			
6	Describe what it is like to grow up there	◉	◉	◉	◉		
7	Describe the culture (that is, the rules of getting along together)	◉	◉	◉			

* Based on time spent on each
◉ Single test item or point of credit on a test item

When you are using a test constructed by someone else, such as a published achievement test, you can determine its content validity for your purposes based on the correspondence between the content outline of the test and your objectives. Construct a content map for your class and then examine the test items and see whether their content and number reflect your content map. Put in a dot for each item as shown in Figure 7-2 and see how well the test fits your map. Examples of a good fit and a poor fit are shown in Figure 7-3.

Keep in mind that the content validity of a test may not be the same for any two teachers; each teacher determines his or her own content map. One teacher's objectives and hence instruction may be more closely related to what the test was designed to measure than another's. Thus, the same test does not always display the same degree of content validity.

Applying the Content Validity Criterion

To test for content validity you need two things: (1) the test itself, and (2) the list of objectives of which that test is presumably a measure. Place these

Figure 7-3
A Content Map Compared for Two Tests: One High and One Low in Content Validity

Objectives	Units of Importance					
	1	2	3	4	5	6
1	◉	◉				
2	◉	◉	X			
3	◉	◉	◉	X		
4	◉	X				
5	◉	◉	◉			
6	◉	◉	◉	◉	X	X
7	⊗					
8						

High Content Validity

Objectives	Units of Importance					
	1	2	3	4	5	6
1	◉	⊗	⊗			
2	X	X	X			
3	◉	◉	X	X		
4	◉	◉	⊗	⊗		
5	◉	X	X			
6	◉	X	X	X	X	X
7	⊗	⊗				
8	⊗	⊗				

Low Content Validity

◉ Test item that measures a given objective.
⊗ Test item that does not measure a given objective.
X Given objective for which a necessary test item is missing.
Bold line indicates outline of content map.

two side by side; then ask yourself if you have measured performance on each objective. There should be no objective for which there are no items on the test (unless you are using some other measurement strategy for one or more of the objectives). There should be no items on the test for which there are no objectives. If you find items on the test for which you have no objective, then either remove those items or rewrite them so that they conform to an objective on your list. (You may also consider modifying your list.) It is important to try to achieve consistency.

Correspondence to Intended Behavior.   You will notice from the list of questions on page 130 that the three components—action verbs, conditions, and criteria—have been set forth for evaluating the extent to which your items are consistent with your objectives. Of these three, action verbs typically cause the greatest difficulty. Often, the action verb in the objective will specify one kind of performance and the corresponding item will measure a different kind of performance. For example, the action verb requires the student to *demonstrate* something and in fact the test item asks him or her to *identify* something. Because a student can identify something does not necessarily mean he or she can demonstrate it. If the objective deals with demonstration, the corresponding test item must provide for such an operation.

The best strategy would seem to be to specify your objectives and then design, through the use of content mapping, a test and testing situation valid for measuring those objectives. **Let the objectives be the elements that are fixed and the test items the elements that are flexible enough to be fitted to the objectives, rather than the other way around.**

Correspondence to Conditions and Criteria.   The same kind of matching of objectives and test items must be demanded in terms of conditions and criteria. Those conditions set forth in the objective as the conditions under which the action or performance must occur should be the conditions provided in the items to measure that objective. If the objective specifies that the student is to be given a map of the United States, then such a map must be provided in the items to measure that objective. Criteria must be handled in the same manner. If the objective specifies that the student's description of topography will include mention of at least six of the mountain ranges present, then the item measuring that objective should be a free response or essay-type of item and should be scored in terms of the criterion as it was stated in the objective.

DOMAIN-REFERENCING

As we have seen, a test's content validity is dependent on the consistency between the conditions specified in each objective and the manner in which that objective is measured. As the items written to measure an objective become more representative of that set of performances that the objective calls for (otherwise known as the objective's **domain**), the test on which these items appear becomes more content valid.

Writers of achievement tests are encouraged to engage in domain-referencing to increase the content validity of their tests. The problem that the item writer faces is that objectives, even good ones, are not item specific; that is, given an objective, a rather large number of items can usually be written. How does the writer know which one to write so that his or her resulting test will be high in content validity and have clear interpretability? The answer to this question may be to define and describe the domain or class of items that might be written in terms of the range of characteristics that these items might have.

If we have an objective such as determining the volume of an irregular solid using a water displacement procedure, we could develop a statement of the item domain or item form by specifying in detail the characteristics of the irregular solid, the equipment provided, the instructions given to the student, the form of his or her response, and the possible different outcomes that the student might encounter within the range or domain of the objective. Using this kind of detailed information about the conditions under which the performance will be measured, the item writer can know and precisely describe the population of items (that is, *all* the items) that might be written to measure the objective. The item writer can then randomly or representatively select items from this population of items in order to insure that the items chosen are representative of that population and hence that (1) the items are content valid, and (2) the performance of students on those items can be interpreted to reflect their likely performance on the whole population of items and thereby the degree of proficiency on the objective itself.

Hively (1973) has designed an approach called the **item form** that can be used for constructing appropriate test items for given objectives. The item form allows the test item to be referenced to the objective's domain.

The item form has six categories that provide the basis for constructing one or more items for a given objective. These categories are

1. response description
2. content limits
3. item format
4. criteria
5. test directions
6. sample test item

Response description refers to the **action** part of the objective and **criteria** to the **criteria** part. **Item format** refers to the **conditions** part of the objective and the type of test item to be used. **Test directions** and **sample test item** are obvious in meaning. Most difficult of the six parts of the form to construct is the **content limits,** which refers to the range of instances of the conditions or givens that will be accepted as suitable for the objective.

Content limits specify the objective's **domain**. Putting all the parts together yields the following example.

1. **Response description:** To be able to add fractional expressions in sequence.
2. **Content limits:** No more than four fractional expressions; mixed numbers and fractions will be used; only denominators to be used are between 2 and 8, inclusive, except 7 which is excluded; all answers are greater than one and reducible.
3. **Item format:** One sequence of fractional expressions per item. Students should show their work and fill in their answers in the spaces provided.
4. **Criteria:** All fractional answers should be reduced and converted to mixed numbers. Conversion of fractions to lowest common denominator form should be shown.
5. **Directions:** Below is a list of fractional expressions. Add them up. Show all your work. Express your answer as a mixed number with lowest denominator possible.
6. **Sample item:** $\frac{7}{8} + 1\frac{1}{8} + \frac{3}{4} + \frac{1}{2} = $ _____.

Domain-referencing as described above is a considerable undertaking, probably well beyond that which can normally and reasonably be expected of teachers. What is reasonable to expect is that teachers will exercise care and devote effort to describing the conditions of the objective so that they will at least have a conception of the domain from which items may be drawn. By being sensitive to at least the major dimensions of that domain, teachers can write items with sufficient levels of content validity to allow them to justify the interpretations they make based on them.

WHAT MAKES TESTS INVALID?

If basing tests on objectives makes them valid, then lack of an objective base leads them to be invalid. However, lack of validity comes in guises other than a lack of correspondence of test items to objectives. Consider three of the more important ones:

1. You never provided suitable instruction on the objective.
2. Students are responding to their own internal predispositions to respond, rather than to the items.
3. The test items and the students are on different cultural wavelengths.

Testing What Was Never Taught

At the two extremes of achievement testing we have "teaching for the test" and "testing what was never taught." A content valid achievement test represents testing for what was taught (assuming, of course, that instruction has been geared to the objectives). However, in some respects the test must be independent from what was taught; the student must be able to transfer or apply his or her learning to unfamiliar material. The learning must have been provided for, but the situation in which it is to be manifested must be new in that test items have not been singled out for practice during instruction.

Sometimes when you sit down to construct a test you may feel a mischievous urge to spring some surprises on your students. If you spring too many surprises, you will end up with a test that has little to do with what you taught. This situation is shown in Figure 7-4. A test need not be mundane; the students should not be told in advance what the test items will be; but their instructional experiences should bear directly on the material to be covered in an achievement test or it cannot be considered a content valid measure of what students *should have learned.*

Response Sets

On some kinds of tests students can decide what conclusions they want you, the test maker, to draw about them or they can figure out what you want to hear. This practice is known as **faking.**

One form of distortion is called **acquiesence.** This occurs when students respond with a pattern, such as true-false-true-false, or true-true-true . . . , rather than actually attempting to identify the correct response choice in each and every case. Such a response pattern is often prompted by disinterest or hostility or by test items that are consistently too difficult to answer. Students who have the tendency to overselect the "true" response choice are referred to as "yeasayers."

Cultural Bias

Culture is, among other things, a wavelength of communication. Teachers communicate largely in their cultures to students whose cultures overlap to greater or lesser degrees with their own. Tests also reflect a culture, usually that of the test maker. We may say that a test always measures two things: a set of objectives, and an ability to function in the culture in which it is written. If students are in a different culture or on a different wavelength

Figure 7-4
Relation between Testing and Teaching

SIMILARITY BETWEEN TEST AND INSTRUCTION

New Objectives New Items	Same Objectives New Items	Same Objectives Same Items
Test of Something Else	Valid	Part of Instruction (Practice)

from that of the test, the test may lack content validity for them as a measure of its objectives. However, we may also say that the greater the content validity of a test based on its representing its objectives, the greater the likelihood of its overall content validity. Hence, cultural bias is potentially a greater threat to the content validity of broader, more general tests, such as standardized achievement tests, than it is to good teacher-built tests. Test publishers usually screen their achievement tests to try to minimize the chance of culturally biased items. Teachers should be careful not only to screen their own test items but their objectives as well.

Where achievement items are not based on the known opportunity to learn (that is, the availability of school-based instruction), they may be measuring more culturally-based opportunities to learn, thus introducing cultural bias. By virtue of their generality, published tests may often be measuring outcomes that are tied in their likelihood of occurrence to cultural experience. Items about sports, for example, may be biased against girls. Tests with cultural bias lose content validity accordingly unless their purpose is to measure outcomes related to culture.

VALIDITY AND THE TEACHER

The kind of validity most often considered by the teacher is whether the test "looks" as if it measures what the teacher intends to measure with it. We don't usually credit enough importance to this kind of informal judgment, which is called **face validity.**

If the students taking a test feel that it is invalid, this may affect the way they respond to the items. If teachers feel that a test is "unfair," they may reduce its value by indirectly communicating their misgivings to the students. If parents feel that a test is not valid, they may successfully push to have the test removed.

While the "naked eye" is thus an important judge of a test's validity, it is not ultimately the best judge. We might say that content validity, a measure of a test's fit to its objectives, is really a *structured* form of face validity. Content validity is judged by "eye" rather than by statistics, but the judgment is aided by the application of stated objectives.

In choosing or using published tests, teachers should check the test manual to see whether objectives are available and whether they are the desired ones. (Since test manuals are often difficult to interpret, teachers may want to seek the assistance of a staff member with testing experience, a school psychologist, for example.) Teachers should question the content validity of standardized achievement measures for their own use in much the same way they should challenge and subsequently demonstrate (at least to themselves) the content validity of their own tests.

It is virtually impossible to judge the content validity of any achievement test, teacher-built or published, *unless you know the purpose or objectives that the test is intended to measure.* An achievement test should reflect what a teacher wants a student to have learned and thus presumably has taught. (Reexamine Figures 2-1 and 2-7 in Chapter Two showing the systems approach—it is relevant to the point being made here.)

We might simplify the relationship between objectives, teaching, and tests as follows:

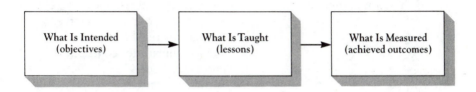

If a test is a measure of what is intended, and what is intended is actually taught, then achievement on the test will tell you the extent to which students have profited by instruction. If the test results indicate that many students have profited from instruction, those that did not may have been inattentive, poorly motivated, ill-prepared, or unable to relate to the instruction. You can also use test results to evaluate your teaching; if test scores indicate that few students profited from instruction, the instruction itself may have been at fault.

Proficiency Test

1. The most important consideration in determining a test's content validity is
   a. the vocabulary level of the test items.
   b. whether its purpose is psychometric or edumetric.
   c. whether it measures outcomes that are consistent with its objectives.
   d. the extent to which students have improved from pretesting to posttesting.
2. List four questions that can be used to determine the content validity of a given test item.
3. You have three objectives that you want to measure. Describe how you would use a content map to build a content valid test of these objectives.
4. Draw a diagram of a content map for a test of four objectives with total content validity. (Use a dot with a circle around it to indicate a test item that measures a given objective.) Make two of the objectives twice as important as the others.
5. In most cases the minimum number of items necessary to measure each objective is _____.
6. On the left, four standards are listed for judging the content validity

of a unit test in a high school humanities course. On the right, questions are listed for applying these standards. Match each item on the left with an appropriate question on the right.

a. Fits objectives.
b. Reflects action verbs.
c. Utilizes conditions.
d. Employs criteria.

i. Does the number of items reflect the relative importance of each part of the unit?
ii. Does each item reflect the "given" in its corresponding objective?
iii. Would this test be suitable for a similar humanities course in another school?
iv. Is the item format appropriate for what the student is asked to do?
v. Are the answers judged to be correct or incorrect according to terms stated in the objectives?

7. Determine the content validity of the first seven items of this test for measuring the first three objectives of this chapter.
8. Domain-referencing requires as its primary prerequisite that
    a. objectives have been labeled as to cognitive or affective area.
    b. behavior to be measured by a set of test items has been specified.
    c. items have been classified as knowledge, comprehension, application, analysis, synthesis, or evaluation.
    d. items have been written to be representative of that set of performances an objective calls for.
    e. the acceptable level of performance has been defined in absolute terms.
9. Domain-referencing helps insure that the items chosen are not too difficult for students to answer correctly.
TRUE   FALSE

10. Check those factors below that can affect a test's content validity.
    a. Response bias.
    b. Student motivation.
    c. Conditions of test administration.
    d. Testing for skills not in the objectives.
    e. Specific cultural factors.
    f. How much sleep a student has had the night before.
11. You have just finished teaching a unit on oceans and have covered the names, descriptions, locations of the oceans, and the resources they provide. Your students are third graders in a small school in rural Tennessee. You are now constructing your end-of-unit test and have written the items below. Unfortunately, some of these items are invalid. Match those that are invalid on the right with the reason for invalidity on the left.

a. Different cultural wavelength.
b. Testing what you never taught.
c. Acquiesence response bias.

i. What are the names of the five oceans?
ii. Write a poem describing your feelings as you watch the sun rise over the ocean.
iii. Which ocean is the largest?
iv. What is the southern-most land mass on the planet Earth?
v. The weight of all the water in the oceans is 100 million tons. (TRUE   FALSE)

Test Reliability

OBJECTIVES

- Define reliability, a test criterion, as test accuracy or consistency over time and items.
- Identify the standard error of measurement and its relationship to test reliability.
- Identify and contrast five different types of test reliability, namely (a) Kuder-Richardson Formula 21, (b) parallel item agreement, (c) split-half (including the Spearman-Brown Formula), (d) alternate forms, and (e) test-retest.
- Name overall sources of test variability and sources of error, and give examples of each.
- Identify ways of building reliability into a test, namely using a sufficient number of items, targeting, controlling conditions of test administration, controlling for general or specific skills, setting intermediate levels of difficulty, and following item writing rules.
- Describe four checklist procedures that teachers can use to determine and improve the reliability of a test, namely (a) determining parallel item agreement, (b) using item analysis, (c) examining student response patterns, and (d) improving reliability of scoring.

NO MEASUREMENT IS PERFECT

No measurement instrument or procedure is perfect. Neither a mechanical device such as a voltmeter nor a human device such as a test gives a result that is a perfect reflection of the property being measured. If you measured the same thing twice under the same conditions you would not get the *exact* same measurement each time. However, given an accurate measuring procedure, the values you would get if you measured twice would probably be so close that you could not easily tell them apart. Measure the length of this page with a twelve-inch ruler. Now do it a second time; the result is probably the same as the first. Given a less accurate measuring procedure, the values you get if you measure twice will not be as close. Try measuring the page with a pencil instead of a ruler. Does the page measure the same number of pencil lengths each time?

When you measure some property of an object or person, you are attempting to discover the *true value* of that property. In measuring the length of the page, you were attempting to find out how long the page actually is, that is, its *true* length (sometimes referred to as *actual* length). When you read its length off the ruler, you were discovering its measured or *obtained* length. But are the two not the same? No, they are not because all measurement contains errors. If you were to measure the length of the page say one hundred times, and then average all of the measurements, that average would be about as close to the true length as you are likely to get using a ruler. It might be possible to improve the accuracy of the measurement by using a more finely calibrated ruler, but, even so, the measured or obtained length and the true length would not be exactly the same.

Consider now a teacher-built test to measure achievement or learning. The teacher is really interested in how much the student has learned, that is, the learning score. To determine that score, the teacher must construct a measuring instrument—a test. However, because the test results reflect not only how much the student has learned but also how accurate a measuring instrument the test is, the score for each student is a less than perfect measure of how much he or she has learned.

Because teachers do not want to come to conclusions about student performance (or anything else for that matter) based on the scores of inaccurate tests, they want to build tests that are as accurate as possible. But since no test can be absolutely perfect, it is important to know how accurate a test is in order to know how much confidence to place in its results. The term *reliability* is used to designate a test's accuracy. Reliability indicates the degree to which a test is consistent in measuring whatever it does measure— the degree to which the test measures the same thing time after time and item after item. **Consistency over time and items is basic to the concept of reliability.**

When a test is given to a group of students, or to the same student more than once, there is variability or variance in the scores (that is, the scores are not all the same; they differ). Part of this variability is a true variability in the property being measured; part reflects error in the test. The next section will consider the relationship of error in the test to its reliability.

The Standard Error of Measurement

If we call the information we want out of a test its **signal** (that is, the true score), what we get when we use the test is a **signal-plus-noise.** Many factors contribute to this noise or inaccuracy. At the moment, let us restrict ourselves to only those noise factors that are likely to be present to some degree each time the test is given; that is, those noise or error factors that are within the test itself. We evaluate the magnitude of that error by determining the **standard error of measurement.** The standard error of measurement is the standard deviation of the differences between students' true scores on the test and their obtained or measured scores. (That is, it is the square root of the sum of the differences between each obtained score and its corresponding true score squared, divided by the number of scores. It is a reflection of the *average* amount of variation between true scores and obtained scores.)

Consider the previous discussion of measuring a page length one hundred times and averaging the one hundred measurements. If a test were given one hundred times, and if we averaged or obtained the mean score of the one hundred (by adding the one hundred scores and dividing by one hundred), we would have a pretty good approximation of the true score. The degree or amount to which the one hundred scores varied around this mean or average would indicate the standard error of measurement of the test.

If we accept the mean score on the one hundred tests as representative of the true score, then the standard error of measurement tells how close each measured score is to the true score and hence how accurate the test can be. Obviously the larger the standard error of measurement, the less accurate the test.

As we have said, though, all the variance in a set of scores cannot be considered error. Some of it is true variance based on the fact that students will actually vary on the property being measured. Though it is obviously important to have a measure of a test's accuracy, it is equally obvious that it would be impractical to give a test one hundred times to obtain the standard error of measurement. Instead, test accuracy is typically expressed not as the standard error of measurement, but as a reliability coefficient. **The reliability coefficient is that portion of the variance in test scores that is not the result of errors of measurement.** It is, in fact, one minus the error variance (the square of the standard error of measurement) divided by the total test score variance.[1] As we increase error variance relative to total

---

[1] This formula is not typically used for calculating reliability, only for representing the relationship between the standard error of measurement and test reliability. Reliability is usually determined using the procedures described in the next section.

variance, we decrease reliability; as we decrease error, we increase reliability. The goal of the test builder, therefore, is to decrease the error in the test, that is, the standard error of measurement.

The questions we must now ask are how can reliability be determined and how can it be improved?

FIVE PROCEDURES FOR ASSESSING RELIABILITY

It is not difficult to imagine a content outline (page 44) for which any of one hundred tests would be appropriate, although few teachers would welcome the task of having to prepare that many. Most teachers simply prepare one test for a given situation. But if you had developed one hundred tests rather than only the one you did develop, how do you know that scores of students on the one would be the same as their averaged scores on the one hundred? Moreover, even in the case of the single test, how do you know that students would obtain the same score each time if it were given one hundred times? That is, how do you know that the test gives you a consistent measure of the property being measured? **The extent to which a particular test gives a consistent and accurate representation of the property being measured by that test is a function of the test's reliability.**

As we have said, reliability is an indication of the accuracy and consistency of a test based, at least in theory, on the degree of true variability in the total variability of test scores. Reliability can thus be thought of as the ratio of the signal to the combination of signal-plus-noise. The more noise (or error variance) a test picks up, the less reliable it is.

The impracticality of giving one hundred tests for the same content outline, or the same test one hundred times, has led to the development of other procedures for assessing the reliability of a test. Each of these procedures represents a way of estimating the probability that the obtained test score is the same as the true score (or actual amount of the measured quality) possessed by the test taker. Five such procedures for estimating a test's reliability will be described, all but the second of which utilize the correlation coefficient as a statistical indicator of reliability.

Kuder-Richardson Formula 21 (K-R 21)

Instead of comparing scores on different administrations of a test to determine that test's reliability, it is far easier to estimate reliability by comparing scores on the test's items, in essence considering each item as a test in itself. If the test items show a high degree of agreement, then you can presume the test is an accurate or consistent measure. (You cannot say, however, what the test is a consistent measure of, based on this estimate; that is a question of validity. But whatever that test is measuring, if a high degree of agreement on students' item scores is obtained, you can only conclude that the test is *consistent*, hence, reliable.)

K-R 21 is a simple way of approximating the degree of agreement or correlations among items on a test. It is shown below.

$$\text{reliability} = \frac{n}{n-1}\left(1 - \frac{\overline{X}(n - \overline{X})}{ns^2}\right)$$

$\overline{X}$ represents the mean or average score on the test by the class; s represents the standard deviation of a set of obtained test scores—a measure of the variability of a group of scores around a mean. The letter n stands for the number of items in the test.

The reliability of a test can vary between 0 and 1.00. A reliability of 0 indicates that a test has no reliability and hence is an inadequate test for making any judgments about students. (Such low reliabilities are quite rare since they indicate that a test measures nothing but error.) A reliability of 1.00 is a perfect reliability, indicating a perfect or error-free test (also an unlikely occurrence). Published tests usually require test reliabilities of .85 or above when based on the agreement among test items while teacher-built tests are usually considered adequate with reliabilities of .60 or above.

Imagine that you have just given your students a twelve-item test on which each item is scored as either right or wrong (items must be scored in this manner if K-R 21 is to be used). Your class of ten students has obtained the following scores:

12	9
11	7
10	6
9	5
9	2

Since these scores add up to 80 and since there are ten students, the mean score would be 8.0 (80/10). The square of the standard deviation (s^2), also called the **variance,** is obtained by subtracting each individual test score from the mean to get a deviation score, squaring each deviation score, adding the squares (which add to 82 in this example), and dividing by the number of scores to give a variance (of 8.2 in this example).

If we put these values into the K-R 21 formula we come out with a reliability of .73,[2] which would be considered adequate for a teacher-built test with as few as twelve items. You can see that as n, the number of items in the test increases, the reliability would increase also (assuming the other values stayed the same) since the fraction to be subtracted from 1 becomes smaller.

---

[2]reliability $= \left(\dfrac{12}{12-1}\right)\left(1 - \dfrac{8(12-8)}{12(8.2)}\right) = (1.09)\left(1 - \dfrac{32}{98.4}\right)$

$= (1.09)(1 - .33) = 1.09(.67) = .73$

Let us try one more example in order to make a point. Consider the following ten scores on the twelve-item test.

$$\begin{array}{cc} 12 & 11 \\ 12 & 11 \\ 12 & 10 \\ 11 & 10 \\ 11 & 10 \end{array}$$

These scores have a mean of 11.0 and a variance (s^2) of 0.6; putting these numbers into the K-R 21 formula yields a reliability value of less than zero. (Normally, the reliability value cannot go below zero but the K-R 21 formula is an approximate rather than an exact one—producing its greatest distortion on scores that appear in the above pattern.)

Why does the first pattern (or as we say in technical terms, **distribution**) yield a much higher reliability than the second, at least in terms of the K-R 21 formula? The answer is important for our consideration of reliability. The K-R 21 formula is based on the assumption of what is called a **normal distribution** of test scores; that is, of the greatest frequency of scores occurring in the center of the distribution, about the mean, and a progressively decreasing frequency of scores as one moves to the extremes. This distribution is represented by what is commonly known as the bell-shaped curve.

Consider the distribution of scores as shown in Figure 8-1. Distribution *a* shows the scores in the first example, in which the K-R 21 reliability was .73. Distribution *b* comes from the second example, having essentially a zero reliability in terms of the K-R 21 formula. Distribution *c* is an ideal

Figure 8-1
Three Distributions of Test Scores: (a) the first example (b) the second example (c) a normal distribution

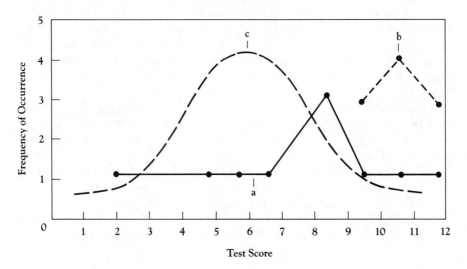

version of a normal distribution, representing the distribution of true scores in the total population. As the obtained distribution of scores approaches the normal or presumably true score distribution, the reliability approaches 1.00.

If, however, the instruction has been successful, it is not totally unlikely that a distribution such as *b* will result. Does this mean that tests on which most students succeed are unreliable and therefore unworthy for use? The answer may be *no*! For classroom tests of the type on which consistent success or the successful demonstration of *proficiency* by all students is the goal (what we will call criterion-referenced tests in the next chapter), another type of reliability determination than that provided by K-R 21 would be more suitable (described below). However, for tests whose scores are to be evaluated on a comparative or relative basis (and for which normal or bell-shaped distributions will be obtained) K-R 21 provides a simple way to calculate test reliability.

Parallel-item Reliability

Parallel-item reliability can be thought of as being suitable for tests on which proficiency by a large segment of the class is expected to be demonstrated (that is, criterion-referenced tests). **Parallel-item reliability is based on the determination of consistency of performance by students across items that are intended to measure the same objective.**

Let us say, for example, that the twelve-item test referred to earlier is an attempt to measure performance on four objectives and so three items have been written for each objective. In essence, then, each item in a three-item set can be considered to be a measure of the same thing—the particular objective that that three-item set has been written to measure. If students have acquired proficiency on that objective, they should get all three items right. If they have not acquired proficiency on that objective, they should get all three items wrong (assuming that all three items have been randomly sampled from the same domain and hence measure the same thing with approximately the same degree of difficulty). Where the characteristic pattern is for students to get one or two items right and two or one wrong, the mini-test of that objective can be considered to be low in parallel-item reliability.

Parallel-item reliability can be assessed by simply counting. Let us examine the performance of the ten students on the twelve-item test. The array of item scores has been laid out in Figure 8-2. You can see from the array that there is considerable consistency of performance across each three-item set. The only exception to this is item six (in the set of items for objective two). Six of the ten students got item six wrong. However, all ten students got items four and five right, indicating that adequate proficiency on objective two had been attained. On this basis, we can conclude that item six is not parallel to items four and five and should be rewritten. Given this

Figure 8-2
An Array of Item Scores by Ten Students on a Twelve-item Test (X's indicate incorrect responses; blanks indicate correct responses)

Students/Items	Objective One			Objective Two			Objective Three			Objective Four		
	1	2	3	4	5	6	7	8	9	10	11	12
1												
2					X						X	
3								X				
4					X							
5												
6					X							
7					X					X		
8					X							
9												
10			X		X							

change, it would be safe to conclude that the twelve-item test had high parallel-item reliability.

Split-half Reliability

Another form of reliability based on parallelism is split-half reliability. **Split-half reliability is based on the equivalence of performance by students on each half of a test.** However, it must be pointed out that split-half reliability is primarily applied to norm-referenced tests and so represents a variation on the use of the K-R 21 approach.

For purposes of calculating split-half reliability, a test is divided arbitrarily in half, one half containing the odd-numbered items, the other the even-numbered items. Now, instead of having one score for the total test, you have two scores—one for each half of the test. The two half-test scores can then be correlated with one another across the group of students who took the test, yielding a split-half reliability coefficient.[3]

The correlation coefficient that results from comparing the two half-test scores, however, describes the reliability of only half of the test rather

---

[3] A correlation can be regarded as the degree to which students maintain their same relative positions on two tests or two sets of test items. If there is little change, that is, much correspondence, the correlation will be high. If there is much change, that is, little correspondence, the correlation will be low.

than the whole test. Since the test user will be using the whole test, it is that reliability which is important. To calculate the reliability of the whole test given the split-half reliability, the **Spearman-Brown Formula,** given below, can be used.

$$\frac{\text{reliability of}}{\text{total test}} = \frac{2 \times \text{reliability of half test}}{1 + \text{reliability of half test}}$$

In many cases, one of the reliabilities of published tests reported in test manuals is a split-half reliability that has been corrected by the Spearman-Brown Formula. Teachers, however, may find the parallel-item reliability procedure, described in the preceding section, more useful since their tests are often of the criterion-referenced type.

Alternate-form Reliability

Another kind of reliability based on parallelism is alternate-form reliability. **Alternate-form reliability is based on the equivalence of scores on two tests that are intended to be substitutable measures of the same thing.** Sometimes test publishers publish two forms of a test—Form A and Form B, Form 1 and Form 2, or a long form and a short form. If a group of students takes both forms and their scores on each form closely correspond, the test can be said to have alternate-form reliability. You can then use the forms interchangeably, a particularly important feature if you are going to use them to measure pupil growth (that is, to compare scores on the two tests with time or instruction intervening).

Test-retest Reliability

Test-retest reliability, as the name implies, is determined by giving students the same test twice. It **is based on the extent to which students' scores on each of two administrations of a test correspond.** Since consistency is the hallmark of reliability, a test that yields similar scores on each of two administrations with no significant events intervening is a highly reliable one.

There are, however, three shortcomings to the test-retest procedure. The first is that it is most difficult to minimize the significance of events intervening between the two test administrations; thus the two test administrations must occur close together in time. The second shortcoming is that many factors can affect the performance of students on a test each time it is taken and hence reduce its reliability. (These factors will be discussed in a later section.) When a test is given on two different occasions, these factors have two opportunities to influence the results (moreover, different error sources may be operating each time), increasing the assessment of a test's unreliability and making test-retest reliability a severe estimate of reliability.

The third shortcoming to test-retest reliability is that its determination requires that students undergo two testings (a problem shared with the determination of alternate-forms reliability). Unlike split-half reliability or K-R 21 reliability which only require a single testing—and that would have been carried out anyway, test-retest reliability forces the test developer to use two parallel testing sessions within a short time span.

Because of the above three shortcomings, test-retest reliability determinations occur infrequently. That is unfortunate because this approach tells us about a test's consistency over time rather than its internal consistency as the other procedures do. Since consistency over time seems basic to the concept of reliability, more use of test-retest reliability would seem desirable. (When this approach is used, lower reliability coefficients must be expected because of the above-mentioned shortcomings.)

SOURCES OF TEST VARIABILITY

Recall that a test's reliability is that portion of the total variation in test scores that does not result from errors of measurement. Consequently, it is worthwhile examining variability in test scores to try to distinguish between true variability on the variable in question and variability that represents or contributes to test unreliability. Knowing the sources of errors of measurement may help us to reduce them and hence improve test reliability.

Overall Sources

Thorndike (1949) identified four general sources of test variability, shown in Figure 8-3. The first category, **lasting and general characteristics of the individual,** includes the general characteristics of the test taker that the test is attempting to measure along with other general characteristics he or she may have. IQ, aptitude, and reading tests, for example, each attempt to measure a general characteristic of the individual. However, on achievement tests, which attempt to measure specific characteristics, general characteristics constitute a source of measurement error or bias. When we are trying to measure how much a student has learned, variability based on a general ability, such as reading skill, serves only to confuse the issue. However, where the effect of general abilities on a test of specific skills is constant across the test, the reliability of that test will be unaffected. It is validity that will be lessened. Where reading skill affects performance on some items more than others, it will affect a test's reliability.

We have all known people who were good test takers. This general characteristic, while not an objective of any specific test, has led these people to perform well on almost every test they took. Other people are test-anxious and characteristically perform poorly on tests even though they can demonstrate proficiency on the test content in a nontest situation. Thus, lasting and general characteristics include some that we want to measure and others that reduce the accuracy of the test for its intended purposes.

Figure 8-3
Sources of Test Variability*

I. Lasting and general characteristics of the individual
  1. General skills (for example, reading)
  2. General ability to comprehend instructions, testwiseness, techniques of taking tests
  3. Ability to solve problems of the general type presented in this test
  4. Attitudes, emotional reactions, or habits generally operating in a situation like the test situation (for example, self-confidence)
II. Lasting and specific characteristics of the individual
  1. Knowledge and skills required by particular problems in the test
  2. Attitudes, emotional reactions, or habits related to particular test stimuli (for example, fear of high places brought to mind by an inquiry about such fears on a personality test)
III. Temporary and general characteristics of the individual (systematically affecting performance on various tests at a particular time)
  1. Health, fatigue, and emotional strain
  2. Motivation, rapport with examiner
  3. Effects of heat, light, ventilation, and so on
  4. Level of practice on skills required by tests of this type
  5. Present attitudes, emotional reactions, or strength of habits (insofar as these are departures from the person's average or lasting characteristics—for example, political attitudes during an election campaign)
IV. Temporary and specific characteristics of the individual
  1. Changes in fatigue or motivation developed by this particular test (for example, discouragement resulting from failure on a particular item)
  2. Fluctuations in attention, coordination, or standards of judgment
  3. Fluctuations in memory for particular facts
  4. Level of practice on skills or knowledge required by this particular test (for example, effects of special coaching)
  5. Temporary emotional states, strength of habits, and so on, related to particular test stimuli (for example, a question calls to mind a recent bad dream)
  6. Luck in the selection of answers by guessing

---

*Reprinted from R. L. Thorndike, *Personnel Selection,* 1949, by permission of John Wiley & Sons, Inc.

Then there are **lasting and specific characteristics of the individual** that often relate to specific items on a test. An item in which automobiles are used for purposes of illustration would be more closely attended to by car buffs while items relating to sports would favor the athletically inclined. On tests of general abilities, specific characteristics constitute undesirable sources of variability because they reduce reliability. However, on tests of specific characteristics such as achievement tests, specific characteristics represent the goal or objective of the measurement.

Temporary and general characteristics of the individual include those that are operating at the particular time when the test is taken. Everybody has a bad day and it is unfortunate to have to take a test on such a day. A recent death in the family, for example, or a failure in the heating system in the testing room will affect test performance. Such characteristics contribute to those portions of a test's variability that constitute errors of measurement since they do not relate to the true variability in the property being measured.

Finally, there are **temporary and specific characteristics of the individual** like good luck at guessing, pretest coaching, a look at last year's test, or problems in concentrating because of street noises or the murmuring of the student sitting at the next desk. These too reduce reliability.

Error Sources

We can trace many of the sources of variability in test performance to the test itself. The **number of test items** will affect test performance. Very short tests provide a very limited sample of performance on which to judge the lasting and general characteristics of an individual while very long tests produce fatigue, inattention, and other temporary and general characteristics. Longer tests do, however, minimize the effect of success based on guessing.

Then, too, there is the **quality of test items**. Bad items may be too easy, or too difficult, or too unrelated to the test's target area and hence quite susceptible to the various temporary, general, or specific characteristics of the individual other than those that the test is attempting to measure. Since a test is just a collection of items, the test's characteristics will be based on the nature and number of the items. These are the only two variables in the test itself, both of which can be controlled by the test maker.

Conditions of test administration affect test performance and hence test reliability by having differing effects on different test takers. Temporary and general characteristics of the individual are largely the result of the conditions of test administration. Performance on most any test given in a hot room will suffer, for example, and confusion or noise will also affect test performance and hence reliability of a test.

Conditions of scoring are also a source of variability and thus error. Where scoring varies from test to test—as may be true for essays—error variance is introduced which interferes with the process of obtaining a true picture of the skills and competencies or other characteristics of students.

These sources of test variability can be used as a basis for identifying ways and means of reducing that portion of the variability that is caused by errors of measurement (primarily the temporary ones) and thus increasing reliability.

STRATEGIES FOR BUILDING RELIABILITY INTO A TEST

If you can identify those factors that affect test performance over and above the single factors you are interested in measuring, you can construct reliable tests by controlling the extraneous factors to the greatest extent possible. Some recommended procedures for accomplishing this are discussed below.

Including Enough Test Items

A longer test is generally more reliable than a shorter one because it provides a larger and hence potentially more representative sample of a student's performance. Imagine a course with ten objectives and a final exam with ten items—one per objective. If a student were to make a careless error on one item, or if one item occurred in an unfamiliar context causing the student to miss it, you would conclude that the student had not learned one of the objectives. This conclusion would not reflect the student's failure; it would reflect the test's failure. Similarly, if a student had guessed correctly on an item, or glanced at his or her neighbor's paper, it would be inaccurately concluded that the student attained proficiency on that objective. If the test were doubled to twenty items—two per objective—or tripled or quadrupled, the effect of these sorts of errors would be reduced. Careless errors and guessing would still occur but their effect on the conclusions drawn from the test would be lessened. It is recommended that no fewer than two items per objective be included and more where possible. If test length becomes a problem, tests should be constructed to measure fewer objectives.

Targeting Items

Items must be written for a goal or objective. Each item represents an attempt to measure some particular outcome or quality. To the extent that the overall objective of a test can be broken down into subobjectives, the more likely it is that the test items can be made to correspond. Thus, the content outline approach presented in Chapter Three not only contributes to test validity but to test reliability as well. It is easier to write ten pairs of items—two per objective—than it is to write twenty items for a single broad course objective. Subdividing helps the test writer write targeted, hence specific, items, increasing the likelihood that items within a cluster are measuring the same property. Since reliability is based on item correspondence or agreement, targeting helps insure reliability, particularly in the case of tests of specific skills such as achievement tests.

Controlling for General or Specific Skills

While the total or overall effect of reading level on an achievement test relates to a test's validity, the variability in the reading level of items within a test relates to its reliability. On tests of specific skills, such as achievement tests, reliability is likely to be higher if the effects of general skills such as reading level are kept constant. Thus, if the test is a measure of something other than reading skills, you should attempt to write all items at approximately the same reading level to avoid introducing variability across items based on an internal characteristic of the test itself.

In any test of specific skills, general skill requirements must be kept relatively constant across items. Reading is the most common of these skills but presumably test items must be consistent in relation to a person's attitudes or self-concept unless these are the qualities measured by the test. Constancy should also be applied to specific characteristics such as interests or particular competencies but this is particularly hard to do. Because all test items must have content, it is hard to control the extraneous variability in item performance that such content, when not intrinsic to the quality being measured, will introduce.

Setting Difficulty Level across Items at Intermediate Levels

Items that are too easy or too difficult do not adequately represent the domain of the objectives being measured. Moreover, where difficulty levels vary greatly from item to item, the internal consistency of a test is not likely to be high. According to Lord's (1952) findings, test reliabilities are highest when item difficulties fall into the 50 to 75 percent range (that is, when 50 to 75 percent of the test takers get an item right). While different groups of students may vary in their success on a test, overall difficulty levels between 50 and 60 percent would seem most suitable for reliability purposes.

However, very easy items may serve motivational purposes such as bolstering student confidence or making students feel comfortable with a test. Some easy items may be included, but the bulk of items should be of intermediate difficulty to give the test good reliability.

Controlling the Conditions of Test Administration

Wherever possible, test administrators should take care to control as many of the conditions of test administration as they can. It is wise to think of a test as more than just the written items. Tests include instructions and the conditions under which testing is to be conducted.

Testing conditions should be such as to avoid creating any extra and unnecessary stress for students beyond that normally experienced in a test situation. Distractions, as well as the teacher's direct intervention, should be kept at a minimum. The physical environment should be made as comfortable as possible. If conditions vary widely from testing to testing, the results of the test will reflect these variations and hence will be less reliable than if conditions remain the same.

USING TEST RESULTS TO IMPROVE A TEST'S RELIABILITY

The preceding sections have dealt largely with the concepts of test reliability, the types of test reliability (for example, Kuder-Richardson Formula 21, split-half, and so forth), sources of test unreliability, and procedures for constructing more reliable tests. Beyond following the recommendations for building their tests to be reliable, it is also possible for teachers to use test results to *improve* upon the reliability of their tests. These procedures for increasing reliability based on the results of testing are outlined as follows:

Is My Test RELIABLE?

1. Are there paired or parallel items that agree:
   a. Do students who get one item of a pair (per objective) right also get the other right and those who get one wrong get the other wrong?
   b. Have nonparallel items been rewritten?
2. Is item performance consistent with test performance:
   a. Is each item consistently passed by students who do well on the total test?
   b. Have inconsistent items been removed?
3. Are all items clear and understandable:
   a. Have student responses been used as a basis for evaluating item clarity?
   b. Have ambiguous items been removed or rewritten?
4. Have scoring procedures proved to be systematic and unbiased:
   a. Have multiple scorings yielded consistent results?
   b. Are scoring criteria and procedures as detailed and as suitable as they can be?

Remember that reliability deals with the question of **accuracy**. A test is an instrument, a measuring device, a scale. If it does not measure some quality accurately and consistently, it is not a reliable instrument. The question is not what it measures, but *does it measure it consistently*. It will not be very consistent if it is sensitive to factors that go up and down from moment to moment, day to day, and item to item. If a test is not consistent within itself, that is from item to item, it holds little possibility of being consistent over time. Thus, for improving reliability we focus on first determining and then improving the consistency of a test from item to item.

Agreement between Parallel Items

Examining agreement between parallel items is a practical way for teachers to assess the reliability of their tests. After you have given a test, go back and look at the performance on the pairs of items per objective by each student and see how many students displayed the same performance on each of the two parallel items in each pair. If the items in each pair are consistent with one another, the majority of students should have gotten both of the items in any pair right or wrong. Those instances where students got one right and one wrong in a pair indicate that the two items are not consistent; they are, in fact, nonparallel items.

Therefore, as a two-item mini-test, those pairs lacking agreement or consistency would detract from reliability. Item pairs in which up to a third or more of the students get one right and one wrong should be reexamined. These items should be rewritten as a pair, or at least one member of such inconsistent pairs should be rewritten.[4]

Item Analysis

After a test has been administered, an analysis of the relationship between item scores and total test scores, called **item analysis,** very often reveals items that are inconsistent with the total test or parts of it. The pattern of item scores shown in Figure 8-2 was used as a basis for determining the inadequacy of a specific item; that item was found not to relate to other items presumably measuring the same quality. The test writer would then rewrite or revise the bad item or items, thereby increasing the reliability of the total test. It is highly recommended that test writers, be they teachers or commercial test writers, reexamine the results of a test by means of an item analysis (or at least an examination of item results) in order to identify the bad items. **Item analysis is the procedure by which individual item performance by a group of test takers is compared to their performance on the total test.** It may be facilitated by preparing an array of responses by individual students to individual items as shown in Figure 8-2.

The purpose of item analysis is to make each item consistent with the total test. To do item analysis, take the performance on an item by each individual and the performance on the total test by each individual and examine this relationship across a number of individuals.[5] You would then choose those items on which student performance corresponded most closely to total test performance. If you start with one hundred items and want to end up with a test of fifty items, initially try all one hundred and then keep the fifty items having the closest correspondence to the total test score. That would give you the most reliable test.

---

[4]This procedure is based on the presumption that a test will be used more than once. If you go to the trouble to make better tests, it would be wasteful to use them once and throw them away. You may not want to use each test time after time after time, but you may want to build up a test-item file from which you can select items for reuse.

[5]When this procedure is done statistically, the relationship between item scores and total test scores across individuals is expressed as a correlation coefficient.

You can also separate the students who have taken the test into high and low scorers and compute item discriminability and item difficulty (or easiness) using the following formulas:

$$\text{Item Discriminability} = \frac{\text{No. of top } \frac{1}{3} \text{ who get item right}}{\text{No of top } \frac{1}{3} + \text{No. of bottom } \frac{1}{3} \text{ who get item right}}$$

$$\text{Item Easiness} = \frac{\text{No. of top } \frac{1}{3} + \text{No. of bottom } \frac{1}{3} \text{ who get item right}}{\text{Total no. in top } \frac{1}{3} + \text{bottom } \frac{1}{3}}$$

Identify the top third scorers and bottom third scorers as a convenient subset of the total class and examine their performance on each item. Good items will have discriminability values around 1.0 and easiness values around 0.5 indicating that all of the top third scorers got the item right and all of the bottom third scorers got it wrong. If all of the students in both high and low thirds get an item right, it will have an easiness score of 1.0 and a discriminability of 0.5. Those are poor items.

Making Items Clearer and More Understandable

You can use student responses on a qualitative basis for making decisions about good items and bad items and for improving bad items. Just by looking at the answers students generate on completion items or the patterns of accepting and rejecting response choices on multiple choice items (that is, which ones are chosen and which ones are not), you can learn a lot about which items are good and which items are poor and why the poor ones are poor.

Many teachers score tests very automatically, simply by grading the number of items right and items wrong and computing the total score. They do not look at responses and rarely count the number of times each distractor or wrong answer in a multiple-choice situation is chosen by students and compare it to the number of students who chose the right answer. A single distractor that is chosen more often than the right answer, or a distractor or option that no one chooses may be interpreted by the students in a different way than you had intended it to be. Or you may have miskeyed an item, that is, included a distractor that is as good or better an answer than the one keyed correct. That is the kind of item that has to be changed to improve test reliability. Particular distractors may require revision. If many such misinterpretations occur, consistency would be poor. It is also worthwhile to examine item difficulty based on overall student performance on an item in order to detect those that may be too easy or too difficult.

In addition to carefully and systematically examining student response patterns on items, it is helpful to discuss the items with students after they take the test. (Discussion of the items with colleagues is also helpful.) Such discussions may help point out sources of ambiguity and misunderstanding and suggest ways that problem items can be revised to overcome their shortcomings.

Reliability of Scoring Procedures

Often in education human beings are the measuring instruments. Other than in multiple choice or true–false or matching tests, which can be scored objectively and automatically, it is human judgment that determines the accuracy of answers.

On an essay test, for example, the teacher reads the responses and makes judgments about students' competency or proficiency. What would happen if the teacher were to read that essay a second time? Would the same judgments of performance be made? If the judgments the second time are different from the first, who is to say which is more accurate? Maybe some of the essays were read late at night when the teacher was tired, while the remainder were read in the morning when the teacher was more alert. Or perhaps the teacher read the name of the student before reading the response and because of the difficulty in making the judgments that the scoring of essay responses requires, was influenced by expectations based on the student's past performance and apparent ability. When your unconscious biases or expectations affect your scoring consistency, your reliability as a scorer suffers.

To determine the reliability of your scoring you must do some rescoring. If you can, score every essay item twice. If not, compromise; try to read some proportion of the essay questions twice and establish your own scoring reliability. The minimal number that is usually considered necessary for reliability is one out of five. Try to read one out of every five essays twice to see how close you come the second time to the judgments you made the first time. If you set up scoring criteria (as described below), scoring can be done much more quickly. If you know exactly what you are looking for and how much you are going to weigh the different criteria, you can score all the essays and rescore 20 percent of them in the time it might have taken you to score them once without explicit criteria.

In performance testing or behavior measurement you are dealing with questions of judgment and should use reliability observers when possible. You need not necessarily use a second observer for every test or observation (that is, you need not collect two full sets of data), but you should include a second observer for one out of every five observations or make it yourself a second time. If you bring in another person to serve as a reliability observer, be sure that both of you are there at the same time so the two of you will be observing the same behavior, but also be sure to make your judgments independently. The comparison between the two sets of judgments can then serve as an indication of the reliability of these judgments. You may also want to practice first with the other observer to increase the likelihood that you can get reasonably good reliability with respect to that person.

Here are some suggestions about how to improve your reliability as a scorer. First, cover the students' names before you score so that you cannot be influenced by your expectation of them. This is called **scoring blind.**

Second, structure your response key as much as you can in terms of what answer you are looking for, how many points you will give for organization, content, creativity, problem solution, and rationale. The more scoring specifications you can generate and write down (and hopefully communicate to students so they know what the criteria are), the more likely it is that you will be able to make these judgments consistently, time after time, student after student.[6] Refer to pages 91–97 for a more thorough discussion of these points. (Also see pages 46–48 on test-item specifications.)

Proficiency Test

1. We use the term reliability to designate
   a. the fit between a test's objectives and its items.
   b. the extent to which test scores predict future learning success.
   c. the degree to which the test measures the same thing time after time.
   d. the meaning of the scores on a test.
   e. the absence of cultural bias.
2. The reliability of a test can be used to express the extent to which it gives a consistent measurement across items.
   TRUE   FALSE
3. The standard error of measurement on a test is
   a. a measure that increases as the accuracy of a test increases.
   b. the difference between predicted scores and obtained scores.
   c. a measure of true variance of test scores.
   d. the difference between true scores and obtained scores.
4. The reliability coefficient is that portion of the variance in test scores that is the result of errors of measurement.
   TRUE   FALSE
5. Match the type of reliability at left with its definition at right.
   a. Kuder-Richardson 21   i. consistency of performance across
   b. Parallel item   items that are intended to measure
   c. Split-half   the same objective

---

[6]Where multiple judges are used simultaneously, as in the judging of diving competition as described on page 104, the two most extreme judgments (that is, the highest and lowest) are discarded each time to increase scoring reliability. The performance score is obtained by averaging the judgments of the remaining judges.

d. Alternate form

e. Test-retest

    ii. consistency of performance across different tests that are intended to measure the same objectives

   iii. consistency of performance across different administrations of the same test

   iv. consistency of performance across the odd-item and even-item segments of a test

    v. approximation of the correlations among all the items on a test

   vi. approximation of all the correlations among half the items on a test

6. For each of the illustrations below, identify the type of reliability depicted.
   a. After the students completed the test, it was divided into two parts and two separate scores were calculated for each student. Correlating the two scores yielded a coefficient of .89.
   b. The test had two items for each objective. On 90 percent of the objectives, students either got both the items measuring that objective right or both wrong.
   c. When a formula was used to approximate the extent of variability in students' test scores not reflecting error, the resulting coefficient was .85.
   d. The first period English class took the test on Monday and again on Friday. Scores on the two testings were correlated to provide a coefficient of .86.
   e. The test came in Form A and Form B. Students were given both forms and their scores on each correlated to get a coefficient of .84.
7. According to Thorndike, there are four categories of individual characteristics that serve as sources of test variability. Name and give an example of each of the four.
8. You are administering a test to measure how much students have learned from a unit on primate biology. Below are factors that will affect how well students do on your test. Some of these factors contribute error variance, some true variance. Write E next to those that contribute error variance and T for true variance.
   a. how well the student paid attention to what was taught
   b. how much the student dislikes taking tests
   c. how much of the information in the unit the student learned
   d. whether the student can read all the words in each item
   e. whether the student understands the test instructions
9. Check those suggestions next that one should follow to build reliability into a test.

    a. write items of intermediate difficulty levels

    b. target items to the content outline

    c. write all items at the same reading level

    d. offer the poorer students rewards to heighten their attention

    e. follow item writing rules when preparing items

    f. write items in different areas of interest

    g. avoid variations in testing conditions

10. The _____ (shorter, longer) a test is, generally the more reliable it is.

11. You have constructed and administered an achievement test on the events leading up to World War I. You plan to use this test again next year and so would like to improve its reliability.

    a. Describe how you would conduct and use item analysis for this purpose.

    b. Assume that the test was a multiple choice test. Describe how you could use student response patterns as the basis for revising to improve reliability.

    c. Assume that the test was an essay test. Describe how you could improve the reliability of scoring.

12. Describe how you would use parallel item agreement to improve the reliability of this proficiency test.

9

Measuring Achievement with Published Test Batteries

OBJECTIVES

- Identify and describe the types of skills and competencies measured by survey achievement batteries (general achievement in language arts, reading, mathematics, social studies, science, and study skills).

- State similarities and differences between standardized and teacher-built achievement tests on various test criteria.

- Distinguish between achievement and intelligence test items in terms of specificity.

- List and explain rules to follow in administering published achievement test batteries.

WHAT DO STANDARDIZED ACHIEVEMENT TESTS MEASURE?

Standardized achievement tests enjoy a widespread use in the public schools of this country. Many school systems administer these tests once a year to all students (or at least to all elementary school students). The first question that must be dealt with in understanding standardized achievement tests and their role in the schools is what they measure.[1]

General Achievement in Reading

Reading skill is generally measured in terms of vocabulary, word analysis, and reading comprehension.

Vocabulary.   In vocabulary tests, respondents are given a definition or synonym and asked to **identify the word that is a synonym or that fits or completes the definition.**[2]

- If you tear a piece of paper, you
  rip it   cry about it   stain it
       o   o   o
- You could best describe an *extrovert* as being
  o pensive   o outgoing
  o exuberant   o self-conscious

Word Analysis.   This type of test at early grade levels requires a student to correctly identify a word that he or she hears—more specifically, to **distinguish a word given orally from potentially confusable forms.** Items often require both listening and reading ability, together with the ability to distinguish from among confusable forms.

- SAID (read aloud by teacher)
  seed   sod   sad   said   (seen by student)
   o   o   o   o

At the later elementary grades, this test may also deal with the similarities between sounds in words, asking the respondent to **select a word that has the same sound as the underlined part of a given word.**

- r<u>h</u>yme   happy   rich   pile
                      o   o   o

For older students word analysis items also often require students to **select the sound that is the same as a designated part of a given word:**

---

[1]The description of achievement tests in this chapter is based largely on an analysis of the major achievement batteries.

[2]All examples are patterned after actual achievement test items. Unless otherwise specified, the first sample item in a pair is an early elementary item (grades 1–3) and the second item, a middle school or junior high item (grades 7–9). At the lower levels, test items and answer choices are read aloud by the teacher while students have answer choices before them. Answers to sample items appear at the bottom of page 172.

- The underlined sound in *particular* (pẽr-tik′ yoo-lẽr)
  - o rhymes with the *a* in *fan*
  - o is pronounced like the *a* in *play*
  - o has the *e* in *penny* sound
  - o has the *u* sound in *curtail*

As you can see from the various illustrations, word analysis focuses on the sounds and structure of words.

Reading Comprehension. Reading is sometimes measured in part by determining whether the student can **identify the word that fits a given picture.** A first grade item might look like this:

-
  - o bat
  - o mat
  - o but

At higher grade levels, a story is provided, which the student reads. He or she must then **identify the correct answer to a question based on the content of the given story.** A fifth grade item might be as follows:

- The sea otter who lives in the Pacific Ocean is covered with a coat of beautiful and valuable fur. Between 1700 and 1910, hunters and trappers tried to kill the otters. They would then skin them and sell their fur. In order to protect the otters from being wiped out, a law was passed in 1910 that said that people couldn't kill otters.

  People killed sea otters
  - o because it was fun to do.
  - o to get their fur.
  - o to keep them from eating up all the fish.
  - o to keep them from spreading.

  From the story we can tell that
  - o all the settlers were so greedy for fur that they would do anything to get it.
  - o you can't buy an otter fur coat today.
  - o by 1910 there was a danger that no otters would be left.
  - o between 1700 and 1910, more otters were caught than any other furry animal.

General Achievement in Language

A considerable number of the items in achievement batteries are devoted to the measurement of language skills—for example, spelling, mechanics (or grammar), and usage.

Spelling. In the multiple-choice, machine-scorable format of published test batteries, respondents cannot be tested for spelling by having them actually construct the spelling of a word. Hence, a form or forms of the word must be given (often in a sentence that the person administering the test reads aloud), and then the respondent is asked to **choose the correct spelling of a given word or indicate whether a given spelling is correct or incorrect.**

- Don't you *believe* me? believe (read aloud by teacher)
  believe   RIGHT   WRONG   (seen by student)
              o   o

Another format is to give all but one correctly spelled word and ask the respondent to **distinguish the incorrectly spelled word from the correct ones.**

- Which word is spelled incorrectly?
  o temperature   o athletic
  o sophmore   o religion

Mechanics.   Language mechanics focuses on aspects such as punctuation, capitalization, and sentence structure. For example, the respondent is given an unpunctuated or uncapitalized sentence and asked to **identify the correct punctuation or correct capitalization for each part of the given sentence.**

- Did you find the book I left at your house
        .   ,   ?   "
        o   o   o   o
- Which word in the sentence should start with a capital letter?

  The boys all laughed at jimmy.
         o   o   o   o   o

Students may also be asked to **distinguish between complete and incomplete sentences.**

- No matter how much he tried.
  complete sentence   incomplete sentence
         o   o

Usage.   Language usage or expression items ask students to **select the right form of a word or phrase to complete or rewrite a sentence in standard, written English,** or to **distinguish between proper and improper usage of words.**

- Which of the following is a correct standard sentence?
  o My friend she get hurt.

o She were at the doctor's.
o I felt sorry for her.
■ Yesterday, we _____ a president for our club.
o choosed
o choose
o chose
o will choose

General Achievement in Mathematics

In addition to language skills and reading, mathematics is a common component of standardized achievement batteries. Most batteries subdivide
mathematics into two or three components with a variety of labels. For our
purposes we will use the terms *computation*, *concepts*, and *applications* to
describe achievement in mathematics.

Mathematics Computation.   This type of test deals with the respondent's ability to **add, subtract, multiply, divide, determine equals and un-
equals, take square roots,** and perform basic mathematical or arithmetic
operations in general.

■ $12 - 4 =$ _____   16   9   8   7
                               o   o   o   o
■ The lowest common denominator of ⅓, ¼, and ⅙ is
   6   12   13   24
   o   o   o   o

Mathematics Concepts.   Math concepts are more difficult to define
than computation because they cover a wide area of mathematical understanding. In essence, these items require the respondent to **demonstrate an
understanding of the basic rules, laws, or definitions of math by making
identifications that involve these rules, laws, or definitions.** (Moreover,
the computation level in concept problems is kept low so as not to confound
the measurement.)

■ What number is three hundred seventy-two?
   327   372   30027   30072
   o   o   o   o
■ What is the reciprocal of the integer y?
   y^2 $1 - y$ $1/y$ $y - 1$
   o   o   o   o

Mathematics Applications.   In math applications respondents must
**demonstrate an understanding of math principles and operations by solving
problems involving these principles and operations.**

- You can buy three jelly beans for a nickel and six pieces of gum for a dime. What is the cost of twelve jelly beans and twelve pieces of gum?

  15¢   20¢   40¢   70¢
   o   o   o   o

- Rosa drove her car at a speed of forty miles per hour. At this rate, how far could Rosa drive in a half-hour?

  20 miles   25 miles   40 miles   80 miles
     o   o   o   o

General Achievement in Social Studies

Social studies, or social science as it is alternatively called, is an area often measured in standardized achievement batteries (but not so commonly as reading, language, or mathematics). Test items measure (1) the acquisition and retention of factual information, (2) the application or interpretation of either given or retained information, and (3) the use of specific skills such as map and graph reading. Respondents are called upon to **identify the correct piece of factual information regarding history, geography, or culture,** as illustrated in the following item for third graders:

- The largest of the fifty United States in terms of area is

  o Texas.   o California.
  o New York.   o Alaska.

Seventh graders might be asked

- Which of the following people was *not* an inventor?

  o Thomas Edison   o Alexander Bell
  o John D. Rockefeller   o Robert Fulton

In another kind of item, respondents are called upon to **identify the choice that represents the correct interpretation of a social science problem or situation.** Fifth graders, for example, might be asked

- Which of the following could be considered a political slogan?

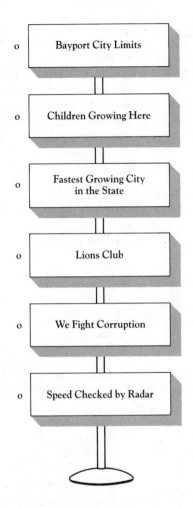

Finally, students are asked to **demonstrate the application of specific skills in areas such as map reading and figure interpretation,** as the following second grade item illustrates:

- The first picture shows a symbol for a factory. Which one of these three maps shows a place where factory products are made?

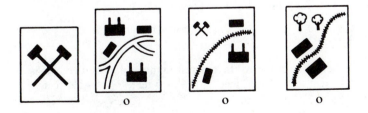

General Achievement in Science

Science items, like social studies items, require respondents to (1) **identify the correct fact, label, or phenomenon,** (2) **identify the correct explanation or application of a principle to the solution of a problem or description of a phenomenon,** and (3) **demonstrate the application of specific skills such as graph reading.** These are respectively illustrated by the following three examples for the fourth, eighth, and sixth grades, in that order.

- Which planet is farthest from the sun?
   o Pluto   o Mars
   o Uranus   o Saturn
- Two balls, A and B, are dropped from the roof of a building at the same time. Both balls are made of solid steel. Which of the following three pictures accurately shows them reaching the ground?

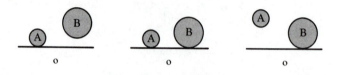

- The class members each wrote their height on the blackboard, and the graph at the top of the next page was made of their heights.

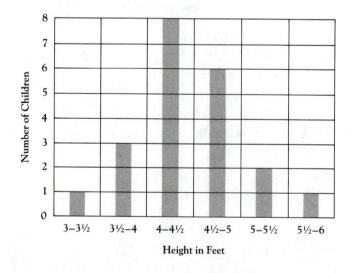

The height common to the greatest number of class members is
3½–4 feet   4–4½ feet   4½–5 feet   5–5½ feet
   o   o   o   o

General Achievement in Study Skills

Some achievement tests provide separate subtests to measure what is called study skills. Others include this area in subtests like science or social science, some may not include it at all. Study skills refers to a student's ability to **identify the correct information from printed and graphic materials.** Presumably if a student has learned how to use a library and reference sources contained in it, such as a dictionary, encyclopedia, atlas, and so forth, he or she will be able to correctly identify information taken from these sources. The last examples for both social studies and science illustrate measurement of study skills within a subject area test. Some additional examples of study skills items from the fifth grade level appear below. (The first two illustrate library skills; the third is a map reading item.)

- Which of the following books would you look in to find a history of commercial fishing?

  atlas   encyclopedia   dictionary   almanac

  o   o   o   o

- im·me·di·ate (i·mē′di-it), *adj.* 1. occurring or accomplished without delay; instant: an *immediate reply.* 2. pertaining to the present time or moment: *our immediate plans.* 3. having no time intervening: *the immediate future.* 4. having no object or space intervening; nearest or next: *in the immediate vicinity.*

  Which of the above definitions fits the use of the word *immediate* in this sentence?

  Because I am in a hurry, I must have an *immediate* answer.

  1   2   3   4

  o   o   o   o

- According to the map shown below, in what direction must you go to get from the airport to the lake?

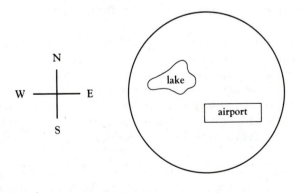

  o northeast   o northwest
  o southeast   o southwest

General Achievement in Listening

Some current achievement test batteries include the measurement of listening comprehension—the ability to **identify the correct response to a question based on information presented orally.** While the question or story itself is only given orally, the answer choices may be given in pictorial or written form or they may be given orally as well. The example below (sixth grade level) illustrates one of these formats.

(Read by teacher and not seen by student)
- Blair and Jackie are in the second grade. They often work together. They are working on a project together now. This project is for their teacher.
  Which statement is based on the story? (The statements are read by the student.)
  o Blair is doing most of the work on the project.
  o Jackie keeps bothering Blair when she is trying to work.
  o Some second grade students do projects for their teachers.
  o The library is a good place to work on a project.

Why These Tests Are Called Standardized

It is useful to examine the procedures that a standardized achievement test battery goes through to earn the label *standardized.* In the next section we will compare standardized achievement tests with teacher-built tests.

Tryout, Item Analysis, and Revision.　The first two steps in the construction of a standardized achievement test are the same as those in the construction of a teacher-built test, that is, the developing of a content outline and the writing of items. In the case of the standardized test, more than one person may write the items. Here the selection of content or objectives is based on an examination of existing curriculums and textbooks used throughout the nation.

As part of its development, the standardized test is tried out on a sample of students, not to measure their achievement but to determine the properties of the items themselves. The results of the tryout are then used to eliminate items that are too easy, too hard, ambiguous, poorly worded, or inconsistent with the majority of like items. Some decisions are based on statistical results while others are based on comments by teachers and students. After the item writers see the results of the tryout and subsequent

Answers
rip it, outgoing, said, pile, as the *u* sound in *curtail*, bat, to get their fur, by 1910 there was a danger that no otters would be left, right, sophmore, ?, jimmy, incomplete sentence, I felt sorry for her., chose, 8, 12, 372, 1/y, 40¢, 20 miles, Alaska, John D. Rockefeller, we fight corruption, 3, pluto, 2, 4–4½ feet, encyclopedia, 1, northwest, some second grade students do projects for their teachers.

analysis, they can tell which items are poor. The poor items are eliminated since more items are used in the tryout than would be needed in the final instrument.

For example, the following item was contained in the original version of a social studies test.

- Ponce de Leon was
   a. a governor of precolonial Florida.
   b. the discoverer of the fountain of youth.
   c. a conqueror of Mexico.
   d. a famous pirate.

The tryout results showed that choice *b* was the most frequent choice but the correlation between getting this item right and total score on the test was quite low. A close examination of choice *b* revealed that it inadvertantly contained a trick. While Ponce de Leon is most well-known for his search for the fountain of youth (and hence his name is closely associated with it), he never succeeded in *discovering* it and hence cannot be called its *discoverer*. He was, however, a governor of precolonial Florida—a fact that most people do not know. The item would have been better if choice *a* had been "discoverer of Puerto Rico" (which is wrong) and *b* "seeker of the fountain of youth" (which is right).

Similarly, tryout and item analysis makes it possible to construct a test that is internally consistent, reasonably free of ambiguity, and graded in terms of item difficulty (if that is the goal).

Uniform and Widespread Use and Reuse. As the test items are being developed, a set of standard instructions for their administration is also being written to insure that time limits and other procedural requirements remain constant from use to use; thus administrative procedures as a differential source of influence on students' test scores are eliminated.

All of this "standardization" is predicated on a major characteristic that differentiates the published achievement test from the one the teacher builds, that is, the matter of reuse. Often teacher-built achievement tests are used only once and, on those rare occasions of reuse, are used again by the same teacher or perhaps the same school, while standardized achievement tests are constructed for multiple use in varied schools across the country. Clearly, if an achievement test were to be used but once, there would be little value to its improvement or standardization, but multiple and repeated use gives these processes value.

The Existence of Norms. The feature of standardized achievement tests that probably has gone furthest to earn them the label of "standardized" is the availability of comparison data in the form of **norms.**[3] When teachers

---

[3] Norms and their use are described in the next chapter.

administer their own achievement tests, they usually discard the results after they have used them to evaluate the students who took the test, but standardized achievement test data are collected and used to provide a relative basis for the interpretation of test scores. Hence, when you give a standardized achievement test, it is possible to compare or reference the performance of students in terms of members of a specific norming group who have taken it before them. It is also possible to compare their performance to all those in their own district who have taken the test in the past or who have taken it at the same time. Widespread test use contributes to the availability of concurrent data, both nationally and locally. (The interpretation of norm-referenced, standardized achievement test scores will be discussed on pages 184–195.)

After a standardized achievement test is constructed and edited, its developers administer it to a national sample of students who will serve as the norming group. This presumably representative group will serve as the basis for the establishment of national norms on the test, clearly marking the test as a "standardized" one. The same process will also be gone through for each test revision.

COMPARING STANDARDIZED AND TEACHER-BUILT ACHIEVEMENT TESTS

School achievement can be measured by either a teacher-built test or a standardized test. Teachers use their own tests to measure the achievement of their own students on their own objectives. School districts use standardized tests to get a broader view of student attainment throughout the district. While teacher-built tests may be given as often as daily or weekly, a standardized achievement test battery will probably only be given once, or at most, twice a year. It should be useful to compare the two types of tests on the test criteria of content validity, reliability, and usability.

Content Validity

Content validity, as you will recall, refers to the fit of a test's items to a set of given objectives. The better the fit between what a test measures and what a teacher wants it to measure, the greater the content validity of that test.

We can assume that teacher-built achievement tests have a high degree of content validity since teachers build them themselves. Standardized achievement tests on the other hand are more general; since they are intended for wider use, their coverage must be broad enough to cover the objectives of many teachers. The content validity of standardized achievement tests depends on to what extent a field of study has uniform and commonly agreed upon objectives. In a field like high school industrial arts where local curriculums may vary widely, standardized achievement tests will be low in content validity. In first grade reading, on the other hand, where objectives from school to school are similar, content validity will be higher.

When teachers give their own tests, they know that the material or objectives to be tested have been covered in class. However, a standardized achievement test may be given *before* some of the objectives it measures are taught. In other words, these objectives may be in the curriculum but not yet taught. This happens because most standardized test levels cover more than one year of work while teacher-built tests cover much smaller segments. Hence, standardized tests will be valid only in a general sense.

Standardized achievement tests are based largely on the content in standard textbooks in the subject area for each grade level. Where teachers follow the content of the standard textbook—as is frequently the case, especially at the elementary level—standardized achievement tests will be higher in content validity. Test manuals for each of the major standardized achievement batteries report item content categories by level for each item on each test. This tells you the topics measured in each subtest and the numbers of the specific items that measure each topic.

The content validity of standardized achievement tests will be increased when either (1) teachers are given a list of the content categories for each subtest at the beginning of each school year, or (2) teachers go through the content coverage table before the test is given and indicate those areas or categories that have been covered in class. For instance, if "modifiers as a sentence part" has not been taught in language arts, responses to items that measure modifier-use on standardized achievement tests can be expected to be wrong, thus reducing the content validity of the instrument for measuring this objective.

It would seem then that standardized achievement test batteries are valid for the general purposes for which they are used but should not be considered measures of the attainment of each teacher's own objectives.

Reliability

Reliability is one of the greatest strengths of standardized achievement test batteries. Because item analysis and revision based on item analysis are steps in the development of these tests, it is possible to eliminate or improve inconsistent items to achieve a high degree of internal reliability. Internal reliabilities reported for published achievement batteries that approach the upper limit of 1.00 are highly acceptable.

While the reliabilities of teachers' tests typically are neither calculated nor reported, the fact that their tests are not usually analyzed or revised suggests that reliabilities much in excess of .65 would not be expected. However, it must be pointed out that high reliabilities do not overcome other deficiencies. A test that lacks content validity for a specific teacher's purposes will not provide useful results regardless of its reliability.

Usability

Although test publishers provide highly specific instructions for the administration of standardized achievement tests, they are inevitably more difficult to administer than teacher-built tests. Teacher-built tests, except perhaps for mid-terms or finals, are confined to a single class period and hence do not disrupt the schedule. Standardized achievement tests take three or more hours to complete—usually in multiple sittings—and so usually necessitate an alteration in the schedule for an entire school or school district. Moreover, the infrequent use of standardized tests makes their administration special to both teachers and students. With understanding and a high degree of cooperation, standardized test administration can be minimally disruptive. But, when teachers and students alike fail to understand the value of these tests, the level of disturbance increases accordingly.

COMPARING STANDARDIZED ACHIEVEMENT AND INTELLIGENCE TESTS

What intelligence or mental ability tests measure may be better understood by examining the kinds of test items (that is, the kinds of performances) found in them. The items used in a test serve as the best operational definition of intelligence as used within that test. After examining a test's items, you can determine for yourself what the test seems to be measuring.

A comparison of the types of items used in IQ or mental ability tests and those used in achievement tests reveals the IQ items to be more general and less dependent upon specified prior experience. The difference is one of degree.

Intelligence Test Items

Verbal Items: Examples

Word Substitution

- Which of the words below is the best substitute for the italicized word in the following sentence?

He was a good doctor, but alcohol was his *ruin*.

a. plague   c. fate
b. undoing   d. destiny

Synonyms

- Which word means the same as the given?

TEMPERAMENT

a. angriness   c. hostility
b. popularity   d. disposition

Word Classification

■ Which word does not belong?

a. horse   c. mosquito
b. flower   d. snake

Verbal Analysis

■ Which word should go in the blank space to fulfill relationships that call for it?

COLD:HOT   UP: _____

a. down   c. low
b. high   d. under

Word Class

■ Into which one of the four classes does the given word best fit?

PALM

a. plant   c. tree
b. flower   d. leaf

Verbal Relations

■ Which alternative pair comes nearest to expressing the relation of the given pair?

BIRD:SONG

a. fish:water   c. pianist:piano
b. person:speech   d. horse:ranch

Figural Items: Examples

Recognition of Objects

■ What is the object?

Figure Matching

- Which alternative (at the right) is most nearly like the test object (at the left)?

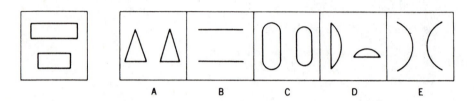

Figural Relations

- What kind of figure should appear in the cell with the question mark?

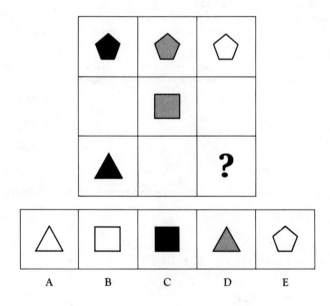

Spatial Visualization

- Diagrams I and II show two steps in folding a square piece of paper and cutting a notch in a certain location. Which alternative shows how the paper would look when unfolded?

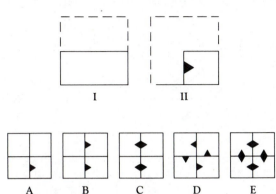

Hidden Figures

- Which of the five simple figures at the top is concealed in each of the item figures?

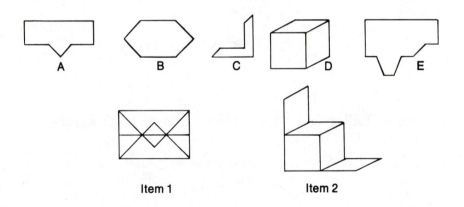

Identical Figures

- Which figure in the row is exactly the same as the one at the left?

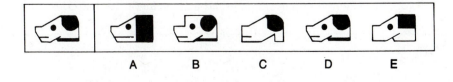

Recognition of Figural Classes

■ Which figure does not belong to the class determined by the other three figures?

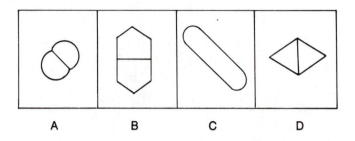

| A | B | C | D |

Intelligence tests appear to measure the reasoning process while achievement tests measure the acquisition of a specific body of knowledge represented by a lengthy and detailed set of objectives. Achievement tests are designed to correspond more closely to the school curriculum than intelligence tests and, therefore, do not measure processes not covered in school such as visual orientation and visual categorization (as intelligence tests usually do).

The greatest degree of correspondence between achievement tests and intelligence tests is that both typically measure basic usage of words (called "vocabulary") and numbers (not illustrated here). The difference, even in these two areas, is that achievement test measurement of them is related to their corresponding coverage in the school curriculum while in intelligence tests, the items are chosen on a more general basis and more of the same type of item is offered.

ADMINISTERING A STANDARDIZED ACHIEVEMENT TEST

For very young children standardized achievement tests are given orally. Thereafter, except for the instructions, they are usually read by the students. For all standardized tests, certain general rules can be established for administration:

1. **Familiarize yourself before the testing date with all instructions for administration.** This means reading the Teacher's Directions for Administering carefully and completely so that you know exactly what to do. For example, some standardized achievement test batteries

---

Answers

b, d, b, a, c, b; airplane, c, a, c, 1—a, 2—d, d, c.

come with practice tests that are to be given a few days before the actual testing. Had you not read the directions thoroughly you might not have known about this and hence might have overlooked it.

2. **Make sure all students have everything they need to take the test and no more.** Students must have number-2 lead pencils, test booklets, and answer sheets. They should not have books or papers out other than scratch paper when allowed.

3. **All information called for in the Pupil Information Box must be filled in by the student.** This information typically includes name, date of birth, grade level, sex, teacher, and school. For younger students, the teacher usually fills in this information.

4. **All test instructions, both general and specific, must be clearly given by the teacher to the students exactly as called for in the directions.** For example, students are told to mark only one answer for each item and to erase an answer completely if they decide to change it. Giving more or fewer instructions may cause variability in student performance and render the norms unusable for that testing.

5. **Time limits must be adhered to exactly.** Standardized achievement tests are almost always timed tests. The test directions tell you precisely how much time is allowed per test. Use a watch with a second hand to be sure that students start and stop each test exactly on time. If students complete a test ahead of time, they may not go on to the next test. If time runs out before they are finished, they must stop nevertheless.

6. **Make sure that all students know how to take the test.** Answer any questions by reading again appropriate instructions. Make sure, particularly, that all students know how to mark their answer sheets.

7. **Monitor the test taking from various points in the room.** Check that all students are following directions. Be available for questions about procedures.

8. **Make sure the students take the testing seriously.** The students should not be frightened by testing, but they must take it seriously. Teachers should prepare but not scare students by explaining the test's purpose to them in advance. They will be more likely to take it seriously if you take it seriously. Give it the same importance as you would your own final exam. Show that you feel the results will help students; do not show annoyance with the administration for wasting your time. The students will sense your feelings and behave accordingly.

Proficiency Test

1. A statement or brief story is read aloud by the teacher. A question based on the story is then read aloud along with four answer choices. The student must identify the correct answer choice. This procedure is used on an achievement test to measure

   a. reading comprehension.
   b. word skills.
   c. language mechanics.
   d. listening comprehension.
   e. vocabulary.
2. Many standardized tests measure three aspects of achievement in
   mathematics: computation, concepts, and applications. Below are
   three sample items. Which of the three aspects does each measure?
   a. You place $50 in a savings account that earns simple interest at the
      rate of 4½ percent per year. At the end of one year, your bank bal-
      ance would be
      $52.50 $52.00 $52.75 $52.25
   b. $\sqrt{14} =$ 4.0   3.8   3.5   3.0
   c. 10^4 is   1,000   10,000   100,000   1,000,000
3. Consider the comparison between a teacher-built achievement test,
   such as a mid-term, and a standardized achievement test. Which of
   the test criteria (content validity or reliability) do you think most
   favors the teacher-built test (at least ideally) and why?
4. Continuing with the consideration in item 3, which of the test criteria
   most favors the standardized achievement test and why?
5. There is a clear and distinct separation between what an intelligence
   test measures and what an achievement test measures.
                      TRUE   FALSE
6. Below are two categories of tests. Which one is most dependent upon
   specified prior knowledge?
   a. group verbal-type mental ability tests
   b. general achievement batteries
7. Cite two reasons why it is important to familiarize yourself with *all*
   instructions before administering a standardized test.
8. List four *other* important rules to follow in test administration.

Interpreting Test Results

OBJECTIVES

- Define the test interpretability concept of (a) norm-referencing, (b) norms, and (c) norming group.
- Identify and contrast four kinds of normative scores, namely: (a) standard score, (b) stanine score, (c) percentile rank, and (d) grade-equivalent score.
- Identify characteristics of norm-referenced tests, namely: (a) item revisions, (b) standard instructions, (c) norms and interpretation based on them. Identify their strengths and shortcomings.
- Identify characteristics of criterion-referenced tests, namely: (a) based on objectives, (b) designed to be valid, (c) measuring performance, (d) using predetermined cutoffs.
- Describe the use of four criteria for determining the interpretability of a test, namely: (a) relation of scores to performance, (b) definition of acceptable performance, (c) diagnostic and evaluative value, (d) useful relative information.

WHAT IS INTERPRETABILITY?

Interpretability has to do with what the scores on a test mean; that is, what they tell us about the test taker with respect to the characteristics being measured. Interpretability provides us with a basis for understanding information conveyed by the test score. Not only should a test measure what we want it to measure, but it should provide the results in a form we can understand and use.

The result of a test is called a **raw score.** The question of interpretability is how can we interpret or understand what the raw score means? Is it high? Is it low? Is it good? Is it adequate? The raw score is only a number; its meaning is based on interpretation. For example, a student gets thirty items right on a forty-item chemistry test. What does this tell us? Would that performance be sufficient to pass the course? To go on to a more advanced course? To become a chemist? Unless a test provides us with a basis for interpreting—that is, unless a test provides us with a **point of reference**— it is not a useful test.

There are two types of reference points that can be applied to interpreting a test. The first is to relate a student's test score to the scores of other students on that test. We call this **norm-referencing.** The second is to establish an external standard and relate the student's test score to it. We call this **criterion-referencing.** These are the different bases for interpretability described below.

NORM-REFERENCING

Teachers are often called upon to interpret the scores of tests that are norm-referenced—that is, **tests for which information about the relative performance of a specific group of people is available.** (We call this information **norms.**) In order to understand norm-referencing, it is necessary to know about norms—that is, the kinds of scores in which they are expressed (standard scores, including stanines, percentile ranks, and grade equivalents).[1]

Norms

Norms are sets of scores based on the test results of an external reference or standardization group; that is, persons who take the test for the express purpose of providing comparative data for interpretation. Norms, therefore, represent a set of test results obtained in order to help interpret the results of scores from future testings.

We may represent norms as (1) **standard scores,** which reflect the deviation of test scores from the mean score of the norm group; as (2) **percentile ranks,** which tell us what percent of the norming group scored at or below

---

[1]While teachers may do some norm-referencing of their own on a small scale, because of its computational aspects and data requirements, norm-referencing is primarily done by testing companies.

a particular score on the test; or as (3) **grade equivalents,** which tell us the school grade at which the given score is typical, or average, for members of the norming group. Each of these represents a way of expressing relative scores, that is, of transforming the raw or obtained scores based on the distribution of scores of the norming group. Let us first discuss the norming group and then consider the three types of normative scores.

Norming Groups. Basically, there are two types of norms: **local norms** and **national norms,** each reflecting a different kind of norming group. National norms are the more common and provide for the widest generalizability. These norms are based on what is called a cross-national sample, or people sampled from all parts of the country—providing representation for all regions. Local norms, on the other hand, may represent a single state or community or school. Results based on local norms are limited in interpretation to just that locale from which the local norming group was drawn. However, in relating an individual's performance to the performance of other individuals with similar experiences, local norms may be more useful than national norms.

Norms are often separated by age or grade and, where appropriate, by sex. Achievement test norms, for example, are typically presented separately for students at each individual grade for which the test is appropriate. Stanines or percentile ranks presented for an eighth grader will be based only on the scores of other eighth graders as a norm-reference group.[2]

Different norming groups (or breakdowns of norm by group) are relevant for different kinds of tests or uses of tests. Norms for different occupational groups or for groups with different educational majors are relevant in certain circumstances. The Graduate Record Examination and the Miller Analogies Test, for instance, provide norms for graduate students in the different disciplines so that chemistry majors, for example, can be compared to a national sample of chemistry majors; similarly for psychology majors, education majors, and so on. The use of specific norming groups allows for the comparison and evaluation of a student's score in terms of "like" people—that is, those who share some past experience in common or who have some developmental comparability. Information on many variables such as age, grade, sex, interests, region, IQ level, socioeconomic status, school type and so forth aids test interpretation because it indicates how a person performed relative to a group into which he or she fits well. Given a person's raw score on a test and a full set of test norms, it is possible to interpret the score relative to any norming group available. However, where only individual normative test scores are presented, as is typically the case with achievement and aptitude test results, interpretations are restricted to the predesignated norming group.

---

[2] Grade equivalent norms, however, are based on the average scores obtained by students across a number of grade levels.

Standard Score

A standard score is a score expressed in terms of its deviation from the mean score of the norming group. Rather than being absolute like a raw score, a standard score indicates the relative status of an individual within a group, that is, how his or her raw score compares to the mean raw score of the norming group. In one group of students a raw score of 50 may be high relative to the other scores while in another group it may be low. By converting the raw score to a standard score we can express and interpret the score relative to the other scores to judge its "highness" or "lowness." Standard scores are thus one form of norm-referencing.

Standard scores are based on the assumption of a normal curve as shown in Figure 10-1. (Recall that we encountered the normal curve or normal distribution in Figure 8-1 in our discussion of reliability.) The normal curve represents an idealized distribution of test scores on a test, but one that fits the occurrence of most psychological and physical traits in the population. It is characterized by a predominance of scores in the middle range of the distribution with progressively fewer scores as we move toward either end. In other words, many more people score at the average on a trait than at the extremes.

The mean of the normal distribution in Figure 10-1 has been designated as 0 standard deviations, and vertical lines have been drawn to indicate distances from the center in terms of standard deviation units. A standard deviation unit is one unit of variability in test scores, designated by the Greek letter sigma (σ) or by s.d. Recall that the standard deviation represents approximately the average of all differences between obtained scores and the mean. The greater the differences between scores, the greater the standard deviation.

Notice that 68.3 percent of all scores on the normal curve fall within one standard deviation of the mean ($\pm 1\sigma$). The percentage of scores falling within three standard deviations of the mean ($\pm 3\sigma$) is 99.9 percent or virtually all the scores. If a person obtained a score of 45 on a test, with the distribution of scores having a mean of 40 and a standard deviation of 5, that score would lie exactly one standard deviation unit above the mean ($+1\sigma$). A score of 35 ($40 - 1\sigma$) would fall at -1σ. A score of 30 ($40 - 2\sigma$) would lie two standard deviations below the mean (-2σ), and so on.

All standard scores are based on standard deviation units. In each case, the mean and the standard deviation unit for the distribution are set by the person norming the test at some predesignated number. When the mean is set at 0 and the standard deviation at 1, the resulting score is called a **z-score**; a predesignated mean of 50 and standard deviation of 10 yields a score called a **T-score**. The Wechsler IQ scores use a preset mean of 100 and standard deviation of 15 while the Scholastic Aptitude Test of the College Boards (CEEB) has a mean set at 500 and a standard deviation of 100. These scores are all illustrated in Figure 10-1. Using the preset mean

Figure 10-1
The Normal Curve, Percentile Scores, and Types of Standard Scores*

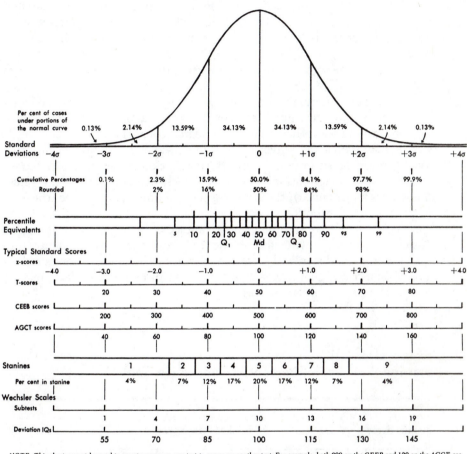

NOTE: *This chart cannot be used to equate scores on one test to scores on another test. For example, both 600 on the CEEB and 120 on the AGCT are one standard deviation above their respective means, but they do not represent "equal" standings because the scores were obtained from different groups.*

---

*From Test Service Bulletin No. 48, January, 1955, The Psychological Corporation, New York.

and standard deviation based on the distribution of test scores for the norming group, a given set of raw test scores can be converted to standard scores.

Again, the reason for converting raw scores to standard scores is to represent the scores on a relative basis within the test group itself. Neither the order of the scores nor the distribution of the scores is changed by this procedure, but the scores themselves are restated in terms of a standard, predesignated scale. Given standard scores, we can interpret them in terms of each test taker's relative standing. In other words, we state the score in such a way that we can tell its relative size.

Stanine Score

Another relevant type of standard score is the **stanine score,** based on dividing the normal curve into nine divisions.[3] (The term *stanine* was formed by combining the words *standard* and *nine*.) The stanine score is a standard score with a mean of five and a standard deviation of two. As a result, each stanine, except for the first and ninth, is one-half a standard deviation unit in length (see Figure 10-1).

Stanine scores are easy to calculate using the conversion scale given in Figure 10-2.

Scores can be normalized or standardized into approximate stanine scores by a counting procedure rather than by the computational procedure required for determining the other types of standard scores (like the z-score or T-score). Raw scores are converted to stanine scores by forcing them into a roughly normal distribution. Unlike the conversion to z-scores and T-scores, which leave the distribution of raw scores unchanged (only the score values themselves are changed), the conversion to stanine scores changes the original raw score distribution to an approximately normal distribution.

The stanine score has the great advantage of being easier to determine and easier to interpret (the latter being true because it is a single-digit score) than other types of standard scores. However, because each score represents a band on a continuum rather than a point, stanine scores are less precisely stated than other standard scores.

Figure 10-2
Stanine–Raw Score–Percentile Conversion Table

Stanine Score	Approximate Percent of Ranked Raw Scores		Percentile
9	Top	4%	96–99
8		7	89–95
7		12	77–88
6		17	60–76
5		20	40–59
4		17	23–39
3		12	11–22
2		7	4–10
1	Bottom	4	0–3

---

[3] Presumably nine divisions were originally chosen because nine is the largest number of one-digit categories possible and single-digit scores are easier for data processing.

Percentile Rank

A percentile rank describes the relative standing of a raw score in a sequence of scores; it tells us what percent of the test takers scored lower and what percent scored higher. Again look at Figure 10-1. Note the part labeled "percentile equivalents" which represent percentile points on the distribution. The person who gets the middle or **median (Md)**[4] score has done as well or better than 50 percent of the test takers and hence is at the fiftieth percentile. Thus, the percentile rank is not based on the absolute size of a score but on its relative standing. It is usually computed as the percent with a lower raw score plus one-half of those with the same raw score. It is important to emphasize that the percentile rank reported by the publisher of a test represents the percentage of students with lower scores and not the percentage of items answered correctly.

A pupil profile report on the Stanford Achievement Test appears in Figure 10-3. Note that both percentile ranks **(PR)** and stanines **(S)** are provided for scores based on both national and local norming groups, although only the former appear in this particular case. When compared to a national sample of fourth graders who took this test at the time of its standardization (the norming group), the student whose achievement is reported in Figure 10-3 scored particularly high in the social science and using-information areas and at about an average level in the other areas. This is shown graphically in the charting of percentile ranks.

Since norms are provided for an entire grade level, and achievement occurs continuously throughout the grade level, normed scores will be partly dependent on when the test is taken. The student reported on in Figure 10-3 took the Stanford Achievement Test early in the grade (specifically, in October). Further experiences in the grade may not produce any measurable effect on the particular form of language arts subtests used if scores are high relative to the norm group. Such is a limitation of percentile ranks where you are typically limited to a single grade level within which to make comparisons even though (1) test taking may occur at different times throughout the grade for different school districts, and (2) some students are performing at levels closer to students in other grade levels than to students in their own.[5]

Figures 10-4 and 10-5 show tables of norms for a portion of a specific grade level as taken from each of two published achievement tests. With these tables it is possible to convert an individual raw score into a percentile rank, thereby providing test score interpretability without recourse to standard score calculations. Tests such as these provide test takers with both

---

[4]The median score is the middle score in the sequential ranking of scores; the mean score is the mathematical average of scores. They are seldom the same except in the perfect or ideal normal distribution.

[5]Those deficiencies may be somewhat overcome by using grade equivalents in addition to percentile ranks.

Figure 10-3
Pupil Profile Report on the Stanford Achievement Test*

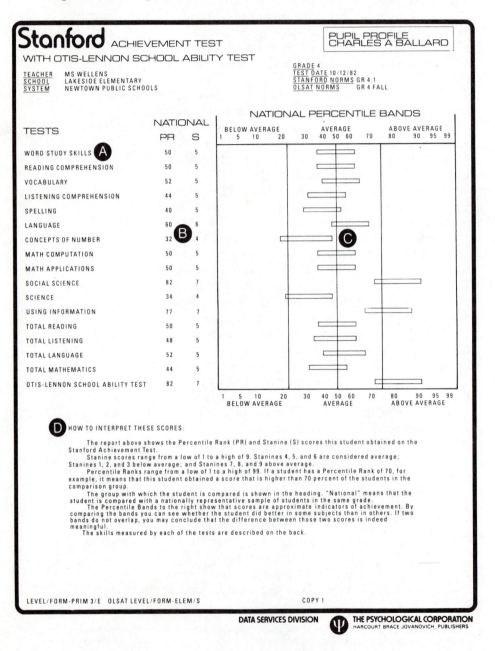

their standard score and their percentile rank, each of which relates their test score to the scores of a norming group. The percentile rank gives the test score a high degree of interpretability on a relative basis since without it, it is hard to determine the quality of a student's performance.

Grade-equivalent Score

Norm-referenced scores on achievement tests can be expressed in a form other than percentile ranks or stanine scores, which as we have seen, are based on the comparison of present scores to those already obtained on the test by a norm group of the same age and grade level. An alternative approach is to compare a student's score to scores across a number of grade levels and identify the grade level at which the given score is most similar to that of the norming group average. Such a procedure results in **grade-equivalent scores.**

To obtain a score that represents an average or typical performance take the standard scores or raw scores of norming groups at each grade level and compute the average or mean. Any student getting one of these average scores on a test (that is, average for the norming group at that grade level) would be assigned the grade-equivalent score of that grade level. If the score corresponded to the average of the beginning fourth grade norming group, the grade-equivalent score would be 4.1; if it corresponded to the average for the beginning fifth grade norming group, the grade-equivalent score would be 5.1; and so on. The greater likelihood is that actual scores will fall between these norming group averages rather than directly on one. To deal with this, the score range between the average standard or raw score for each grade level norming group and that of the succeeding one has been arbitrarily divided into ten equal parts based on a ten-month school year and the necessary but possibly false assumption of uniform growth over time. Thus, if a student gets a score halfway between the average for the fourth grade norming group and the fifth grade norming group, the grade-equivalent of that score would be 4.6. If the score is at the upper limit of fourth grade average performance, the grade-equivalent score would be 4.9. (Most achievement tests are normed at .1, .6, or .9 within grade levels.)

Figure 10-5 shows the grade-equivalent scores for Total Reading on the Metropolitan Achievement Tests (1986 edition), each in terms of its corresponding raw score, percentile rank, stanine, and standard score. Grade-equivalent scores are provided by the publisher based on administrations of the test given either once, or twice in this case (in October and April) for each elementary grade level. (All grade-equivalent scores are based on these administrations.) If the middle raw score among students at grade level 2.1 (that is, in October of the second grade) falls between 60 and 62 for Total Reading on the *Primary 2* test as Figure 10-5 shows it to be, then any students who obtain raw scores between 60 and 62 on this test can be assigned a grade-equivalent score of 2.1. They are performing at the same level as the middle child at this grade level on this test. They may, in fact, be first

Figure 10-4
Spring (Mar. 1 or after)/Percentile Norms for First-Grade Pupils*

Spring GRADE **1**   Spring GRADE **1**

Spring (Mar. 1 or after)/Percentile Norms for First-Grade Pupils

%-ile Rank	Test Li	Test WA	Test V	Test R	L-1	L-2	L-3	L-4	Total L	W-1	W-2	Total W	M-1	M-2	M-3	Total M	Complete Battery C	Basic Battery C	%-ile Rank	Stanine
99	41	45	38	43	45	45	52	48	45	43	41	41	42	40	32	36	38	39	99	
98	39	43	37	41	44	44	50	47	43	41	39	39	39	37	30	34	36	37	98	9
97	38	41	36	39	43	42	48	46	41	40	37	38	37	36	29	32	34	35	97	
96	37	39	35	38	42	40	46	45	40	39	35	36	36	35	—	31	33	34	96	
95	35	38	34	36	41	39	44	44	38	37	34	35	35	34	28	—	32	—	95	
94	34	37	33	35	40	38	43	43	37	36	33	34	34	33	27	30	—	33	94	
93	33	36	—	34	39	36	42	42	36	35	32	33	33	32	—	29	31	32	93	8
92	—	35	32	33	38	35	41	41	—	34	—	—	32	—	26	—	—	—	92	
91	32	34	31	32	37	34	40	40	35	33	31	32	31	31	—	28	30	31	91	
90	31	33	—	—	—	—	38	39	34	32	30	31	—	—	25	—	—	—	90	
89	—	32	30	31	36	33	37	38	33	—	—	—	30	30	—	27	29	30	89	
88	30	—	—	—	35	32	—	—	—	31	29	30	29	—	24	—	28	29	88	
87	—	31	29	30	34	31	36	37	32	30	—	29	28	29	—	—	—	—	87	
86	29	—	—	—	—	—	35	36	—	—	28	—	—	—	—	26	27	28	86	
85	—	30	28	29	33	30	34	35	31	29	—	28	—	28	23	—	—	—	85	7
84	28	—	—	—	32	—	33	—	—	—	27	—	27	—	—	25	—	27	84	
83	—	29	—	28	—	29	32	34	30	28	—	27	—	—	—	—	26	—	83	
82	27	—	27	—	31	—	—	—	29	27	—	—	26	27	22	—	—	—	82	
81	—	28	—	27	30	28	31	33	—	—	—	—	—	—	—	24	—	—	81	
80	—	—	26	—	—	—	30	32	28	26	26	26	—	—	—	—	25	26	80	
79	—	27	—	26	29	27	—	—	27	—	—	25	25	26	—	—	25	26	79	
78	—	26	25	25	28	26	29	31	—	25	25	—	—	—	—	—	—	—	78	
76	25	—	—	—	27	—	28	30	—	—	—	24	24	25	21	23	24	25	76	
75	—	25	—	—	—	25	27	—	29	26	—	24	—	25	—	—	—	24	75	
74	24	—	24	24	26	—	26	—	28	25	24	24	—	—	23	—	23	24	74	
73	—	—	—	—	25	24	25	27	—	—	—	23	23	24	—	22	—	—	73	
72	—	24	—	23	—	—	—	—	—	—	—	23	—	—	20	—	23	—	72	
71	23	—	23	23	24	—	24	26	—	23	23	—	—	—	—	22	—	—	71	
70	—	—	—	—	—	—	—	—	24	—	—	—	—	20	—	—	—	—	70	
69	—	23	—	—	24	—	24	26	—	—	—	22	22	—	—	—	22	23	69	
68	—	—	—	—	—	23	—	25	—	—	—	—	—	23	—	—	—	—	68	
67	22	—	22	22	23	—	23	—	25	22	22	—	—	—	—	21	—	22	67	6
66	—	—	—	—	—	—	—	24	—	—	—	—	—	—	21	—	—	—	66	
65	—	22	—	—	—	22	22	—	22	—	—	21	21	22	—	—	—	—	65	
64	—	—	—	—	22	—	—	23	—	21	—	—	—	—	—	—	—	21	64	
63	21	—	21	21	22	—	—	—	—	21	21	—	—	19	—	—	21	—	63	
62	—	21	—	—	—	21	21	22	21	—	—	—	20	21	—	20	—	—	62	
61	—	—	—	—	21	—	—	—	—	—	—	—	—	—	—	—	—	—	61	
59	20	20	20	—	20	20	20	21	20	20	20	20	—	20	—	—	20	20		
	19	20	19	19	19	19	19	20	19	19	19	19	19	19	19	—	19	19		
	18	18	18	18	18	18	18	—	18	18	18	18	18	18	18	18	18	18		5
	17	17	17	17	17	17	17	16	17	17	17	17	17	17	17	17	17	17		
	16	16	16	16	16	16	16	15	15	16	16	16	16	16	16	16	16	16		
39	15	—	15	15	—	—	—	14	16	—	—	—	—	—	—	—	—	—	39	
38	—	15	—	—	—	—	15	—	—	—	15	15	—	15	16	—	—	—	38	
37	—	—	—	—	15	15	—	13	—	15	—	—	—	—	—	—	15	15	37	
36	14	—	14	14	—	—	—	—	—	—	—	—	15	14	16	—	15	—	36	
35	—	14	—	—	—	—	14	12	15	—	14	—	—	—	—	15	—	—	35	
34	—	—	—	—	—	—	—	—	—	14	—	14	—	13	—	—	—	14	34	4
33	13	—	13	13	14	14	—	—	—	—	—	—	14	—	—	—	14	—	33	
32	—	13	—	—	—	—	13	11	14	13	13	13	—	12	15	14	—	13	32	
31	12	—	12	—	12	—	—	—	—	—	—	—	13	—	—	—	13	—	31	
30	11	—	11	11	—	13	12	10	—	12	12	12	—	11	—	13	—	12	30	
29	—	—	—	—	—	—	13	—	11	—	13	—	—	—	15	—	—	—	29	
28	—	—	12	—	—	13	—	14	—	13	—	13	—	12	—	14	—	13	28	
27	12	12	—	12	—	—	—	—	—	—	—	—	—	—	—	—	—	—	27	
26	—	—	—	—	13	—	—	10	—	—	12	—	13	—	—	13	—	—	26	
25	11	—	11	—	—	—	—	—	K9	12	—	12	—	11	—	13	12	—	25	
24	10	11	10	11	12	12	12	—	—	—	—	11	—	14	—	—	11	—	24	3
	—	10	—	10	11	11	11	K8	—	11	11	—	12	10	—	12	—	11		
	K9	—	—	K9	10	—	10	10	12	10	10	10	11	K9	13	12	11	10		
	K8	K7	K8	K8	K9	10	K7	K6	11	K9	K9	K9	10	K8	12	11	10	—		
10	K7	K6	K6	K7	K8	K9	K6	K5	10	K8	K8	K8	—	K7	11	10	K9	K9	10	
9	K6	K5	K5	K6	K7	K8	K8	—	K7	K7	K7	K8	K9	K7	11	10	—	K8	9	
8	K5	K4	K4	K5	K6	K7	K7	K4	K6	K6	K6	K7	—	K6	10	K9	K9	K7	8	2
7	K4	K3	K3	K4	K5	K6	K6	K9	K5	K5	K5	K6	K8	K5	K9	K8	K8	K7	7	
6	K3	K2	K2	K3	K4	K5	K5	K2	K8	K4	K4	K5	K7	K4	K8	—	K7	K6	6	
5	K2	K1	K1	K2	K3	K4	K4	K1	K7	K3	K3	K4	K6	K3	K8	—	K6	K5	5	1
4	K1	K0	K1	K2	K1	K2	K2	K1	K7	K1	K2	K3	K5	K2	K7	—	K5	—	4	

Figure 10-5
A Sample Norms Table Taken from the Metropolitan Achievement Tests. Percentile Ranks (PR), Stanines (S), Grade Equivalents (GE), and Scaled Scores (SS) Corresponding to Primary 2-Form L Raw Scores (RS)—Spring of Grade 2*

TOTAL READING									
RS	PR	S	GE	SS	RS	PR	S	GE	SS
105	99	9	PHS	734	52	22	3	1.9	529
104	99	9	PHS	711	51	20	3	1.9	527
103	99	9	9.7	686	50	20	3	1.9	526
102	99	9	8.0	671	49	19	3	1.9	524
101	98	9	7.2	660	48	17	3	1.8	522
100	97	9	6.8	652	47	17	3	1.8	521
99	96	9	6.1	644	46	16	3	1.8	519
98	95	8	5.8	638	45	15	3	1.8	518
97	93	8	5.6	633	44	14	3	1.8	516
96	92	8	5.2	628	43	13	3	1.7	514
95	90	8	4.9	623	42	13	3	1.7	513
94	88	7	4.8	619	41	12	3	1.7	511
93	86	7	4.6	615	40	11	3	1.7	509
92	85	7	4.4	612	39	11	3	1.7	508
91	83	7	4.1	608	38	10	2	1.7	506
90	81	7	3.9	605	37	9	2	1.6	504
89	79	7	3.7	602	36	8	2	1.6	502
88	77	7	3.6	599	35	8	2	1.6	501
87	76	6	3.5	597	34	7	2	1.6	499
86	74	6	3.4	594	33	7	2	1.6	497
85	72	6	3.3	591	32	6	2	1.5	495
84	70	6	3.2	589	31	6	2	1.5	493
83	68	6	3.1	586	30	5	2	1.5	491
82	66	6	3.1	584	29	5	2	1.5	490
81	65	6	3.0	582	28	4	2	1.5	488
80	62	6	3.0	579	27	4	2	1.5	486
79	60	6	2.9	577	26	4	2	1.4	484
78	59	5	2.9	575	25	3	1	1.4	481
77	57	5	2.9	573	24	3	1	1.4	479
76	55	5	2.8	571	23	3	1	1.4	477
75	54	5	2.8	569	22	2	1	1.4	475
74	52	5	2.7	567	21	2	1	1.3	473
73	50	5	2.7	565	20	2	1	1.3	470
72	48	5	2.6	563	19	2	1	1.3	468
71	47	5	2.6	561	18	1	1	1.3	465
70	45	5	2.5	559	17	1	1	1.2	463
69	44	5	2.5	558	16	1	1	1.2	460
68	42	5	2.4	556	15	1	1	1.2	457
67	41	5	2.4	554	14	1	1	1.1	454
66	39	4	2.3	552	13	1	1	1.1	451
65	38	4	2.3	551	12	1	1	1.1	447
64	36	4	2.2	549	11	1	1	1.0	443
63	35	4	2.2	547	10	1	1	K.9	439
62	33	4	2.1	545	9	1	1	K.8	435

(continued)

Figure 10-5 (continued)

RS	PR	S	GE	SS	RS	PR	S	GE	SS
61	32	4	2.1	544	8	1	1	K.7	430
60	31	4	2.1	542	7	1	1	K.6	425
59	29	4	2.0	540	6	1	1	K.6	419
58	29	4	2.0	539	5	1	1	K.5	412
57	27	4	2.0	537	4	1	1	K.4	404
56	26	4	2.0	535	3	1	1	K.3	393
55	25	4	2.0	534	2	1	1	K.1	378
54	24	4	1.9	532	1	1	1	PK	353
53	23	4	1.9	531					

graders or third graders but their score of, say, 61 on the second grade test falls in the range of the middle scorer in the 2.1 grade level of the norming test group. Thus, they would be assigned a grade-equivalent score of 2.1, meaning that they are scoring on the *Primary 2* test at the middle level for beginning second graders.

If a student gets a raw score of 101 for Total Reading on the *Primary 2* test, that would be classified as a grade equivalent of 7.2 (second month of seventh grade; see Figure 10-5). That would not mean that this second grader was ready for seventh grade since the performance was measured on a test of second grade content.

Since students are not tested and retested every month of school, but are typically tested once or twice, actual empirical data for use in assigning grade equivalents are available for only one or two months within each grade level. To get the grade-equivalent scores for the other eight or nine months in the school year, interpolation is used to prepare conversion tables as shown in Figure 10-5. Keep in mind that these interpolated grade equivalency figures are determined by dividing the interval between empirically-determined scores by 10, a process that automatically assumes that equal learning occurs each month.

When students take an achievement test such as the Metropolitan Achievement Test, their raw scores (the actual numerical scores they obtain—usually the number of right answers) are transformed into standard scores based on the scores of the norming group. The standard scores can then be "transformed" into grade-equivalent scores for purposes of additional interpretability. If a child has just begun the fourth grade and obtains a grade-equivalent score of 3.5, this indicates that the child is scoring on this one test at the average level of students halfway through the third grade rather than at the average level of his or her grade-mates (beginning fourth graders).

Grade equivalents are not comparable across subtests of a battery for students who are well above or below average for their grade. A student whose percentile rank position within his or her grade is the same in all subtests may have grade equivalent scores in the different subtests varying by five or six months of score. Furthermore, grade equivalents (like percentile ranks) are not of equal size across the scale. At the extremes, a single point of raw score may make several months of difference in grade equivalents, whereas at the middle, an increase of one raw score point may make only one month of difference. Finally, grade equivalents cannot be interpreted literally. If a second grade student obtains a math computation score of 4.8, that does not mean he or she can be moved immediately into the fourth grade.

Thus, each type of normed score has its advantages and limitations. Each serves a different purpose, and most publishers of standardized tests provide all the different kinds. In general, **stanines and percentile ranks are most appropriate for comparing scores across different subtests; standard scores are used most often to compare scores across levels and forms of the same subtest; grade equivalents may be helpful in evaluating students' grade placement or progress in school.** Interpreting the same raw score in various ways increases perspective.

Standardized Tests

Those tests whose interpretability is based on norm-referencing, are known by three general characteristics.

First, **the items on a standardized test have been analyzed and refined.** In other words, the items on a standardized test are not necessarily the originals. They have been tried out and the results of the tryout analyzed. Based on the analysis, poorer items have been deleted or revised so that the items that remain are reasonably effective (in separating high scorers from low scorers, or in other ways). Similarly, scoring keys and answer choices have been revised to eliminate ambiguity.

Second, **the instructions for administering a standardized test have themselves been standardized or formalized.** Standardized tests are accompanied by manuals that include a specific set of instructions for test administration, thus increasing the likelihood that whenever the test is administered, it will be administered in the same manner. In other words, for the test results to be comparable from time to time and from place to place, the instructions given the test takers have to be the same, the amount of time allowed the same, and so on.

Finally, **standardized tests are accompanied by norms that permit interpretation of test performances relative to a national population of test takers.** It is this last feature—that standardized tests are norm-referenced—that is the most critical. It is this feature that provides a standardized test with its interpretability, for it is the norms that enable a test performance to be evaluated by comparing it with a large number of preexisting test performances, those of the norming group.

In Summary

The basic value of norms is to indicate how high or low a student's score is, independent of the difficulty of a test, by comparing it to scores of others on the same test over a period of years. Standard scores, stanine scores, percentile ranks, and grade-equivalent scores are normative or relative versions of raw scores. They tell about performances and characteristics of test takers relative to the performances and characteristics of other test takers in a reference testing group. If a test was hard—it was hard for all; if easy—easy for all. Norm-referenced scores thus help us to (1) interpret individual scores by comparison to group data, and (2) make conclusions based on test scores, therefore, somewhat independent of the failings or weaknesses of the test. This latter point is worth amplifying. We may not be sure whether a particular test is too easy or too hard; to compensate for the test's possible inexactness we use it not as an absolute measure of capability but as a way of determining the relative capabilities of students one to the other.

Two shortcomings of norms must be kept in mind. First, people, cultures, and societies change over time and norms can become dated and no longer reflect the types of performances of which people are capable based on the pattern of their experiences. As educational practices change, old norms can pose a serious problem and lead to misinterpretation. Second, an emphasis on the relative interpretation of tests tends to obscure the relation between the content of those tests and any bearing on the past or future reality of the test takers. If the test results are to have any bearing on evaluating the educational past or determining the educational future of a student, norms should not be seen as a substitute for content validity.

Moreover, there are times when we are interested in the absolute value of a score rather than the relative one. For this purpose we now turn to criterion-referenced tests.

CRITERION-REFERENCING

Thus far in this chapter on test interpretation, only norm-referencing has been considered—only the interpretation of test scores on a relative basis. Standardized or published tests are usually norm-referenced because they are typically designed by someone other than their user and are constructed in such a way as to have their primary meaning in terms of how different groups perform on them. It is possible, though, to interpret scores on some tests in terms of how many items students get right regardless of how this number compares to group performance. In such cases we say that the test represents a performance criterion and that students who get every item right or some predetermined number of items right are capable of the total performance demanded by the test. We call such an approach **criterion-referenced.**

Teacher-built tests are criterion-referenced when (1) performance on them is linked or related to behavioral referents and (2) they have been designed and constructed on such a basis. In other words, the test, by design, must furnish information about a student's ability to carry out certain performances in absolute terms or, if you prefer, measure the degree of proficiency attained by a student on a given set of objectives.

If the test is one of adding and subtracting fractions, we must have some basis for saying that a student knows how to add and subtract fractions if he or she can correctly complete all the items on the test. If no student can pass the test, and if it truly has a behavioral or performance criterion, then we must conclude that no student has met the proficiency criterion for the skill being tested.

To be justified in considering a test to be criterion-referenced, we might go through steps such as the following in its construction and referencing.

1. Prepare a content outline listing the skills and knowledge that the test is an attempt to measure (this is the content outline prepared as a basis for content validity—see pages 42–46).
2. Identify the performances (measurable objectives) of which the test taker should be capable assuming that he or she has acquired proficiency in the skills and knowledge measured by the test.
3. Identify the domain that each objective defines; write items according to the specifications of that domain, and randomly select at least two per objective to make up the test (refer to *domain-referencing* on pages 134–136 and to test-item specifications on pages 46–48).
4. Validate the fact that the skills and knowledge measured by the test are in fact prerequisite to the performance objectives identified in step 2; this is perhaps the most variable aspect of the process since the validation begins with the application of one's own judgment (that is, establishing face validity) and extends to include the judgment of a group of experts or actual data obtained by giving the test to a group that has demonstrated proficient performance to see whether they possess the skills and knowledge on the test.
5. Decide upon or determine a criterion or cutoff score showing the test performance a person must obtain to indicate sufficient proficiency in the skills and knowledge to be able to perform the criterion behaviors.

The important features of criterion-referenced tests, therefore, are that

- they are based on a set of behavioral or *performance* objectives which they are an attempt to measure;
- they are designed to have a high degree of content validity by virtue of being based on objectives;
- they represent samples of actual behavior or performance;
- performance on them can be interpreted in terms of predetermined cutoff scores.

It is important to point out that there is not a clear dichotomy between norm-referenced and criterion-referenced tests. They can be thought of as complementary; in fact, it is possible to interpret the same test in either or both ways provided that objectives or discrete content categories are used as the basis for writing items. The essential difference between criterion-referenced and norm-referenced interpretation is that the former is based on predetermined cutoff scores (presumably intrinsic to the required performance itself) while the latter is based on the performance of a norm group (an extrinsic basis for interpretation).

There is an interest in making greater use of criterion-referencing in school achievement testing, both in teacher-built tests and published ones. Criterion-referencing is used by (1) generating or selecting a set of objectives representing the desirable performance outcomes of instruction, (2) designing or finding items to adequately measure each objective (that is, representing its domain), (3) presetting acceptable performance levels,[6] (4) administering the test to students and evaluating their performance in terms of the number of objectives whose performance requirements they can adequately meet.

Criterion-referencing involves the task of writing or finding objectives and items to measure those objectives. While this can be readily done by teachers in their own classrooms, writing the objectives and items required for a district-wide criterion-referenced achievement test is a major undertaking, perhaps more suitable for testing companies than for local school personnel. But even a testing company will find it difficult to prepare a criterion-referenced test on a national or even regional basis since such an approach would sacrifice the targeting of a test to the needs of a particular school system. The fact that local inputs are most necessary for local use but that few local personnel have the time or skill to build district-wide achievement tests limits the availability or practicality of systematically built criterion-referenced achievement tests. However, the increasing availability of *banks* or repositories of performance objectives and test items, the increasing inclination by school administrations to have teachers develop lists of performance objectives for their districts, and the developments by testing companies in this area, have increased the likelihood that criterion-referenced tests will be available and used for measuring school achievement.

Such criterion-referenced tests have the advantage of allowing each school district to target its testing program to its own goals and to monitor goal attainment in an absolute rather than a relative sense. It will not suffice to say that Blair has learned more than Bret. We will have to know the number of goals that each has met in order to certify advancement to new and more complex ones. Considerable help will be afforded by test publishers who offer school test items matched to objectives so that each school can shape and form its own achievement test, geared to the needs of its own students.

A form for reporting criterion-referenced results on an otherwise norm-referenced test (the Stanford Achievement Test) appears in Figure 10-6.

---

[6]It is perhaps somewhat ironic that these levels are mainly set in a kind of normative way, that is, 80 percent of pupils getting 80 percent of the items correct, rather than in a way truly intrinsic to the objective. This may be due to the work required to collect necessary data for an empirical determination and/or to the fact that so little in our world is absolute.

Figure 10-6
Report of Individual and Class Performance on the Stanford Achievement Tests Using Criterion-referenced Scoring and Interpretation*

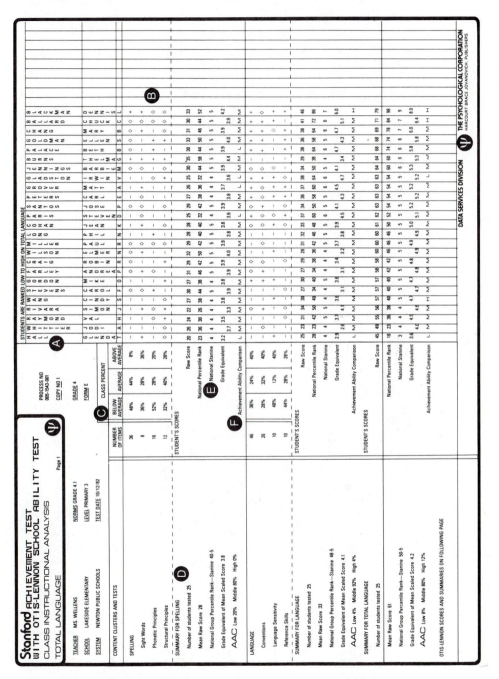

*Reproduced from the *HBJ Service Reports*, SAT-82, copyright © 1982, by Harcourt Brace Jovanovich, Inc. Reproduced by special permission of the publisher.

Not only does this form report individual performance on each objective, it also reports class performance and the comparison of class performance to the performance of students in the national sample. This record enables the teacher to identify individual and class performance on each objective and to evaluate these results relative to those nationwide.

DETERMINING A TEST'S INTERPRETABILITY

By applying the concepts of interpretability described on the previous pages a teacher can determine a test's interpretability. To assist the teacher the checklist questions below are offered.

Is My Test Interpretable?

1. Do I know how the scores relate to relevant performance:
   a. Is my test referenced in terms of some criterion (for example, my objectives)?
   b. Can I tell what a high score and a low score mean? Or, can I report the specific objectives on which proficiency has been demonstrated?
   c. Can the results for an individual student be used as a specific indication of level or degree of proficiency?
2. Do I know what defines acceptable performance:
   a. Have I preestablished cutoff scores (passing grade for example) and if so, on what basis?
   b. Do I have some concrete and verifiable way to say whether a particular performance suffices in terms of objective specifications of acceptability?
3. Does the test provide diagnostic and evaluative information:
   a. Does it tell me the areas in which a student needs help?
   b. Does it tell me the areas in which the class needs help?
   c. Does it tell me the areas in which instruction needs improvement?
4. Does it provide useful relative information:
   a. Does it provide the kind of data that I can compare meaningfully with results of past and future testings?
   b. Can the results be interpreted on a norm-referenced basis if that is desired?

The question of interpretability boils down to how you tell what a score on a test means. After all, it is only a number. Usually it is the number of items right. What does that information convey? Has the student demonstrated proficiency on the objectives being measured? Does the student have the ability to move to the next level of performance? Does he or she have the capability to perform skills at a level required for beginning employment in some occupation? In itself, a test score tells you very little; to be useful, test scores must be interpreted.

Relation of Test Scores to Relevant Performance

If a test is based on a set of objectives and if the objectives themselves have some validity, then the score on a test should tell us something about a student's ability to perform in the test area. A **criterion-referenced test** should provide information about students' degree of proficiency in the objectives of which the test is a measure. A high score on the test should be indicative of achievement of objectives and a low score of lack of achievement. You may think, perhaps, that the test items are too easy or too hard and hence not a fair measure of achievement. If your test has already met the criteria of validity and reliability, it is likely that the items are adequate for assessing achievement and thus you can conclude that test success reflects achievement of objectives.

To adequately interpret achievement, it may be helpful not to restrict yourself to the total test score. Since a criterion-referenced test is like a collection of mini-tests, each measuring a single, but related objective (and each containing a minimum of two, but preferably many more, items), achievement can be described by reporting the specific objectives that each student has demonstrated proficiency on by virtue of passing the appropriate mini-test. Thus, instead of having to decide how high a score must be to be considered "high," you would simply list for each student the name of each objective on which he or she has demonstrated proficiency along with (if desired) an indication of the level of proficiency attained. Interpretability of such a test is primarily based, therefore, not on the total test score but on indications of degree of proficiency attained for each objective of which the test is a measure. Since the objectives represent our real interest, and criterion-referenced tests measure achievement of objectives, we can focus our test results and interpretations on the very learning we are interested in enhancing. However, be cautious in interpreting results on mini-tests containing as few as two items.

Defining Acceptable Performance

Must a student pass every item that measures a given objective to be judged competent on that objective? That is, how are we to interpret performance on each mini-test? Because of variability on item difficulty and the appearance of various types of unsystematic errors, it is not unreasonable to allow some room for error. Each teacher must decide what the acceptable margin of error will be for each objective. Often, test performance can first be examined in order to facilitate this judgment. However, if items that seem to be too difficult are replaced or revised during the establishment of reliability, the remaining margin of error can be made as small as 10 to 20 percent to allow for unsystematic errors.

The amount of error that can be tolerated is proportionate to the number of items used to measure a particular objective. Where a single item, or even two items, are used, proficiency will require 100 percent success. In order to allow for 20 percent error, a minimum of five items would be required to measure an objective. In that case, it would be necessary to answer only four out of five correctly (80 percent) to indicate proficiency. Where fewer items are used, the 80 percent criterion could be used for evaluating total test performance (across related objectives) but not performance on individual objectives.

Diagnostic and Evaluative Information

Test results provide a basis for drawing conclusions about learning and teaching. A useful test not only tells you about student achievement but also tells about instructional effectiveness. If you examine individual performance, you should be able to determine each student's degree of proficiency on each objective. Where proficiency is sufficient, progress can continue to new learning areas. Where proficiency has not been demonstrated, remedial instruction aimed directly at those objectives can be instituted. In this way, a test can have diagnostic value. Test performance not only serves to certify success but to provide the kind of information that will make it possible to overcome failure.[7]

Where instruction is of a group nature, test results must be applicable to judgments of group progress. If group success has largely been attained, then instruction on new material can begin. If group gains have been minimal, then remedial instruction should be provided before instruction can progress to new areas.

Finally, the interpretable test gives you information on the adequacy of instruction. If proficiency on a particular objective has not been demonstrated by many students, it is probably because instruction in this area has been less than successful. Frequency breakdowns of student performance using a table such as the one below may be helpful. When the number of students who do not show proficiency reaches or exceeds the number who do show proficiency you can probably conclude that instructional experiences were insufficient for achievement of this objective. Changes in lesson plans or learning materials for teaching this objective should be seriously considered for subsequent instruction to augment or replace those currently in use.

OBJECTIVE 1

Number of students showing proficiency	Number of students not showing proficiency

---

[7] As the number of items per objective increases, so too does the reliability with which these objectives are measured. In order to use test results for individual diagnostic purposes, reliabilities must be high; hence, such tests should probably have at least four or five items per objective. This can usually be accomplished by keeping the number of objectives measured by a test to a maximum of five.

Useful Relative Information

Test results also represent a source of relative information about student performance. That is, we can evaluate a student's performance by comparing it to the performance of other students. In the largest sense, this is called norm-referencing. To use the concept of norm-referencing in your own classroom, place the total scores of all your students who are taking (or who have taken) the test in rank order going from the highest score to the lowest, and then assign each score a rank starting with 1 for the highest. You can then assign each score a percentile rank or convert it to a stanine score (using the procedures described earlier in this chapter), or simply separate scores into the top fifth, second fifth, middle fifth, fourth fifth, and lowest fifth (corresponding, perhaps, to the grades A, B, C, D, and F) with approximately one-fifth of the scores in each category.

You must now decide whether this kind of information is useful in interpreting test scores in addition to or in place of the criterion-referenced concept of proficiency on objectives relative to some intrinsic standard. (On aptitude tests, for example, relative information is considerably easier to interpret than absolute information because specific objectives or subtopical content areas do not have quite as much independence and meaning as they do in achievement or performance areas.) However, a comparative look at test scores does represent a way to provide them with some meaning at least in relative terms. Where you are less sure about the properties of your test, the normative or comparative approach is recommended. Where you have more confidence in the meaning of your objectives and the validity with which your test measures them, criterion-referenced interpretation is the more informative of the two approaches for evaluating students.

Proficiency Test

1. Norm-referenced interpretation relates a person's test score to _____ on that test by other people.
2. Define, in one sentence each, (a) norms, and (b) norming group.
3. For each of the illustrations below, identify the type of score depicted, that is, standard score, stanine score, percentile rank, or grade-equivalent score.
   a. Bobbie's score on the test was higher than 82 percent of the students in the norming group at the same grade level.
   b. Although Bobbie is in the fourth grade, her test score was as high as the average fifth grader on the fourth grade test.
   c. Bobbie's test score was two standard deviation units above the norming group average score for her grade level.
   d. Bobbie's test score fell into a band of scores of the norming group that was represented by the score of 7.
4. Match the description on the right with the type of score on the left.
   a. raw score   i. one of nine scale scores
   b. percentile rank   reflecting performance

c. stanine
d. grade equivalent
e. standard achievement score
f. anticipated achievement score
g. item performance

relative to a norming group
ii. the number of items the student got right
iii. report of scores on each individual test item
iv. a score in standard deviation units that reflects the distance from the norming group mean
v. the percentage of students scoring lower
vi. the number of students who took the test
vii. a score based on the performance of students of the same age and IQ
viii. a score expressed as grade level of median norm group student who achieved it

5. At the beginning of second grade, Deedie took a standardized achievement test in reading. Each of the following represents a different type of score, that is, a different way of reporting Deedie's performance on the reading test. Label the type of score that each represents.
   a. 2.7
   b. 85
   c. 61 right
   d. 1.5 S.D.
   e. 7
6. Check all of the statements below that are characteristic of standardized tests.
   a. items are purposely written to include ambiguity
   b. formal instructions for administration are provided
   c. scores are best interpreted in terms of the number of correct responses
   d. items have been analyzed and refined
   e. norms are available for score interpretation
7. Name one strength or advantage and one shortcoming or disadvantage of norm-referencing a test.
8. Percentage figures are used in both criterion-referenced tests and in norm-referenced tests. Describe the difference between performances reported as 85 percent on a criterion-referenced test and 85th percentile on a norm-referenced test.
9. Check all of the statements below that are characteristic of criterion-referenced tests.
   a. measure samples of actual performance

    b. scores do not relate to absolute proficiency

    c. based on objectives

    d. interpreted in terms of predetermined cutoffs

    e. reflect performance relative to other students.

10. You have just administered a math test to your sixth grade class. Describe how you might interpret individual scores in terms of (a) relevant performance, and (b) acceptable performance.

11. How would you use the test results obtained in item 9 (a) to identify ineffective instruction, and (b) to provide useful relative information about student performance?

Getting the Most from a
Testing Program

OBJECTIVES

- Describe the test item file as a strategy for improving teacher-built tests.
- Describe the individual applications of test data to include (a) monitoring and certifying student progress, (b) diagnosing individual strengths and weaknesses, (c) prescribing instructional experiences, and (d) providing student feedback.
- Describe and demonstrate the classroom applications of test data to improve instructional procedures.
- Describe the program and system applications of test data to determine the proficiency of the system through the use of system output measures.

A TEACHER-BUILT TESTING PROGRAM: THE TEST ITEM FILE

Since teacher-built tests constitute a major portion of the school testing program, obviously strategies for improving teacher testing would be desirable; one major strategy is the development of a test item file. A test item file is a collection of test items each of which has been shown to possess the qualities of validity and reliability and can be reused. A curriculum or a textbook is not used once and then discarded. Why, then, should a test be used once and discarded? (To some extent, reusing a test may pose a security problem, but one that can be solved.)

If we consider the typical teacher-built test as being potentially high in content validity and reasonably easy to interpret (with, however, limited reliability) and the standardized test as being somewhat the reverse, then the best strategy would be to seek a middle ground: teacher tests with increased reliability and standardized tests with greater content validity and easier interpretation. But why has little been done to improve teacher testing? The reason is that teacher tests *are* typically used once and then discarded, and test improvement demands test reuse.

A test item file works as follows. Teachers prepare test items to fit their instructional objectives (as illustrated in Chapter Three) and use these items in their classroom tests. Test results are then used to evaluate the items themselves in terms of the criteria of validity and reliability. Poor items are discarded; good items are retained. Each item, along with the objective it measures, is put on an index card and kept in a card file. Each time you want to test for proficiency on a particular set of objectives, you can construct a test largely from items in the file. The date that an item is used should appear on the back of the card. By mixing up items, adding new ones every testing period, and not reusing items in successive testings, the security problem could be minimized. (A sample test item file card appears in Figure 11-1.)

When you consider the curriculum resources available to teachers and the amount of training teachers receive in utilizing these resources, and then consider how few resources, if any, are made available to assist teachers in testing, the difference is considerable. Teachers are encouraged to develop their own resources by developing individual test item files and by pooling their test item files on a school, grade level, or even district basis.

Teachers' committees should also be formed to examine and review published achievement tests and identify those that are most appropriate for a particular school, grade level, or district.

OVERALL FUNCTIONS OF TESTING

It is possible for a school district to be involved to some degree in each of the following types of testing.

Figure 11-1
A Sample Test Item File Card: Front (above) and Back (below)

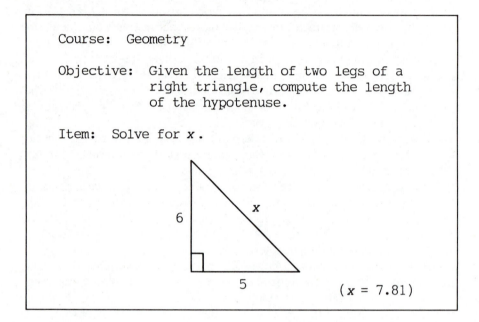

Course: Geometry

Objective: Given the length of two legs of a
            right triangle, compute the length
            of the hypotenuse.

Item: Solve for x.

6

x

5

$(x = 7.81)$

Date Used	Results	
11/84	Disc = .87	Ease = .50[*]
11/85	Disc = .78	Ease = .64
11/86	Disc = .80	Ease = .62

---

[*] Indices of discriminability and easiness (see page 158).

- teacher testing for the achievement of knowledge and comprehension (Chapter 4)
- teacher testing for the development of problem-solving skills (Chapter 5)
- teacher assessment of students' performance competencies and behavior (Chapter 6)
- standardized testing of achievement in reading, language arts, mathematics, science, social studies, and study skills (Chapter 9)

The purposes for which these types of tests can be applied are also numerous but consist basically of the following three types: (1) **individual applications,** (2) **classroom applications,** and (3) **system applications.** All three rely on individual data, but in classroom applications these data are pooled to provide information about classroom effects, and in system applications these data are pooled to provide information about school effects, grade level effects, and district effects. All three types of applications emphasize the instructional improvement value of test data as illustrated in Figure 11-2.

The rest of this chapter will describe the many aspects of individual, classroom, and system applications of test data in the school testing program. Since individual applications are the more traditional, and are more the role of the teacher, they will be described first.

INDIVIDUAL APPLICATIONS OF TEST DATA

There are basically four broad areas in which test data can be applied to individual student needs. These are: (1) monitoring and certifying student progress, (2) diagnosing individual strengths and weaknesses, (3) prescribing instruction, and (4) providing student feedback. Each will be described next.

Figure 11-2
The Role of Testing in Program Improvement

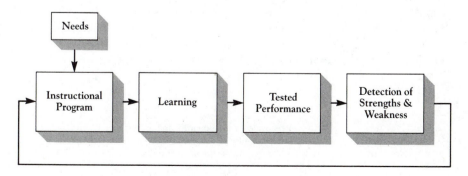

Monitoring and Certifying Student Progress (Grading)

Teachers have to monitor a student's progress to certify learning and to prescribe instruction. The most common measures of student learning are teacher-built tests and standardized achievement tests.[1]

Teacher-built Tests.   The success with which teachers' tests evaluate student progress depends on the extent to which these tests meet the criteria of validity and reliability. It cannot be overemphasized that the quality of decisions about individual student progress will vary as a function of the quality of the tests on which these decisions are based.

It is recommended that teachers do their recordkeeping of test performance in terms of objectives and that testing be undertaken for the degree of proficiency on each objective. Figure 11-3 shows a sample recordkeeping system for a class of twenty-two. Names of the students are listed down the side of the chart and the objectives across the top. There is, then, one box for each student's performance on each objective. The entry in this box could be the date on which adequate proficiency on that objective was demonstrated or a number indicating *degree* of proficiency attained.[2] Where adequate proficiency was not attained, the box would be left blank.

This recordkeeping procedure is based on the objective as the unit of analysis rather than on content area, test, book chapter or the like. Since the teacher's tests are designed to measure degree of proficiency on specific objectives (at least if the position laid out in this book is followed), it makes sense to utilize the objective as the unit of analysis for recordkeeping and evaluating as well. All of the objectives listed do not have to be cognitive in nature. Objectives describing attitudes and behavior (the affective domain) can be included as well. Moreover, among cognitive objectives, all do not have to deal with the acquisition of knowledge. Objectives dealing with cognitive skills such as analysis and synthesis are also quite appropriate. (Refer to Chapter Three for a description of the relationship between objectives and tests designed to measure them.)

This procedure for certifying student proficiency presents three possible ways for dealing with individual differences in performance. One is to **allow students to proceed through instruction at their own rate** so that individual capability will be reflected in terms of the number of objectives on which a student has acquired proficiency. A second is to **measure degree of proficiency based on the percentage of items measuring the objective that the student answers correctly.** A third is to **distinguish between objectives in terms of their complexity or difficulty** with more capable students concentrating on the more difficult objectives.

---

[1]Of course, teachers also use such nontest evidence as homework and observation of classroom performance to assist them in judging individual student learning.

[2]For example, degree of proficiency may be recorded as the number of items used to measure that objective that were passed divided by the number used, such as 6/8 meaning 6 out of 8 were passed.

Figure 11-3
Sample Roster for Recording Students' Performance by Objective

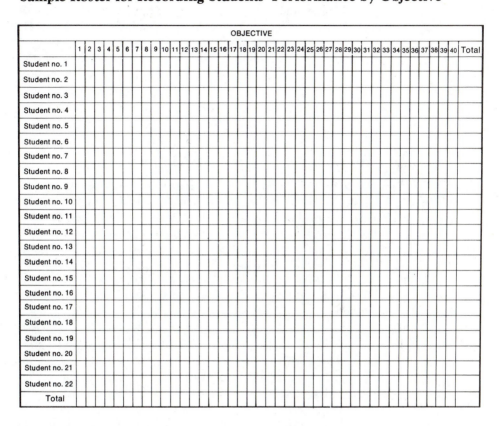

Published Tests.   Norm-referenced standardized tests are typically of less use in evaluating student progress than teacher tests because they do not conform as closely to a teacher's objectives as do his or her own tests. Published criterion-referenced achievement tests are written in terms of specific objectives and hence may be more useful than their norm-referenced counterparts for evaluating or certifying progress made by the student.

To increase the content validity of a standardized achievement test, a teacher would have to go through it and select only those items that relate to his or her specific objectives of instruction; this procedure, however, would negate the norm-referencing and hence make the scores difficult to interpret. Since standardized achievement tests are written for national use, they must be based on a set of objectives that is generally valid and hence not specifically valid for an individual class. While standardized tests have applicability as part of the school testing program, this applicability is only minimal in the area of monitoring and evaluating individual student progress with respect to the objectives of instruction. However, item screening in terms of objectives can be done on published criterion-referenced tests since these are interpreted in terms of objectives rather than norms.[3] Thus, these tests have potential for evaluating in-class learning progress using the kind of recordkeeping scheme shown in Figure 11-3. (Refer also to the report form shown in Figure 10-6 for criterion-referenced reporting.)

When your interest is in evaluating a student's progress relative to the performance of other students rather than relative to objectives, then use a standardized achievement test. A report form such as appears in Figure 11-4 provides grade-equivalent scores which can be used to compare a student's performance to that of his or her grade-mates.

Diagnosing Individual Strengths and Weaknesses

The purpose of diagnostic testing is not to identify students' levels of proficiency on specific instructional objectives but to identify more general levels of learning, performance, and abilities. This kind of testing is concerned with the skills and competencies that students need to have acquired to advance in the learning sequence. Because prerequisites are often hard to identify, diagnostic tests must either (a) survey a wide range of such skills and competencies (thereby having the likelihood of covering all prerequisites) or else (b) measure specific objectives on which proficiency is required before the student can move on to subsequent objectives in the sequence.

At lower levels of instruction, reading and arithmetic are the basic general areas on which much learning is built. Testing students in these areas can provide information about general strengths and weaknesses in individual students. By looking at the performance of each student in the class on a standardized achievement test (see Figures 11-4, 11-5, and 10-3), the teacher can detect potential problem areas before their influence over a child's performance becomes serious. A student, for example, like Charles A. Ballard in Figure 11-4, is performing at or above grade level in all test areas except two, "concepts of number" and "science."[4] If this pattern continues, Charles' mathematics ability may be limited by his difficulty in acquiring math concepts. Certainly, in science he is in need of assistance. Without this test information, Ms. Wellens, Charles' teacher, would perhaps not have known of these two areas of difficulties. Had she already perceived them, the test scores would serve to increase her confidence in her judgment.

Teachers do not, for the most part, build diagnostic tests but depend, instead, upon published ones. Achievement test results in particular can be helpful to teachers in detecting patterns of accomplishment relative to

---

[3] Some test publishers have made certain standardized tests interpretable on a criterion-referenced basis.

[4] Charles' frequent evaluations of "low" on the Achievement Ability Comparison indicate that based on his measured school ability, he would be expected to perform above grade level in virtually all topics.

Figure 11-4
Achievement Test Results for One Student, Charles A. Ballard, in Ms. Wellens' Class*

Stanford ACHIEVEMENT TEST WITH OTIS-LENNON SCHOOL ABILITY TEST

SKILLS ANALYSIS FOR CHARLES A BALLARD

TEACHER MS WELLENS
SCHOOL LAKESIDE ELEMENTARY
SYSTEM NEWTOWN PUBLIC SCHOOLS

GRADE 4   TEST DATE 10/12/82   COPY 1
STANFORD NORMS GR 4.1   LEVEL PRIM 3   FORM E
OLSAT NORMS   GR 4 FALL   LEVEL ELEM   FORM S

TESTS NUMBER OF ITEMS	RAW SCORE	SCALE SCORE	NAT'L PR-S	GRADE EQUIV	ACHIEVMNT ABILITY COMPARISN
WORD STUDY SKILLS 54	35	142	50- 5	4.1	LOW
READING COMPREHENSION 60	49	143	50- 5	4.0	LOW
VOCABULARY 38	29	148	52- 5	4.3	LOW
LISTENING COMPREHENSION 40	31	139	44- 5	3.9	LOW
SPELLING 36	18	143	40- 5	3.8	LOW
LANGUAGE 46	37	148	60- 6	4.6	MIDDLE
CONCEPTS OF NUMBER 34	14	137	32- 4	3.5	LOW
MATH COMPUTATION 42	20	145	50- 5	3.9	MIDDLE
MATH APPLICATIONS 38	19	145	50- 5	4.0	LOW
SOCIAL SCIENCE 44	36	161	82- 7	5.5	MIDDLE
SCIENCE 44	19	130	34- 4	3.3	LOW
USING INFORMATION 40	27	160	77- 7	5.0	MIDDLE
TOTAL READING 114	84	143	50- 5	4.0	LOW
TOTAL LISTENING 78	60	144	48- 5	4.1	LOW
TOTAL LANGUAGE 82	55	146	52- 5	4.2	LOW
TOTAL MATHEMATICS 114	53	143	44- 5	3.8	LOW
BASIC BATTERY TOTAL 388	252	NA²	50- 5	4.0	NA²
COMPLETE BATTERY TOTAL 476	308	NA²	50- 5	4.0	NA²
OTIS-LENNON	AGE	PR-S	84-7	RS = 51	SAI = 116
SCHOOL ABILITY TEST	GRADE	PR-S	82-7		

AGE 9 YRS. 1 MO.

READING SKILLS GROUP—DEVELOPMENTAL

CONTENT CLUSTERS RAW SCORE/NUMBER OF ITEMS		BELOW AVERAGE	AVERAGE	ABOVE AVERAGE
WORD STUDY SKILLS	35/54		√	
Structural Analysis	7/18	√		
Phonetic Analysis—Consonants	16/18			√
Phonetic Analysis—Vowels	12/18		√	
READING COMPREHENSION	49/60		√	
Textual Reading	15/20		√	
Functional Reading	17/20			√
Recreational Reading	17/20		√	
Literal Comprehension	28/30			√
Inferential Comprehension	21/30		√	
VOCABULARY	29/38		√	
LISTENING COMPREHENSION	31/40		√	
Retention	17/20		√	
Organization	14/20		√	
SPELLING	18/36		√	
Sight Words	6/ 8		√	
Phonetic Principles	4/16	√		
Structural Principles	8/12		√	
LANGUAGE	37/46		√	
Conventions	22/26		√	
Language Sensitivity	7/10		√	
Reference Skills	8/10			√
CONCEPTS OF NUMBER	14/34		√	
Whole Numbers and Place Value	8/18		√	
Fractions	1/ 5	√		
Operations and Properties	5/11		√	

WRITING TEST RESULTS:

CONTENT CLUSTERS RAW SCORE/NUMBER OF ITEMS		BELOW AVERAGE	AVERAGE	ABOVE AVERAGE
MATHEMATICS COMPUTATION	20/42		√	
Addition with Whole Numbers	9/12		√	
Subtraction with Whole Numbers	8/ 9			√
Multiplication with Whole Numbers	2/12	√		
Division with Whole Numbers	1/ 9	√		
MATHEMATICS APPLICATIONS	19/38		√	
Problem Solving	9/18		√	
Geometry/Measurement	5/14	√		
Graphs and Charts	5/6			√
SOCIAL SCIENCE	36/44			√
Geography	6/ 6			√
History and Anthropology	6/ 9		√	
Sociology	5/ 6			√
Political Science	3/ 4			√
Economics	8/10			√
Inquiry Skills	8/ 9			√
SCIENCE	19/44			√
Physical Science	4/11	√		
Biological Science	9/18		√	
Inquiry Skills	6/15		√	
USING INFORMATION	27/40			√

DATA SERVICES DIVISION   **THE PSYCHOLOGICAL CORPORATION** HARCOURT BRACE JOVANOVICH, PUBLISHERS ability. Perhaps the most potentially useful tests for diagnostic purposes are the published criterion-referenced tests. Designed to cover a lengthy instructional sequence (which may span two or three school years) they are highly specific about performance on earlier objectives in the sequence. Where earlier failures are blocking current learning, these tests will enable the teacher to detect (that is, diagnose) such deficiencies. Diagnosis of this sort poses two requirements: (1) a criterion-referenced test, that is, a test that measures performance on objectives, and (2) a test that measures performance on objectives that were covered earlier in the sequence, going back as far as can be considered convenient for testing purposes. By looking back in the sequence and finding a minus score on an objective, the teacher may find the basis for a student's current difficulties. Failure to have acquired proficiency on a particular objective may have occurred during the preceding school year when the student had a different teacher from the current one. (Forms such as the one that appears in Figure 10-6 are used to report results on criterion-referenced tests.)[5]

In general, broad deficiencies or strengths can be diagnosed by means of published, norm-referenced tests while specific deficiencies are most easily identified using criterion-referenced tests that extend reasonably far back in a learning sequence.

Prescribing Instruction

To the extent that the curriculum is not fixed, the teacher may prescribe specific instructional experiences for students. In most cases a large part of the curriculum is reasonably fixed with the remainder available for supplementary activities. In other cases, the sequence of instruction is fixed but the rate at which a student can progress may be varied.

To make prescriptive decisions, teachers can make good use of both their own and published tests. In the case of Charles Ballard, for example (cited in the preceding section based on Figure 11-4), his weakness in concepts of number that showed up on his standardized test scores suggests that the teacher have him work on problems involving rational numbers (see Section F of the form). His teacher could use a diagnostic math test in order to pinpoint other areas in which additional instruction might be helpful.

Prescriptions for instruction can also be based on the results of teacher tests in conjunction with the recordkeeping form illustrated in Figure 11-3. The blanks in the form for a particular student indicate the objectives on which he or she has failed to demonstrate adequate proficiency. A teacher's tests should be considerably more than a mechanism for certifying prog-

---

[5]The individual student report form for a standardized test also reports performance in specific content categories and on individual items, thus offering the potential for use as a diagnostic test (that is, a measure of past deficiencies). However, interpretation of results on individual items poses serious problems in terms of reliability. For standardized tests to be used in a criterion-referenced way, interpretations would need to be based on specific content category scores.

ress; tests can be and should be a basic part of the mechanics for indicating supplementary or even primary instruction.

Providing Student Feedback

Although tests are an excellent source of feedback for students, merely providing them with a score that tells only their overall level of performance may be more demoralizing than helpful. The most helpful feedback should be that which tells them which objectives they failed to master and the nature of their mistakes. Test feedback should provide the student with information to help him or her improve subsequent test performance; mere scores can be more of a frustration than a help. Witness the standardized test score report shown in Figure 11-4, a similar version of the upper half of which was sent home with Charles A. Ballard, a fourth grader. How will the information on the upper half of the form help Charles? Since it doesn't tell him exactly where his deficiencies lie, it may produce either frustration or a competitive sense of self-satisfaction.

In order for achievement tests to serve a helpful feedback function for a student, the teacher must be able to point out to that student where his or her errors lie. The teacher cannot do this unless information at this level of detail is available as it is in this illustration (Figure 11-4) on the lower half of the form. Standardized test results have the potential to assist teachers and thereby indirectly assist students (through prescriptive instruction) when teachers have specific performance information available to them rather than just overall scores. However, the major source of student feedback still remains teacher-built tests. To maximize the feedback value of such tests, teachers should do the following.

- **Give a pretest** (that is, the end-of-unit test itself or an alternate form of it prior to the instruction). If pretesting is not viable, at least present the objectives of instruction at the start of an instructional sequence.
- **Return the scored tests themselves, not just the scores.** The scores alone have the same shortcomings as most standardized test score reports, that is, no actual feedback in terms of specific performance on objectives.
- **Return the tests quickly after they are given.** Otherwise students will forget the instructional goals.
- **Clearly indicate errors and bases for scoring on each student's test.** Feedback is based on the discrepancy between what is and what ought to be; your markings on the students' tests should tell them what "ought to be."
- **Test in a warm and accepting atmosphere** rather than a threatening one so that students will believe, accept, and use feedback in a constructive way rather than feel they must defend themselves against it. This usually means giving students at least a second

chance to "pass" the test; it means always projecting the philosophy that tests should serve to help students improve rather than simply to evaluate their performance.

CLASSROOM APPLICATIONS OF TEST DATA

In addition to helping teachers interpret the learning and performance of individual students, test data can be used to help teachers improve upon their own instructional procedures. Let us consider how an examination of the collective test performance of students can be accomplished and how it can be useful.

Using Results of Teacher-built Tests

Consider the sample roster in Figure 11-3. While it was constructed originally to record and evaluate individual student performance, it can also help a teacher to evaluate his or her own performance. The last row of the roster presents the results on each objective accumulated across all the students in the class. By examining the accumulative results on each objective, the teacher can determine those objectives on which additional or different instructional procedures are needed. Suppose, for example, that approximately 80 percent of the students demonstrate adequate proficiency on all but five of the objectives. On these five, only 50 percent of the class at most perform at an acceptable level. The teacher must first examine the objectives themselves and the test items used to measure them to make sure they were not too difficult; but if they seem not to be, the teacher must conclude that the instruction provided for these five objectives was insufficient and provide further or alternative forms of instruction.

The important point is that student performance taken individually reflects upon individual learning but that individual performances can be considered collectively to help tell the teacher, empirically, whether his or her instruction is working as well as it should be.

Using Results of Published Tests

To be able to use standardized test scores to help evaluate classroom instruction, they must be reported for the classroom as a unit. For illustrative purposes, a class summary of scores is shown in Figure 11-5 for Ms. Wellens' fourth grade class. Based on this report, Ms. Wellens' fourth graders appear to be doing average work in most tested areas. In language and social studies, they performed above average. The weakest areas are "concepts of number" and "science" each with about 25 percent performing below average. On the basis of these scores, Ms. Wellens should consider working more intensively with those small groups of seven (not necessarily the same ones) who are performing below average in concepts of number and science and spend less time teaching language and social science.

Figure 11-5
Class Summary for Ms. Wellens' Fourth Grade Class*

TESTS	NUMBER TESTED FOR AAC	MEAN RAW SCORE	MEAN SCALE SCORE	NAT'L GROUP PR-S	GE OF MEAN SS	AAC PERCENT L M H
WORD STUDY SKILLS	28	34	140	25-5	4.0	40 50 10
READING COMPREHENSION	28	47	137	46-5	3.7	36 46 18
VOCABULARY	28	26	135	48-5	4.2	38 40 22
LISTENING COMPREHENSION	28	30	140	38-4	3.7	30 62 8
SPELLING	28	20	141	42-5	3.5	42 50 8
LANGUAGE	28	35	145	56-5	4.4	44 44 12
CONCEPTS OF NUMBER	28	13	130	28-4	3.3	48 30 22
MATH COMPUTATION	28	19	142	48-5	3.6	46 36 18
MATH APPLICATIONS	28	18	140	44-5	4.1	42 40 18
SOCIAL SCIENCE	28	26	150	54-5	4.4	31 41 28
SCIENCE	28	18	127	26-4	3.1	38 60 2
USING INFORMATION	28	29	135	52-5	4.4	37 40 23
TOTAL READING	28	81	140	46-5	3.9	38 48 14
TOTAL LISTENING	28	56	142	48-5	4.1	30 50 20
TOTAL LANGUAGE	28	63	145	52-5	4.0	43 47 11
TOTAL MATHEMATICS	28	51	140	42-5	3.8	45 36 20
BASIC BATTERY TOTAL	242	NA²	NA²	NA²	NA²	
COMPLETE BATTERY TOTAL	286	NA²	NA²	NA²	NA²	
OTIS-LENNON	MEAN RS = 46			MEAN SAI = 107		
SCHOOL ABILITY TEST	N = 28					

Stanford ACHIEVEMENT TEST WITH OTIS-LENNON SCHOOL ABILITY TEST

SKILLS ANALYSIS FOR MS WELLENS

SCHOOL SYSTEM: LAKESIDE ELEMENTARY NEWTON PUBLIC SCHOOLS
GRADE 4 TEST DATE 10/12/82
STANFORD NORMS GR 4.1 LEVEL PRIM 3 FORM E
OLSAT NORMS GR 4 FALL LEVEL ELEM FORM S
COPY 1

OLSAT GRADE NORM ABOVE AVERAGE (7,8,9) 30%
STANINE SUMMARY AVERAGE (4,5,6) 52%
N = 28 BELOW AVERAGE (1,2,3) 18%

CONTENT CLUSTERS	NUMBER TESTED	BELOW AVERAGE	AVERAGE	ABOVE AVERAGE
WORD STUDY SKILLS	28	21%	44%	35%
Structural Analysis		40%	40%	20%
Phonetic Analysis—Consonants		7%	40%	53%
Phonetic Analysis—Vowels		17%	52%	31%
READING COMPREHENSION	28	21%	50%	28%
Textual Reading		23%	54%	23%
Functional Reading		12%	48%	40%
Recreational Reading		18%	44%	38%
Literal Comprehension		19%	50%	31%
Inferential Comprehension		32%	52%	16%
VOCABULARY	28	20%	56%	24%
LISTENING COMPREHENSION	28	8%	68%	24%
Retention		4%	58%	38%
Organization		12%	78%	10%
SPELLING	28	23%	61%	16%
Sight Words		10%	60%	30%
Phonetic Principles		28%	62%	10%
Structural Principles		30%	62%	8%
LANGUAGE	28	18%	57%	25%
Conventions		7%	64%	29%
Language Sensitivity		32%	52%	16%
Reference Skills		15%	55%	30%
CONCEPTS OF NUMBER	28	26%	55%	19%
Whole Numbers and Place Value		22%	58%	20%
Fractions		34%	58%	8%
Operations and Properties		21%	50%	29%

CONTENT CLUSTERS	NUMBER TESTED	BELOW AVERAGE	AVERAGE	ABOVE AVERAGE
MATHEMATICS COMPUTATION	28	23%	51%	26%
Addition with Whole Numbers		23%	51%	26%
Subtraction with Whole Numbers		23%	54%	23%
Multiplication with Whole Numbers		25%	48%	27%
Division with Whole Numbers		21%	52%	27%
MATHEMATICS APPLICATIONS	28	12%	65%	23%
Problem Solving		18%	60%	22%
Geometry/Measurement		10%	65%	25%
Graphs and Charts		8%	71%	21%
SOCIAL SCIENCE	28	22%	56%	22%
Geography		32%	60%	8%
History and Anthropology		24%	55%	21%
Sociology		20%	60%	20%
Political Science		22%	58%	20%
Economics		16%	56%	28%
Inquiry Skills		18%	52%	30%
SCIENCE	28	27%	59%	14%
Physical Science		30%	62%	8%
Biological Science		28%	60%	12%
Inquiry Skills		24%	54%	22%
USING INFORMATION		19%	55%	26%

READING SKILLS GROUPS		TOTAL N = 28		
	N	%		N	%
ENRICHMENT	7	25	VOCABULARY	2	7
DEVELOPMENTAL	14	50	COMPREHENSION	3	11
REMEDIAL	0	0	INCOMPLETE	0	0
DECODING	2	7			

DATA SERVICES DIVISION   THE PSYCHOLOGICAL CORPORATION
HARCOURT BRACE JOVANOVICH, PUBLISHERS

PROGRAM AND SYSTEM APPLICATIONS OF TEST DATA

For purposes of measurement it is convenient to separate educational variables into *input, process, and output.* **Measurable educational inputs are the givens of an educational system**—school budget, facilities, community needs, and the characteristics that students and teachers bring with them into the school system. For students, input would include prior learning and, for teachers, past experience. **Measurable educational processes are the performance characteristics of the system itself**—the teaching behaviors of teachers, the administering behavior of administrators, and the operation of the instructional program. Finally, **measurable educational outputs,** the area of greatest concern in measurement, **are learner achievements, attitudes, and behaviors,** that when taken together reflect upon the inputs and processes of the school. These relationships are shown in Figure 11-6.

The chief focus of educational measurement is on output. In a very real sense, the "products" of education are the students; thus it is important to measure their collective acquisition of skills, knowledges, attitudes, and behaviors. It is important, too, to measure the individual acquisition of these skills, knowledges, attitudes, and behaviors in order to evaluate, facilitate, and certify that growth and progress. Thus, we can distinguish for purposes of educational measurement individual effects and group effects (the latter being the sum of the former and thus representing tendencies) on school input, process, and output.

Measuring Educational Output

While it is difficult to be sure one way of doing something is better than another, we can have considerable confidence in specifying, for example, that high reading performance is better than low reading performance. In

Figure 11-6
Examples of Input, Process, Output, and their Relationship

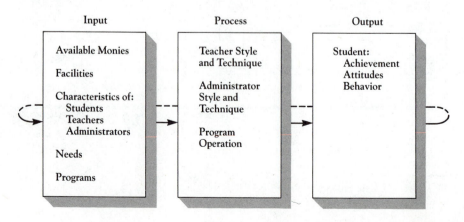

other words, it is easier to attach positive values to outcomes than to processes. People may not be able to agree on the best way to teach children to read, but they can agree that improving their reading skills is a goal of education. Thus, educational outputs rather than processes are appropriate for measuring and evaluating educational effects.

A second reason for focusing on outputs as measures of educational effectiveness is that we are far more adept at measuring output than we are at measuring process (that is, we are much more adept at measuring how students perform than how systems perform). Also, we are an output-oriented society with a tendency to value our processes only if we also value their products. In the final analysis we judge things (and people) by how well they "work."

Basic Subject Outputs. The first area of interest in examining the school's or district's output includes the most basic subjects: language arts and mathematics. The performance of students in these basic subjects can be measured by examining standardized test results such as those appearing in Figure 11-7. On the average, Newtown's fourth graders are performing at or below grade level on more than half of the tests. A look at the "Below Average" stanine results (shown in the bottom row) reveals Concept of Number and Listening Comprehension to be the weakest areas with 22 and 14 percent respectively performing below average.

To better evaluate results like those shown in Figure 11-7, it is helpful to make comparisons. Has the performance of students improved in any area from last year to this year? Has it worsened? Assume that the school was experimenting with a new mathematics workbook series that focused on computation. Achievement test results could be used to answer the following questions: (1) Have the fourth grade students improved their math computational skills during the course of the year while the experimental materials were in use? (2) Are this year's fourth graders, all of whom used the new workbook, performing better than last year's fourth graders, none of whom used the new workbook? (3) Are the fourth graders in Newtown, all of whom used the new workbook, performing better than the fourth graders in Elm City (an otherwise reasonably comparable district with a similar student population), none of whom used the new workbook? Thus, results on a standardized achievement test can be examined across districts, across schools (not illustrated here), across time (following the progress of a class), or across classes (comparing this year's class to last year's) to make the results an interpretable reflection of system or program effects.

The results of teacher tests can also be used as a reflection of system or program effects when examined collectively across students and classes; that is, by keeping track of the percentage of students who acquire proficiency on each objective over the course of the school year. Thus, if the teacher uses Figure 11-3 to monitor the acquisition of individual student proficiency (for purposes of facilitating individual learning) and then sums up the results across students to monitor the effectiveness of classroom instruction, an

Figure 11-7
Achievement Test Results for Newtown Public Schools' Fourth Grade*

Stanford ACHIEVEMENT TEST

ADMINISTRATOR'S DATA SUMMARY FOR NEWTOWN PUBLIC SCHOOLS — PAGE 1 — GRADE 4

SYSTEM NEWTOWN PUBLIC SCHOOLS   TEST DATE 10/12/82   NORMS GR 4 1

	WD STUDY SKILLS	READING COMP	VOCAB	LISTENING COMP	SPELLING	LANGUAGE	CONCEPTS OF NUMBER	MATH COMP	MATH APPL
(scale max)	375	375	375	375	375	375	375	375	375
(A) NUMBER OF STUDENTS FOR STATISTICS N=									
RAW SCORE STATISTICS MEAN (MN=)	36.4	44.4	31.6	31.0	34.5	33.0	16.3	21.7	18.0
STANDARD DEVIATION (SD=)	7.0	6.8	5.9	5.2	4.8	5.2	5.1	5.2	3.7
PERCENTILES P90 - 90th	45.8	52.5	38.8	37.5	39.8	37.8	22.5	28.5	21.5
Q3 - 75th	40.8	48.5	33.9	34.8	37.9	36.4	19.4	25.4	20.2
MEDIAN 50th	35.5	43.4	31.2	30.5	34.2	32.5	16.2	20.7	18.1
Q1 - 25th	30.2	38.1	26.6	26.6	30.2	30.2	12.1	16.6	15.1
P10 - 10th	27.5	35.2	23.5	23.5	27.5	25.5	8.2	14.2	11.5
(B) SCALED SCORE STATISTICS MEAN (MN=)	145.2	139.3	153.2	139.4	149.8	141.2	141.4	147.6	143.9
STANDARD DEVIATION (SD=)	14.5	6.7	12.7	10.4	6.7	9.2	13.0	8.2	7.0
PERCENTILES P90 - 90th	164.0	146.5	170.0	152.5	154.8	148.8	156.0	158.0	150.0
Q3 - 75th	150.5	142.5	156.8	146.2	153.4	145.9	147.9	153.4	147.4
MEDIAN 50th	142.5	137.5	151.2	138.0	147.5	140.0	140.8	145.5	143.2
Q1 - 25th	133.5	133.1	142.6	130.6	144.6	133.6	133.4	140.2	139.1
P10 - 10th	130.0	131.5	136.0	125.5	142.5	128.8	120.8	135.0	133.0
(C) GRADE EQUIVALENT OF THE MEAN SCALED SCORE GE=	4.5	3.7	4.9	3.9	4.5	3.9	3.7	4.3	3.8
GRADE EQUIVALENTS OF SCALED SCORE PERCENTILES P90 - 90th	6.3	4.3	6.3	5.2	5.1	4.7	5.2	5.0	4.6
Q3 - 75th	4.9	3.9	5.0	4.6	4.7	4.3	4.5	5.6	4.2
MEDIAN 50th	4.2	3.6	4.7	3.9	4.3	3.8	3.7	4.1	3.8
Q1 - 25th	3.4	3.2	4.0	3.2	3.9	3.4	3.1	3.5	3.5
P10 - 10th	3.2	3.0	3.4	2.8	3.8	3.0	2.1	3.0	3.0
NATIONAL GROUP PR-S OF THE MEAN SCALED SCORE PR=	66	38	90	36	82	48	34	62	38
S=	6	4	8	4	7	5	4	6	4
(D) NATIONAL PERCENTILE RANK SUMMARY PR SCORES OF 76-99 N	60	15	90	45	30	15	45	120	15
%	16%	4%	24%	12%	8%	4%	12%	32%	4%
PR SCORES OF 51-75 N	135	75	165	120	195	120	120	105	210
%	36%	20%	44%	32%	52%	32%	32%	28%	56%
PR SCORES OF 26-50 N	165	270	105	150	150	225	120	120	120
%	44%	72%	28%	40%	40%	60%	32%	32%	32%
PR SCORES OF 1-25 N	15	15	15	60	0	15	90	30	30
%	4%	4%	4%	16%	0%	4%	24%	8%	8%
NATIONAL NCE SCORE STATISTICS MEAN (MN=)	52.57	45.26	58.29	48.14	54.42	49.55	46.15	54.92	48.06
STANDARD DEVIATION (SD=)	9.73	7.36	15.58	11.70	8.35	8.26	15.33	14.31	8.51
(E) NATIONAL STANINE SUMMARY ABOVE AVERAGE (STANINES 7,8,9) N	56	14	85	42	29	12	39	105	12
%	15%	4%	23%	11%	8%	3%	10%	28%	3%
AVERAGE (STANINES 4,5,6) N	307	348	275	280	346	352	254	245	342
%	82%	93%	73%	75%	92%	94%	68%	65%	91%
BELOW AVERAGE (STANINES 1,2,3) N	12	13	15	53	0	11	82	25	21
%	3%	3%	4%	14%	0%	3%	22%	7%	6%

(F) READING SKILLS GROUP SUMMARY

	N	%
ENRICHMENT	19	5%
DEVELOPMENTAL	169	45%
REMEDIAL	26	7%
DECODING	45	12%

VOCABULARY COMPREHENSION INCOMPLETE

NUMBER OF STUDENTS FOR STATISTICS IS 375

STANFORD LEVEL/FORM   Primary 3/E   DATA SERVICES DIVISION   THE PSYCHOLOGICAL CORPORATION   HARCOURT BRACE JOVANOVICH, PUBLISHERS   PROCESS NO 005-1543-001   COPY 1

*Reproduced from the HBJ Service Reports, SAT 82, copyright © 1982, by Harcourt Brace Jovanovich, Inc. Reproduced by special permission of the publisher.

administrator could sum up the classroom results for an entire school, grade level, or school district to arrive at an appraisal of system effects in the basic subject areas.

In Summary

Whether the purpose of testing is to monitor and improve individual, class, or system performance, the pattern of procedures is largely the same (and has basically served as the theme of this book). In all cases objectives must be specified and tests must be constructed or found to measure those objectives—tests that are valid, reliable, interpretable, and usable. To determine the degree of proficiency that has been attained by the student, class, or system, the test results are compared to the objectives. Where proficiency levels are adequate, no additional evaluation is needed; but where performance is below acceptable levels, test results should be analyzed to provide intensified or alternative programs of instruction to attempt to raise performance to an acceptable level, and further evaluation will be necessary. To monitor, to diagnose, to provide feedback, to facilitate the achievement of proficiency, to certify or grade—these then are the functions of tests in the schools for the teachers.

Proficiency Test

1. You are trying to convince your colleagues to collaborate on the construction of a test item file. Cite three reasons you would use to convince them that the file is a good idea.
2. Describe the steps in establishing a test item file.
3. Individual test results can be very helpful to the classroom teacher. Give an example of how the teacher can obtain and use test data to
   a. monitor and certify student progress.
   b. diagnose individual deficiencies.
   c. decide whether or not to prescribe additional instruction.
   d. provide feedback to students.
4. Construct a sample roster for recording student's performance by objective.
5. Consider the lower half of the class summary of achievement test performance shown in Figure 11-5.
   a. What is the specific content area of greatest strength? How did you determine this?
   b. What is the specific content area of greatest weakness? How did you determine this?
   c. Based on the test results, what changes in instruction would you recommend the teacher make?
6. Describe three ways to determine whether a new instructional procedure being used throughout the sixth grade of a school is effective.

Appendix

A GLOSSARY OF MEASUREMENT TERMS*

Academic Aptitude. The combination of native and acquired abilities that are needed for school learning; likelihood of success in mastering academic work, as estimated from measures of the necessary abilities. (Also called *scholastic aptitude*)

Achievement Age. The performance level or achievement test score expressed in terms of the chronological age group for which a particular performance level or achievement test score is average.

Achievement Test. A test that measures the extent to which a person has "achieved" something, acquired certain information, demonstrated proficiency in certain skills—usually as a result of instruction.

Acquiescence Response Bias. Responding to stimuli other than the test items themselves. This usually takes the form of responding in some systematic pattern such as marking *true* (yea saying) or *false* (nay saying) on every item.

Age Norms. Values representing typical, or average, performance for persons of various age groups.

Alternate-form Reliability. The closeness of correspondence, or correlation, between results on alternate (that is, equivalent or parallel) forms of a test; thus, a measure of the extent to which the two forms are consistent or reliable in measuring whatever they do measure. (See *reliability, reliability coefficient*)

---

* Adapted from A *Glossary of Measurement Terms* (Test Service Notebook 13), prepared by Blythe C. Mitchell, distributed by Harcourt Brace Jovanovich, Inc., and reproduced by permission. It is introduced in part, by the following statement. "This glossary of terms used in educational and psychological measurement is primarily for persons with limited training in measurement, rather than for the specialist. The terms defined are the more common or basic ones such as occur in test manuals and educational journals. In the definitions, certain technicalities and niceties of usage have been sacrificed for the sake of brevity and, it is hoped, clarity. Where there is not complete uniformity among writers in the measurement field with respect to the meaning of a term, either these variations are noted or the definition offered is the one that writers judged to represent the 'best' usage." In addition to the HBJ glossary edited for use here, other measurement terms related to concepts developed in this book have been included.

Aptitude. A combination of abilities and other characteristics, whether native or acquired, known or believed to be indicative of an individual's ability to learn or to develop proficiency in some particular area. Aptitude tests include those of general academic ability (commonly called *mental ability* or *intelligence* tests); those of special abilities, such as verbal, numerical, mechanical, or musical ability; those assessing "readiness" for learning; and prognostic tests, which measure both ability and previous learning and are used to predict future performance, usually in a specific field, such as foreign language, shorthand, or nursing.

Arithmetic Mean. The sum of a set of scores divided by their number. It is usually referred to as the *mean* or *average*.

Average. A general term applied to the various measures of central tendency. The three most widely used averages are the *arithmetic mean* (mean), the *median*, and the *mode*. When the term "average" is used without designation as to type, the most likely assumption is that it is the arithmetic mean.

Battery. A group of several tests standardized on the same sample population so that results on the several tests are comparable. (Sometimes loosely applied to any group of tests administered together, even though not standardized on the same subjects.) The most common test batteries are those of school achievement, which include subtests in the separate learning areas.

Behavior Rating Scale. An instrument used to record judgments about the incidence or nature of the behavior of a given individual or group. Such judgments will be influenced by subjective factors and should be tested for reliability.

Ceiling. The upper limit of performance measured by a test.

Checklist. A list of behaviors, observations, or characteristics, each of which is checked (or answered "yes") by the rater or observer when the item has been judged to have occurred satisfactorily and not checked (or answered "no") when judged not to have occurred satisfactorily.

Chronological Age. A person's age usually expressed in years and months.

Coefficient of Correlation. A measure of the degree of relationship or "going-togetherness" between two sets of measures for the same individuals. The correlation coefficient most frequently used in test development and educational research is that known as the Pearson, or *product-moment* (r). Unless otherwise specified, "correlation" usually refers to this coefficient, but "*rank*," "*biserial*," and others are used in special situations. Correlation coefficients range from .00, denoting a complete absence of relationship, to +1.00, and to −1.00, indicating perfect positive or perfect negative correspondence, respectively. (See *correlation*)

Completion Item. A short-answer test question calling for the filling in of an omitted word or phrase.

Concurrent Validity. See *validity*.

Construct Validity. See *validity*.

Content Outline. A specification of the content covered in a segment of instruction and of the importance of each piece of content. This outline serves as a basis for test item construction.

Content Validity. On achievement tests, an indication of the extent to which the test items adequately represent the objectives that they have been written or selected to measure. It is best established by a comparison of test content with instructional objectives.

Correction for Guessing (correction for chance). A reduction in score for wrong answers, sometimes applied in scoring true–false or multiple choice questions. Such scoring formulas ($R - W$ for tests with two-option response, $R - \frac{1}{2}W$ for three-option response, $R - \frac{1}{3}W$ for four, and so on) are intended to discourage guessing and to yield more accurate rankings of test takers in terms of their true knowledge. They are used much less today than in the early days of testing.

Correlation. Relationship, or "going-togetherness," between two sets of scores or measures; tendency of one score to vary concomitantly with the other, as the tendency of students of high IQ to be above average in reading ability. The existence of a strong relationship—that is, a high correlation—between two variables does not necessarily indicate that one has any causal influence on the other. (See *coefficient of correlation*)

Criterion. A standard by which a test or test performance may be judged or evaluated; a set of scores, ratings, and so on, that a test is designed to measure, predict, or correlate with. (See *validity*)

Criterion-referenced Test. Term used to describe tests designed to provide information on the specific knowledge or skills possessed by a student. Such tests are designed to measure the objectives of instruction. Their scores have meaning in terms of *what* the student knows or can do, rather than in their relation to the scores made by some comparison or norm group.

Criterion Validity. See *validity*.

Culture-fair Test. Culture-fair tests attempt to provide an equal opportunity for success by persons of all cultures and life experiences. Their content must therefore be limited to that which is assumed to be equally common to all cultures, or to material that is entirely unfamiliar and novel for all persons whatever their cultural background.

Decile. Any one of the nine percentile points (scores) that divide a distribution into ten parts, each containing one-tenth of all the scores or cases; every tenth percentile. The first decile is the 10th percentile, the second the 20th, the eighth the 80th percentile, and so on.

Deviation. The amount by which a score differs from a designated reference value, such as the mean, the norm, or the score on some other test.

Deviation IQ (DIQ). An age-based index of general mental ability. It is based upon the difference, or deviation, between a person's score and the typical, or average, score for persons of the same chronological age. Deviation IQs from most current mental ability measures are standard scores with a mean of 100 and a standard deviation of 16 for each defined age group. (See *intelligence quotient*)

Diagnostic Test. A test used to locate specific areas of weakness or strength, to determine the nature of weaknesses or deficiencies, and to yield measures of the components or subparts of a larger body of information or skill. Diagnostic tests are most commonly prepared for reading and mathematics.

Difficulty Index. The percentage of a specified group, such as students of a given age or grade, who answer a test item correctly. (Referred to in this book as *easiness index*)

Discriminability Index. The ability of a test item to differentiate between persons possessing much or little of a certain trait, skill, or proficiency. It is usually derived from the number passing the item in the highest third of the group (on total score) and the number passing in the lowest third.

Distractor. Any of the incorrect choices, or options, in a multiple choice or matching short-answer test item.

Distribution (frequency distribution). A tabulation of the scores of a group of individuals showing the number of individuals obtaining each score, or the number of individuals within the range of each interval.

Domain-referencing. Systematically constructing items to be representative of the full range of possible conditions set forth in the objective for which the items are intended to be a measure.

Equivalent Form. Any of two or more forms of a test that are closely parallel with respect to the nature of the content and the number and difficulty of the items included, and that will yield very similar average scores and measures of variability for a given group. (Also called *alternate, comparable,* or *parallel form*)

Error of Measurement. See *standard error of measurement.*

Essay-type Item. An item that provides test takers with the opportunity to structure and compose their own responses within relatively broad limits. Scoring of an essay-type item often involves the subjective judgment of the scorer, in contrast to a short-answer item, which structures or even includes the correct response, making scoring quite objective.

Extrapolation. In general, any process of estimating values of a variable beyond the range of available data. As applied to test norms, the process of extending a norm line into grade or age levels not tested in the standardization program, in order to permit interpretation of extreme scores. Since this extension is usually done graphically rather than empirically or according to a given mathematical function, considerable judgment is involved. Extrapolated values are thus to some extent arbitrary; for this and other reasons, they have limited meaning.

Face Validity. Refers to the acceptability of the test and test situation by the examinee or user in terms of apparent uses to which the test is to be put. A test has face validity when it appears to measure the variable or objectives to be tested.

Factor. In mental measurement, a hypothetical trait, ability, or component of ability that underlies and influences performance on two or more tests and hence causes scores on the tests to be correlated. The term "factor" strictly refers to a theoretical variable, derived by a process of factor analysis from a table of intercorrelations among tests. However, it is also used to denote the psychological interpretation given to the variable—that is, the mental trait assumed to be represented by the variable, as *verbal ability, numerical ability,* and so on.

Factor Analysis. Any of several methods of analyzing the intercorrelations among a set of variables such as test scores. Factor analysis attempts to account for the interrelationships in terms of some underlying "factors," preferably fewer in number than the original variables, and it reveals how much of the variation in each of the original measures arises from, or is associated with, each of the hypothetical factors. Factor analysis has contributed to an understanding of the organization or components of intelligence, aptitudes, and personality; and it has pointed the way to the development of "purer" tests of the several components.

Faking.   Giving a test response on an affective test that is an intended distortion in an attempt to create an impression. It is more likely to occur when the test taker feels pressure to respond in a particular way, such as when taking an employment test.

Forced-choice Item.   Broadly, any multiple choice item in which the examinee is required to select one or more of the given choices. The term is most often used to denote a special type of multiple choice item used in personality tests in which the options are (1) of equal "preference value," that is, chosen equally often by a typical group, and are (2) such that one of the options discriminates between persons high and low on the factor that this option measures, while the other option measures another factor.

Frequency Distribution.   See *distribution.*

Grade Equivalent (GE).   The grade level for which a given score is the real or estimated average. Grade-equivalent interpretation, most appropriate for elementary level achievement tests, expresses obtained scores in terms of grade and month of grade, assuming a ten-month school year (for example, 5.7). Since such tests are usually standardized at only one (or two) point(s) within each grade, grade equivalents between points for which there are data-based scores must be "estimated" by interpolation. (See *extrapolation, interpolation*)

Grade Norm.   The average test score obtained by typical pupils classified at a given grade placement. (See *grade equivalent, norms, percentile rank, stanine*)

Group Test.   A test that may be administered to a number of individuals at the same time by one examiner.

Individual Test.   A test that can be administered to only one person at a time.

Intelligence Quotient (IQ).   Originally, the ratio of a person's mental age to his or her chronological age, MA/CA, multiplied by 100 to eliminate the decimal. More precisely—and particularly for adult ages, at which mental growth is assumed to have ceased—the ratio of mental age to the mental age normal for chronological age. This quotient IQ has been gradually replaced by the deviation IQ concept. (See *deviation IQ*)

Interpolation.   In general, any process of estimating intermediate values between two known points. As applied to test norms, it refers to the procedure used in assigning interpretive values (such as grade equivalents) to scores between the successive average scores actually obtained in the standardization process. Also, in reading norm tables it is necessary at times to interpolate to obtain a norm value for a score between two scores given in the table; for example, in the table shown here, a percentile rank of 83 (from $81 + \frac{1}{3}$ of 6) would be assigned, by interpolation, to a score of 46; a score of 50 would correspond to a percentile rank of 94 (obtained as $87 + \frac{2}{3}$ of 10).

Score	Percentile Rank
51	97
48	87
45	81

Interpretability.   An indication of what the scores on a test mean and how their meaning is derived or determined. Test interpretation is either *criterion-referenced* or *norm-referenced.*

Inventory Test.   An achievement test that attempts to cover rather thoroughly some relatively small unit of specific instruction or training. An inventory test, as the name suggests, is in the nature of a "stock-taking" of an individual's knowledge or skill, and is often administered prior to instruction. Inventories are also used to measure personality traits, interests, attitudes, problems, motivation, etc. (See *personality test*)

Item.   A single question or exercise in a test.

Item Analysis.   The process of evaluating single test items by determining the difficulty value and the discriminating power of the item, and often its correlation with some criterion.

Kuder-Richardson Formula(s).   Formulas for estimating the reliability of a test that are based on inter-item consistency and that require only a single administration of the test. The one most used, *formula 21*, requires information based on the number of items in the test, the variance, and the test mean. Kuder-Richardson formulas are not appropriate for use with speed tests, that is, tests which measure rate of performance, nor with tests whose items cannot be scored as either right or wrong.

Likert Scale.   An attitude scale in which the test taker is given a series of attitude statements and responds by choosing one of given choices: *strongly agree, agree, undecided* (this choice is not always used), *disagree,* or *strongly disagree.*

Matching Item.   A short-answer test item in which the student must associate an entry in one list with one in another.

Mean.   See *arithmetic mean.*

Median.   The middle score in a distribution or set of ranked scores; the point (score) that divides the group into two equal parts; the 50th percentile. Half of the scores are below the median and half above it.

Mental Ability.   Skills including reasoning, verbal comprehension and fluency, numerical or quantitative ability, and figural comprehension that are influenced by or relate to a learning environment which reinforces or requires them. More traditionally, this has been called *intelligence.*

Mental Age (MA).   The age for which a given score on an intelligence or mental ability test is average or normal. If the average score made by an unselected group of children six years, ten months of age is 55, then a child making a score of 55 is said to have a mental age of 6-10. (See *achievement age, chronological age*)

Mode. The score, or value, that occurs most frequently in a distribution.

Multiple Choice Item. A test item in which the test taker's task is to choose the correct or best answer from several given answers, or options.

N or n. The symbol commonly used to represent the number of cases or observations in a distribution.

Nominations. The procedure of naming choices or preferences. It is often used to identify friendship choices, in which case its results are diagrammed as a sociogram.

Nonverbal Test. A test that does not require the use of words in the item or in the response to it. (However, oral directions may be included in the formulation of the task.) A test cannot be classified as nonverbal simply because it does not require reading on the part of the test taker.

Normal Distribution. A distribution of scores or measures that in graphic form has a distinctive bell-shaped appearance. The graph of a normal distribution is known as a *normal curve*. In a normal distribution, scores or measures are distributed symmetrically about the mean, with as many cases at various distances above the mean as at equal distances below it. Cases are concentrated near the mean and decrease in frequency the farther one departs from the mean. The assumption that mental and psychological characteristics are distributed normally has been useful in much test development work.

Norming Group. Sample on which norms or comparison scores are obtained as part of the process of test standardization. (Also called a *norm group* or *standardization sample*)

Norm-line. A smooth curve drawn to best fit (1) the plotted mean or median scores of successive age or grade groups, or (2) the successive percentile points for a single group.

Norm-referenced Test. Term used to describe tests designed to provide information on the performance of test takers relative to one another. Usually norms for interpretation are obtained from a *norming group*. This type of test is contrasted to a *criterion-referenced test*, which is interpreted on an absolute rather than a relative basis.

Norms. Statistics that supply a frame of reference by which meaning may be given to obtained test scores. Norms are based upon the actual performance of pupils of various grades or ages in the standardization group for the test. Since norms represent average or typical performance, they should not be regarded as standards or as universally desirable levels of attainment. The most common types of norms are *deviation IQ, percentile rank, grade equivalent*, and *stanine*. Reference groups are usually those of specified age or grade.

Objective. An intended outcome of instruction stated in such a way that its attainment can be observed and measured. Objectives serve as the basis for constructing test items. (Also called *behavioral, instructional, measurable, learner*, or *performance* objectives. See *content validity*)

Omnibus Test. A test (1) in which items measuring a variety of mental operations are all combined into a single sequence rather than being grouped together by type of operation, and (2) from which only a single score is derived, rather than separate scores for each operation or function. Omnibus tests make for simplicity of administration, since one set of directions and one overall time limit usually suffice.

Other Two-choice Item.   A short-answer item other than true–false that requires the test taker to classify or categorize objects into one of two categories (such as: a capital city, not a capital city).

Parallel-item Agreement.   A reliability procedure for use with criterion-referenced tests in which performances on the items that were written to measure the same objective are compared and an indication of similarity or dissimilarity in these performances noted. Lack of agreement can then become the basis for item revision.

Percentile.   The percent of cases falling at or below a given or indicated point in the distribution. Thus a score coinciding with the 35th percentile (P_{35}) is regarded as equaling or surpassing that of 35 percent of the persons in the group, and such that 65 percent of the performances exceeds this score.

Percentile Rank (PR).   The expression of an obtained test score in terms of its position within a group of 100 scores; the percentile rank of a score is the percent of scores equal to or lower than the given score in its own group or in an external reference (that is, norm) group.

Performance Test.   A test usually involving some motor or manual response on the test taker's part, generally a manipulation of concrete equipment or materials as contrasted to a paper-and-pencil test. The term "performance" is also used to denote a test that is actually a work sample; in this sense it may include paper-and-pencil tests, as, for example, a test in bookkeeping, in shorthand, or in proofreading, where no materials other than paper and pencil may be required, and where the test response is identical with the behavior about which information is desired.

Personality Test.   A test intended to measure one or more of the non-intellective aspects of an individual's mental or psychological make-up; an instrument designed to obtain information on the affective characteristics of an individual—emotional, motivational, attitudinal—as distinguished from his or her abilities. Personality tests include (1) personality and adjustment inventories that seek to measure a person's status on such traits as dominance, sociability, introversion, and so on, by means of self-descriptive responses to a series of questions; (2) rating scales that call for rating, by one's self or another, the extent to which a subject possesses certain traits; and (3) opinion or attitude inventories. More specifically, category 1 may be called tests of personality orientation, category 2, self-concept, and category 3, attitude scales.

Power Test.   A test intended to measure level of performance unaffected by speed of response; hence one in which there is either no time limit or a very generous one. Items are usually arranged in order of increasing difficulty.

Practice Effect.   The influence of previous experience with a test on a later administration of the same or a similar test; usually an increased familiarity with the directions, kind of questions, and so on. Practice effect is greatest when the interval between testings is short, when the content of the two tests is identical or very similar, and when the initial test taking represents a relatively novel experience for the subjects.

Predictive Validity.   See *validity*.

Product-moment Coefficient (r).   Also known as the *Pearson r*. (See *coefficient of correlation*)

Proficiency Test.   A test designed to determine whether a pupil has acquired proficiency on a given unit of instruction or a single knowledge or skill; a test whose results give information on what a pupil knows, rather than on how his or her performance relates to that of some norm-reference group. Such tests are usually referred to as criterion-referenced tests.

Profile.   A graphic representation of the results on several tests, for either an individual or a group, when the results have been expressed in some uniform or comparable terms (standard scores, percentile ranks, grade equivalents, and so on). The profile method of presentation permits identification of areas of strength or weakness.

Prognosis (prognostic) Test.   A test used to predict future success in a specific subject or field.

Projective Technique (projective method).   A method of personality study in which the subject responds as he or she chooses to a series of ambiguous stimuli, such as ink blots, pictures, unfinished sentences, and so on. It is assumed that under this free-response condition the subject "projects" manifestations of personality characteristics and organization that can, by suitable methods, be scored and interpreted to yield a description of his or her basic personality structure. The Rorschach (ink blot) Technique, and the Murray Thematic Apperception Test are commonly used projective methods.

Quartile.   One of three points that divide the cases in a distribution into four equal groups. The lower quartile (Q_1), or 25th percentile, sets off the lowest fourth of the group; the middle quartile (Q_2) is the same as the 50th percentile, or median, and divides the second fourth of cases from the third; and the third quartile (Q_3), or 75th percentile, sets off the top fourth.

r.   See *coefficient of correlation*.

Random Sample.   A sample of the members of a specified total population drawn in such a way that every member of the population has an equal chance of being included—that is, in a way that precludes the operation of bias or selection. The purpose in using a sample free of bias is, of course, the requirement that the cases used be representative of the total population if findings for the sample are to be generalized to that population. In a stratified random sample, the drawing of cases is controlled in such a way that those chosen are "representative" also of specified subgroups of the total population. (See *representative sample*)

Range.   The difference between the highest and the lowest score on a test by a group of test takers.

Raw Score.   The first quantitative result obtained in scoring a test; for example, the number of right answers, time required for performance, number of errors, or a similar direct, unconverted, uninterpreted measure.

Readiness Test.   A test that measures the extent to which an individual has achieved a degree of maturity or has acquired certain skills or information needed for successfully undertaking a particular new learning activity. Thus a reading readiness test indicates whether a child has reached a developmental stage where he or she may profitably begin formal reading instruction.

Recall Item.   A type of item that requires the test taker to supply the correct answer from memory or recollection, as contrasted with a *recognition* item, in which he or she need only identify the correct answer. For example:

Columbus discovered America in the year _____ .

is a *recall* item. Both *completion* and *unstructured* items are recall items.

Recognition Item.   An item that requires the examinee to recognize or select the correct answer from among two or more given answers (options). For example:

Columbus discovered America in
   a. 1425   b. 1492   c. 1520   d. 1546

is is recognition item. All short-answer item formats other than completion or unstructured require recognition. (See *recall item*)

Regression Effect.   The tendency for students who make extremely high or extremely low scores on a test to make less extreme scores, that is, scores closer to the mean, on a second administration of the same test or on some predicted measure.

Reliability.   The extent to which a test is consistent in measuring whatever it does measure; accuracy, dependability, stability, trustworthiness, relative freedom from errors of measurement. Reliability is usually expressed by a reliability coefficient or by the standard error of measurement derived from it.

Reliability Coefficient.   The coefficient of correlation between two forms of a test, between scores on two administrations of the same test, or between halves of a test (corrected by the Spearman-Brown formula). The three measure somewhat different aspects of reliability, but all are properly spoken of as reliability coefficients. (See *alternate-form reliability, split-half reliability coefficient, Spearman-Brown formula, test-retest reliability coefficient, Kuder-Richardson formula(s)*; see also *parallel-item agreement*)

Representative Sample.   A sample that corresponds to or matches the population of which it is a sample with respect to characteristics important for the purposes under investigation. In an achievement test norm sample, such significant aspects might be the proportion of cases from various types of schools, different geographical areas, and so on.

Scale.   A continuum marked off into numerical units that can be applied to some object or state in order to measure a particular property of it.

Scholastic Aptitude.   See *academic aptitude.*

Semantic Differential.   A bipolar adjective scale used for measuring attitudes toward a given object or stimulus. Scales are labeled with an adjective and its opposite at each end with seven points between as shown below

interesting ___: ___: ___: ___: ___: ___: ___ boring

to reflect the test taker's judgment of the "goodness" (evaluation), potency, activity, or some other more specific property of the given stimulus.

Short-answer Item.   An item for which the correct responses or scoring key may be set up in advance so that scores are unaffected by the opinion or judgment of the scorer. Such an item is contrasted with an essay-type item to which different persons may assign different scores, ratings, or grades.

Skewed Distribution.   A distribution that departs from symmetry, or balance around the mean, that is, from normality. Scores pile up at one end and trail off at the other.

Social Desirability Response Bias.   Giving a presumably unconsciously distorted test response that conforms to the test taker's expectation of what is the most "normal" or socially acceptable response.

Spearman-Brown Formula.   A formula giving the relationship between the reliability of a test and its length. The formula permits estimation of the reliability of a test lengthened or shortened by any amount from the known reliability of a test of specified length. Its most common application is the estimation of reliability of an entire test from the correlation between its two halves. (See *split-half reliability coefficient*)

Split-half Reliability Coefficient.   A coefficient of reliability obtained by correlating scores on one half of a test with scores on the other half, and applying the Spearman-Brown formula to adjust for the doubled length of the total test. Generally, but not necessarily, the two halves consist of the odd-numbered and the even-numbered items.

Standard Deviation (σ, s, S.D.).   A measure of the variability or dispersion of a set of scores based on the square of the deviation of each score from the mean. The more the scores cluster around the mean, the smaller the standard deviation. For a normal distribution, approximately two thirds (68.3 percent) of the scores are within the range from one S.D. below the mean to one S.D. above the mean. The square of the standard deviation is called the *variance*.

Standard Error of Measurement (S.E.M.).   Estimate of the magnitude of "error" present in an obtained score, whether (1) an individual score, or (2) a group measure, as a mean or a correlation coefficient. It is the standard deviation of the difference between obtained scores and corresponding true scores.

Standard Score.   A general term referring to any of a variety of "transformed" scores, in terms of which raw scores may be expressed for reasons of convenience, comparability, ease of interpretation, and so on. The simplest type of standard score, known as a z-score, is an expression of the deviation of a score from the mean score of the group in relation to the standard deviation of the scores of the group. Thus:

$$\text{standard score } (z) = \frac{\text{raw score } (X) - \text{mean } (\overline{X})}{\text{standard deviation (S.D.)}}$$

Adjustments may be made in this ratio so that a system of standard scores having any desired mean and standard deviation may be set up. The use of such standard scores does not affect the relative standing of the individuals in the group or change the shape of the original distribution. *T*-scores have a mean of 50 and an S.D. of 10. Deviation IQs are standard scores with a mean of 100 and a chosen S.D., most often 16. Standard scores are useful in expressing the raw scores of two forms of a test in comparable terms in instances where tryouts have shown that the two forms are not identical in difficulty; also, successive levels of a test may be linked to form a continuous standard-score scale, making across-battery comparison possible.

Standardized Test.   A test designed to provide a systematic sample of individual performance, administered according to prescribed directions, scored in conformance with definite rules, and interpreted in reference to certain normative information. We can further restrict the usage of the term "standardized" to those tests for which the items have been chosen on the basis of experimental evaluation, and for which data on reliability and validity are provided. Typically such tests are commercially published. (See *norm-referenced test*)

Stanine.   One of the steps in a nine-point scale of standard scores. The stanine (short for standard-nine) scale has values from 1 to 9, with a mean of 5 and a standard deviation of 2.

Structured Item.   Any of a number of short-answer items where the correct answer is provided and the test taker must recognize it. (See *recognition item, matching item, multiple choice item, other two-choice item,* and *true–false item*)

Survey Test.   A test that measures general achievement in a given area, usually with the connotation that the test is intended to assess group status, rather than to yield precise measures of individual performance.

T-score.   A standard score scale using a mean of 50 and a standard deviation of 10.

Taxonomy.   An embodiment of the principles of classification; a survey, usually in outline form, such as a presentation of the objectives of education. Two taxonomies are those of the cognitive and affective domains.

Test-retest Reliability Coefficient.   A type of reliability coefficient obtained by administering the same test a second time, after a short interval, and correlating the two sets of scores.

True–False Item.   A test question in which the test taker is given a statement and asked whether it is true or false.

True Score.   A score entirely free of error; hence, a hypothetical value that can never be obtained by testing, because testing always involves some measurement error. A true score may be thought of as the average score from an infinite number of measurements from the same or exactly equivalent tests, assuming no practice effect or change in the test taker during the testings. The standard deviation of this infinite number of "samplings" is known as the *standard error of measurement.*

Unstructured Item.   A short-answer question that can be answered by a word, phrase, or number. It is similar to a completion item except without the blank contained within the item. For example: Who is the author of *Catch-22?* (See *completion item* and *recall item*)

Usability.   An indication of the suitability or practicality of a test as it relates to its intended use. For teachers, this would be classroom use.

Validity.   The extent to which a test does the job for which it is used, that is, measures what it is supposed to measure. (See also *content validity*)

    Concurrent Validity.   The extent to which different tests of the same property are in agreement. Such validity might be evidenced by concurrent measures of academic ability and of achievement, by the relation of a new test to one generally accepted as or known to be valid, or by the correlation between scores on a test and criteria measures that are valid but are less objective and more time consuming to obtain than a test score would be.

Construct Validity.   The extent to which two tests or measures of different but conceptually related properties agree. Tests of personality, verbal ability, mechanical aptitude, critical thinking, and so on, are validated in terms of their construct and the relation of their scores to pertinent external data.

Criterion Validity.   The extent to which a group already proficient or experienced in the quality measured by a test scores higher on that test than before they acquired proficiency or higher than a nonproficient or inexperienced group. For the validation of performance tests, trained groups are compared to untrained groups or groups are compared before and after training.

Predictive Validity.   The accuracy with which a test (such as an aptitude, prognostic, or readiness test) indicates future outcomes (for example, learning success) in a particular area, as evidenced by correlations between scores on the test and future criterion measures (for example, the relation of a score on an academic aptitude test administered in high school to grade point average over four years of college).

Variance.   A measure of dispersion of a set of scores from the mean: the square of the standard deviation.

z-score.   A standard score expressed in standard deviation units having a mean of 0 and a standard deviation of 1.

Answers to Proficiency Tests

CHAPTER 1

1. b
2. False
3. To decide what it is you want to measure.
4. c
5. content validity
6. d

CHAPTER 2

1. An intended outcome stated in such a way that its attainment can be determined; to state desired outcomes, to plan strategies for and produce the desired outcomes, to measure to what extent desired outcomes are being achieved.
2. To store food, to store eating and cooking implements, to prepare meals, to serve meals, to clean eating and cooking implements, to provide a social setting.
3. Instruction, construction of achievement tests.
4. By helping you know what is expected of you; by providing a basis for judging if you are meeting the expectations.
5. c
6. False
7. To be correct, an action verb must have been used and all three parts of the objective provided. For example, *given a map of the United States, the student shall identify by pointing to the longest river system; he or she shall point to the Mississippi-Missouri River.*
8. For example, *given five addition problems, each with two 3-digit numbers, the student shall compute the correct answer for at least four.*
9. b

10. In proper relation to prior, concomitant, and subsequent objectives. Determined by seeing if students who fail it also fail those objectives for which it is a prerequisite or an objective that is prerequisite to it.
11. d

CHAPTER 3

1. a. iii; b. iv; c. i.
2. c
3. c
4. a. False; b. True
5. application
6. *State the names of your state's two senators.*
7. *Create an accompaniment for a familiar melody.*
8. For example, using a jack, removing a tire, putting on a tire, tightening bolts.
9. For example, defining fascism and democracy, presenting examples of fascist governments (or describing principles of fascism), presenting examples of democratic governments (or describing examples of democracy), discussing advantages and disadvantages of fascism in comparison with democracy.

10.

Conditions	Action	Criteria
Three problems, each containing from two to four similar fractions whose sum is neither reducible nor greater than one.	Find the sum.	All three are added correctly.

CHAPTER 4

1. a. state
   b. identify
2. a. iii; b. iv; c. ii.
3. b
4. a. True
   b. False
   c. False
5. ■ Name the first three presidents of the United States in order.
   ■ The first, second, and third presidents of the United States were _____, _____, and _____.
   ■ Washington, Adams, and Jefferson were the first three presidents of the United States in that order.   TRUE   FALSE
   ■ Circle the names of those people who were United States presidents.
       J. Adams
       A. Burr
       P. Henry

T. Jefferson
G. Washington
A. Hamilton
For those circled, indicate which was first, second, and third.

■ Which represents the first three presidents of the United States in the proper order?
   a. Washington, Jefferson, Adams
   b. Washington, Jefferson, Madison
   c. Washington, Adams, Jefferson
   d. Adams, Washington, Jefferson
   e. Adams, Washington, Madison

■ Match the categories on the left with names on the right.
   first president   Adams
   second president   Madison
   third president   Hamilton
                          Washington
                          Jefferson

6. ■ What is the result of adding 7 and 3?
   ■ $7 + 5 = $ _____
   ■ $3 + 2 = 6$ TRUE   FALSE
   ■ Circle the correct additions:
      $2 + 1 = 3$ $9 + 6 = 16$
      $3 + 5 = 7$ $8 + 2 = 11$
      $4 + 4 = 8$ $5 + 6 = 11$

   ■ Which one of the following results when 5 and 6 are added?
      a. 9
      b. 10
      c. 11
      d. 12
      e. 13

   ■ Match the number on the right which, when added to the number on the left, gives 13 as the result.
      1. 4   a. 8
      2. 6   b. 6
      3. 9   c. 9
      4. 5   d. 7
                  e. 4

7. c
8. a

CHAPTER 5

1. a. iv;   b. v;   c. i;   d. ii.
2. True

3. For example, *on occasion, often with little forewarning, certain commodities become short in supply (for example, gasoline in the spring of 1974). What effect do such shortages have on prices? Name at least two possible reasons for such shortages.*
4. For example, *describe five ways that moles, opossums, beavers, and woodchucks are similar and one way that they are different. Use no more than one sentence for your description of each similarity or difference.*
5. For example, *in 300 words or less describe how to use carrots and celery to make a device that tells time. Be as specific as possible.*
6. For example, *evaluate the Treaty of Versailles as a means of solving the problems of aggression. Specify at least five criteria and apply to the treaty in an essay of 400–500 words.*
7. Organization, content accuracy, accuracy of solution, completeness, internal consistency, originality.
8. b; c; e; f; h.

CHAPTER 6

1. See the list of criteria on pages 108–109.
2. For example, *given an analytical balance and a sample substance, demonstrate a procedure for determining the weight of the substance. Given tools, materials, and a plan, construct a bird feeder.* Reason: each objective calls for a real performance or product.
3. For example, *given a piece of construction paper, compass, and pencil, construct an exact equilateral right triangle.*
4. a. Uses compass to lay off equal sides. _____
   b. Uses compass to construct the perpendicular properly. _____
   c. Resulting triangle has equal sides and contains a right angle. _____
   d. Work is neat and construction lines removed. _____
5. For example, *given a ruler, graph paper, and colored pencils, draw the layout of this floor of the school.*
6. For example:
   a. Drawing contains all areas of this floor of the school. _____
   b. All spaces are proportional to actual size. _____
   c. All spaces are correctly located with respect to one another. _____
   d. All spaces are accurately labeled. _____
   e. Drawing is neat. _____
7. Student motivation:
   a. Comes on time.
   b. Volunteers for activities.
   c. Completes assignments.
   d. Asks questions.
   e. Shows enthusiasm.
8. Student:

	NEVER	RARELY	OCCA-SION-ALLY	FRE-QUENTLY	ALWAYS
Comes to class on time.	N	R	O	F	A
Volunteers for activities.	N	R	O	F	A
Completes assignments.	N	R	O	F	A
Asks questions.	N	R	O	F	A
Shows enthusiasm.	N	R	O	F	A

9. For example, the teacher will show well-preparedness in teaching a lesson.
   1. Has a prepared lesson plan.
   2. Is familiar with what he/she wants to do.
   3. Proceeds in a smooth fashion.
   4. Is well-organized.
   5. Knows the content.
   6. Is able to answer questions.
10. Teacher:

	BEHAVIOR ABSENT				BEHAVIOR PRESENT
Has a prepared lesson plan.	1	2	3	4	5
Is familiar with what he/she wants to do.	1	2	3	4	5
Proceeds in a smooth fashion.	1	2	3	4	5
Is well-organized.	1	2	3	4	5
Knows the content.	1	2	3	4	5
Is able to answer questions.	1	2	3	4	5

11. Affective objectives that deal with such behaviors as cooperativeness and involvement should not be neglected; as part of overall student evaluation, rating of such behaviors would be useful.
12. As values are clarified and change, student behavior should also change. (For example, students might become more cooperative or more involved.) Measurement of student behavior would help to determine whether the experimental program was stimulating positive changes in the behavior of students.

CHAPTER 7

1. c
2. Does it fit my objective? Does it reflect the action verb? Does it utilize the conditions? Does it employ the criteria?
3. a. List the three objectives.
   b. Determine how many items you want to write for each based on its relative importance.

c. Draw the map indicating the number of items per objective.

d. Follow the map to construct items.

4.

Objectives	Units of Importance			
	1	2	3	4
1	◉	◉		
2	◉	◉	◉	◉
3	◉	◉	◉	◉
4	◉	◉		

5. two

6. a. i; b. iv; c. ii; d. v.

7. Items 1 and 2 are valid for measuring objective 1; items 3 and 4 are valid for measuring objective 2; item 5 is invalid (no objective); items 6 and 7 are valid for measuring objective 3; and no items among the first seven measure objective 4.

8. d.

9. False

10. a, d, e

11. a. ii; b. iv; c. v.

CHAPTER 8

1. c

2. True

3. d

4. False

5. a. v; b. i; c. iv; d. ii; e. iii.

6. a. split-half
   b. parallel-item
   c. Kuder-Richardson 21
   d. test-retest
   e. alternate-form

7. a. lasting and general characteristics—reading ability
   b. lasting and specific characteristics—knowledge required by particular test items
   c. temporary and general characteristics—fatigue
   d. temporary and specific characteristics—luck (For more examples, see Figure 8-3.)

8. a. T; b. E; c. T; d. E; e. E.

9. a, b, c, e, g

10. longer

11. a. Separate the tests of the high scorers and low scorers and compare the

performance of each group on each item. Take those items on which the two groups had about the same success rate and revise or replace them with ones that correspond more closely to the content of the unit.

b. Identify those items that the majority of students got wrong and find the answer choices that were selected more often than the ones you designated as correct; see if these choices are possibly correct. If they could be considered correct, change them to improve the items.

c. Identify in advance the ideas that must be presented for each item in order to earn different amounts of credit; determine the point allocation per essay response for the different features (for example, organization, creativity); do not look at student names; score one-fifth of the responses twice.

12. This test was designed to measure six objectives with two items per objective; students' performance on each pair of items per objective can be examined and those pairs where half or more of the students got one member of the pair right and one wrong identified; a close examination of the items in these nonparallel item pairs can form the basis for a revision or replacement of at least one member of the pair.

CHAPTER 9

1. d
2. a. application; b. computation; c. concepts.
3. Validity because teachers can build a test to fit their own objectives whereas standardized achievement tests are built around a general content outline.
4. Reliability because revision based on item analysis allows for the elimination of inconsistent items.
5. False
6. b
7. In order to maintain constancy across test conditions from administration to administration, tests must be administered the same way each time. Only familiarity with administrative procedures makes this possible. Some tests have practice tests that are administered in advance. Without familiarizing yourself with these and other procedures, you are likely to overlook an instruction or a stop in the testing procedure.
8. Make sure all students have everything they need to take the test and no more. Make sure each student fills in all information called for in the Pupil Information Box. Clearly give all instructions as called for in the directions. Adhere to time limits exactly. Make sure that all students know how to take the test. Monitor test taking from various points in the room. Make sure students take the testing seriously.

CHAPTER 10

1. scores or performance
2. a. Information about the performance (that is, test results) of a specific group of people on which subsequent test score interpretation is based.

b. The specific group of people on whose test scores interpretation is based.

3. a. percentile rank
   b. grade-equivalent score
   c. standard score
   d. stanine score

4. a. ii;   b. v;   c. i;   d. viii;   e. iv;   f. vii;   g. iii.

5. a. grade-equivalent score;   b. percentile rank;   c. raw score;   d. standard score;   e. stanine score.

6. b, d, e

7. Advantages: enables individual scores to be interpreted by comparison to group data; makes conclusions based on test scores somewhat independent of the failings or weaknesses of the test.
   Disadvantages: norms become dated and no longer reflect the types of performances of which people are capable; an emphasis on the relative interpretation of tests tends to obscure the relation between the content of those tests and any bearing on the past or future (that is, real capabilities) of the test takers.

8. On a criterion-referenced test, 85 percent means that the student has shown proficiency on 85 percent of the objectives or, if the test was of a single objective, on 85 percent of the items. On a norm-referenced test, 85th percentile means that the student has gotten more items right than 85 percent of the students in the norming group at the same grade level.

9. a, c, d

10. a. Report the names of each objective that each student has "passed" rather than reporting simply the total number of items right on the total test.
    b. Consider a student to have "passed" an objective if he or she gets both of the items right that were written to measure proficiency on each objective.

11. a. Make a table displaying the number of students showing proficiency per objective vs. the number not showing proficiency; where the percentage showing proficiency dips below 50 percent, the instruction for that objective must be considered less than completely effective.
    b. Rank order all the test scores (that is, total number of items right) and divide them up in segments such as fifths or pentiles; give each student a number score (1–5), which represents his or her pentile.

CHAPTER 11

1. Teacher-built tests constitute a major portion of the school testing program so it is obviously important to improve them; a test is a resource like a curriculum and hence should be reused; a test-item file results in tests that are more valid and reliable.

2. a. Teacher prepares test items to fit instructional objectives.
   b. Teacher uses items in classroom testing.
   c. Teacher uses test results to evaluate reliability of items.
   d. Teacher discards poor items, retains good ones.

3. a. Make sure the test is valid for measuring the objectives of instruction.

Record the date proficiency on an objective is acquired and the degree of proficiency attained.

b. Select a test that measures objectives in sequence within a wide range, in particular covering objectives that should have been mastered prior to instruction. Examine the student's performance on this test to identify prior objectives on which the student has not acquired proficiency.

c. Determine from test results whether there are any objectives that a particular student has failed to acquire proficiency on (or any students who have failed to acquire proficiency on a particular objective) and provide additional instruction appropriate to that objective.

d. Give a pretest or at least precede instruction by presenting the objectives; give a posttest and return scored tests with minimal delay; clearly indicate errors and bases for scoring; test in a warm and accepting atmosphere.

4. See Figure 11-3.

5. Greatest strength: word study skills–phonetic analysis, consonants (53 percent above average).
Greatest weakness: word study skills–word division (40 percent below average).
Instructional recommendation: in teaching word skills, shift emphasis somewhat from phonetic analysis to word division.

6. Compare the 6th graders using the new instruction before and after to see how much they improve. Compare the end results on this year's 6th graders—who have used the new instruction—with last year's (in the same school) who have not. Compare the end results on this year's 6th graders—who have used the new instruction—with the end results for 6th graders in a comparable school in the district not using the new instruction.

References

Bloom, B. S. (1956). *Taxonomy of educational objectives.* Handbook I: Cognitive domain. New York: David McKay.

Educational Testing Service. (1959). *Making the classroom test. A guide for teachers.* Princeton, NJ: ETS, Evaluation & Advisory Service Series No. 4.

Gagne, R. M. (1974). *Essentials of learning for instruction.* Hinsdale, Ill.: The Dryden Press.

Gagne, R. M. (1985). *The conditions of learning.* (4th ed.). New York: Holt, Rinehart, and Winston.

Hively, W. et al. (1973). Domain-referenced curriculum evaluation: A technical handbook and a case study from the Minnesota Project. Los Angeles: Center for the Study of Evaluation, UCLA Graduate School of Education, CSE Monograph Series in Evaluation No. 1.

Kriege, J. W. (1971). Behavioral objectives: 10 ways to make them count. *Grade Teacher,* Sept. 138–43.

Lord, F. M. (1952). The relation of the reliability of multiple-choice tests to the distribution of item difficulties. *Psychometrika, 17,* 181–94.

Thorndike, R. L. (1949). *Personnel selection.* New York: Wiley.

Tuckman, B. W. (1985). *Evaluating instructional programs.* (2nd ed.). Boston: Allyn and Bacon.

INDEX

Page numbers in italics refer to figures
and boxes; *n* refers to footnotes.